D0615214

IN THE SHADOW OF 'JUST WARS'

From Médecins Sans Frontières in the same collection:

Populations in Danger (London: John Libbey, 1992)

Life, Death and Aid: the Médecins Sans Frontières Report on World Crisis Intervention (London: Routledge, 1993)

Populations in Danger 1995: a Médecins Sans Frontières Report (London: MSF and La Découverte, 1995).

MEDECINS SANS FRONTIERES

edited by Fabrice Weissman

In the Shadow of 'Just Wars'

Violence, Politics and Humanitarian Action

Translations from the French by
Vincent Homolka, Roger Leverdier and Fiona Terry
English text edited by Fiona Terry

Cornell University Press
Ithaca, New York

First published in the United Kingdom by
C. Hurst & Co. (Publishers) Ltd, London

First published in the United States of America by
Cornell University Press

Copyright © 2004 Médecins Sans Frontières

All rights reserved. Except for brief quotations in a
review, this book, or parts thereof, must not be reproduced
in any form without permission in writing from the publisher.
For information, address Cornell University Press, Sage House,
512 East State Street, Ithaca, New York 14850.

ISBN (cloth) 0-8014-4281-8
ISBN (paper) 0-8014-8911-3

Librarians: Library of Congress Cataloging-in-Publication
Data are available.

To François -Jean

Acknowledgments

Dr Jean-Hervé Bradol (President of Médecins Sans Frontières), Rony Brauman, Denis Gouzerh and Marc Le Pape actively participated in this project and their contribution to its publication was invaluable. Loïck Barriquand, Catherine Boucau, Delphine Chedorge, Eric Dachy, Katherine de Rivero, Fabien Dubuet, Anne Fouchard, Karim Laouabdia, Pascal Lefort, Guillaume Le Gallais, Pierre Mendiharat, Catrin Schulte-Hillen, Milton Tectonidis, Fiona Terry, and Jean-Guy Vataux attentively read parts of the manuscript and offered constructive comment. Fiona Terry, the MSF-London team and Katherine Monahan provided indispensable support for the English edition. Aline Leboeuf assisted with research. Finally, this work would not have been possible without the collaboration of all those at MSF, both in the field and at headquarters.

All are warmly thanked.

Paris, September 2003   F. W.

Contents

Part III. Abstention

POINTS OF VIEW

Maps

realised by Abdeljalil Abdesselam

Boxes

The text in boxes was written by Marine Buissonnière, Sophie Delaunay, Fabien Dubuet, Anne Fouchard, Aurélie Grémaud, Caroline Livio and Jacques Péron.

Abbreviations

EU	European Union
FAO	UN Food and Agricultural Organisation
ICRC	International Committee of the Red Cross
IMF	International Monetary Fund
MSF	Médecins Sans Frontières
NGO	Non-governmental Organisation
OCHA	Office of Coordination of Humanitarian Affairs
UN	United Nations
UNDP	United Nations Development Fund
UNHCR	United Nations High Commissioner for Refugees
UNICEF	United Nations Children's Fund
WFP	World Food Programme
WHO	World Health Organisation
WTO	World Trade Organisation

Introduction

The Sacrificial International Order and Humanitarian Action

Jean-Hervé Bradol

A few days after Western forces intervened in Kosovo in 1999 the British prime minister, Tony Blair, delivered a speech in Chicago during which he declared: 'Now our actions are guided by a more subtle blend of mutual self-interest and moral purpose in defending the values we cherish. In the end values and interests merge. If we can establish and spread the values of liberty, the rule of law, human rights and an open society then that is in our national interests too.'[1] Five months later Australian troops landed in East Timor to bring an end to the violence committed by pro-Indonesian militias, and in May 2000 a contingent of British paratroopers arrived in Sierra Leone to assist UN peacekeepers and restore a fragile calm to a country ravaged by ten years of civil war.

---

[1] *Doctrine of the International Community*, Remarks by the British prime minister Tony Blair to the Economic Club of Chicago, 22 April 1999.

Hence Western states conducted three armed interventions in conflict-ridden countries between 1999 and 2000 in the name of democracy and the defence of human rights. This predilection for military action in defence of 'values' as much as interests received fresh impetus from the attacks of 11 September 2001. A combination of universal humanist morality and national security has been cited as justification for Western and US-British interventions in Afghanistan and Iraq. Ethics and politics have become reconciled on the initiative of a handful of *avant-gardist* states that now consider the defence of fundamental liberties throughout the world as an essential component of their national interests. 'If people are really set free to run their countries as they see fit, we will be dealing with a world very favourable to American interests,' declared Paul Wolfowitz, US Under-Secretary for Defense, at the start of 2002.

These developments might appear to offer hope to populations subjected to the most violent forms of oppression. At last the incantatory appeals of humanitarian organisations calling on politicians to 'shoulder their responsibilities', abandon *Realpolitik*, and put an end to massive human rights violations seem to have been heard: first by the UN, whose Secretary-General warned on 20 September 1999, at the very moment when Australian peacekeepers were landing in East Timor, that 'states bent on criminal behaviour [should] know that frontiers are not the absolute defence... that massive and systematic violations of human rights – wherever they may take place – should not be allowed to stand', [2] then by the US, conscious of

---

[2] As quoted in T.G. Weiss, 'The Politics of Humanitarian Ideas', *Security Dialogue*, vol. 31, no. 11, 2000, p. 11.

its 'manifest destiny' and determined, through the 'war on terrorism', to export the doctrine of human rights and 'free-market democracy' – by force of arms and disregarding international law if necessary. In short, we are allegedly witnessing the blooming of a universal moral conscience that mobilises the energies of all towards the continuous improvement of the global human condition – under the banner of the UN for some and the US for others.

Having symbolised this representation of the world, humanitarian organisations are obliged to confront it with the actual suffering they encounter in their work, and to reflect upon the effectiveness of their own actions. To what extent has the proliferation of so-called 'just' wars and the recent enthusiasm for ethical and humanitarian values benefited populations exposed to mass violence? What has been the practical international reaction to the most serious crises of the last five years stemming from the discourse of a 'right to intervene' and the 'war on Evil'? These are the central questions posed by *In the Shadow of 'Just Wars'*, which picks up the thread of a project initiated in 1992 by François Jean.

A project of this nature has to pass from the particular to the general. The first part (Situations) analyses eleven major crises and the international reactions they aroused, while the second part (Points of View) raises some thematic questions affecting humanitarian action. This inquiry is founded on practical experience and highlights the successes but also the most tragic failures of international responses to crisis and their humanitarian components. Given the depth and breath of the competence required, the editor, Fabrice Weissman, has enlisted external as well as internal contributors from a variety of different backgrounds including researchers, academics and journalists.

The selection of the most serious crises is always difficult. What is the best indicator of the severity of a crisis? In terms of human life the mortality rate must be the decisive factor, and for this reason the Ivorian, Nepalese and Israel-Palestinian conflicts are not discussed in this book. The number of victims claimed by these conflicts is clearly less than the countless dead in Chechnya, Algeria, the Democratic Republic of Congo, Colombia, North Korea, Angola, Sudan, Sierra Leone, Liberia, Afghanistan and East Timor. Countries like Burundi, Congo-Brazzaville and Ethiopia could have figured in the book.

By way of introduction this section examines some of the questions that humanitarian actors should ask themselves if they hope to clarify their relationship to political power and improve the quality of their actions. In this spirit of inquiry – and with the aim of improving humanitarian action – we begin by rethinking the meaning of a humanitarian approach before reviewing the principal characteristics of different types of international political responses to crises and their impact on the quality of aid.

From the logic of sacrifice to the humanitarian spirit

The production of order at the international level – just as at national or local levels – demands its quota of victims. The sacrifice of Sierra Leonean and Liberian lives during the pacification of Sierra Leone, like the massacres of prisoners of war in Afghanistan during 'Operation Enduring Freedom' in 2001, reminds us that the construction of a 'better world' invariably comes at a price – the lives of others. Advocates of a new political order, like those who defend the continuation of the existing order, do not deny that some people are condemned, but justify their sacrifice in the name of a better future or the preservation of the benefits of 'civilisation' –   'you can't make an omelette without breaking eggs'. The logic of a culinary recipe ultimately dictates the premature extinction of a part of humanity. The execution of the sentence may take the spectacular form of violent death or – so perfectly integrated into the social landscape that it becomes invisible – slow extinction through denial of the elements essential to survival (water, food, medical care, shelter). It makes no great difference how a society distinguishes the marks of infamy that allow it to separate those who may live from those who can or must die; the human mind, endowed with limitless imagination, can redefine them in accordance with the latest notions of an ideal society. While in certain countries skin colour or the way a particular word is pronounced is enough to provoke a roadside execution, in contemporary Western societies such indicators have been displaced from the surface to the interior of the human body. Today, because of 'biological deviance' (hypocholesterolaemia) or 'behavioural deviance' (obesity), an individual may be refused treatment or medical insurance.

Humanitarian action, as we understand it, directly challenges the logic that justifies the premature and avoidable death of a part of humanity in the name of a hypothetical collective good. 'Are all these deaths really necessary?' is the question we systematically address to political powers. Why? Because we have taken the arbitrary and radical decision to help the people society has decided to sacrifice. In other words, humanitarian action is primarily addressed to those whose right to exist clashes with the indifference or overt hostility of others. It is intended to reach those who are being robbed of life by violence and extreme privation. Consequently, if humanitarian action is to be consistent, it will inevitably clash with the established order. Its subversive dimension becomes apparent when it moves beyond an analysis of material needs and exposes the processes of discrimination that produce victims and prevent efficient protection and assistance programs from being established.

Before delivering aid, humanitarian actors must identify the individuals or populations whose deaths are avoidable, as well as the nature of the crises that engulf them. Identifying the populations genuinely in need of assistance constitutes the first step of humanitarian action. But this is not a simple task because those in need are often hidden from view by political authorities. On many occasions famine victims have been buried near warehouses filled with food. The chapter on North Korea exemplifies this phenomenon, but is sadly reminiscent of other cases such as Somalia in 1992, Southern Sudan in 1998, and Angola.

How can we limit the number of deaths and reduce the suffering caused by the establishment and preservation of order? It is tempting to resort to law because international humanitarian law seeks to 'humanise war' by defining acceptable and unacceptable standards for armed warfare. In the theatre of conflict aid workers are supported by a corpus of internationally recognised rules that draw a line between legitimate and illegitimate sacrifice. By exposing the human cost of violence, aid workers remind belligerents of their failure to uphold the obligations that they have contracted or have had imposed on them. By negotiating the price of sacrifice, aid workers enjoin combatants to respect the lives of non-combatants (civilians, wounded soldiers, prisoners) in the name of an arbitrary, barely respected, and paradoxically consensual international standard that theoretically restricts the use of violence to legally defined necessity, and allows impartial humanitarian organisations to bring relief to victims of conflict. In reality, however, the appeal to law must remain purely opportunistic. We resort to it because it enables us to exert pressure on political authority; it is a means of staving off suffering and death. But the law is also violence. In our experience some of the worst cruelty and privation is found in camps and prisons run by judicial systems or so-called security forces. Before even contemplating recourse to the protection of international humanitarian law, aid workers have invariably been forced to break certain laws as they bring relief – by illegally crossing a border, for example.

War is not the only arena where the death of a part of humanity is played out. Several million people a year die from AIDS compared to hundreds of thousands killed in wars, according to World Health Organisation estimates. In other words, AIDS kills ten times as many people as war does. Moreover, AIDS related mortality represents only one fifth of the annual death toll linked to the deadliest infectious diseases (14 million deaths in 1999 according to the WHO *World Health Report 2000*), even though these diseases can be prevented by vaccination or cured with antibiotics. The first treatments designed to prolong the lives of AIDS patients appeared in the mid-1990s. By 2000 their price had risen to several thousand dollars a year, effectively putting them beyond the reach of most sufferers. High production costs do not account for high prices: due to public pressure, the price of these life-saving drugs was divided by 30 in less than two years yet pharmaceutical companies have not plunged into bankruptcy. Why was so little attention paid to the survival of millions of people until recently? Driven into a corner by the dedicated campaigning of patient and carer organisations, Andrew Natsios, head of the US Agency for International Development, responded with a diatribe worthy of Gobineau, the 19th century advocate of European racial supremacy: 'In many parts of Africa, people do not know what watches or clocks are, they do not use western means to tell the time, they use the sun. These drugs have to be administered in certain sequences at certain times during the day. You say, take it at 10 o'clock, they say, what do you mean, 10 o'clock?' (*Boston Globe*, 7 June 2001)

In terms of the destruction of human life, what difference is there between the wartime bombing of a civilian population and the distribution of ineffective medicines during a pandemic that is killing millions of people? Whatever form social interaction may take, bloodshed has long been regarded as the distinctive criterion of war. But is it enough to isolate war as a distinct social field, the natural territory of humanitarian organisations by virtue of the rights international standards bestow on them in this specific context? In our opinion, no. The distinction between war and peace depends less on the use or otherwise of violence and more on differences between overt violence and hidden violence – the kind that is integrated into the routine reproduction of the social order, with all the intermediate gradations that such a distinction may contain. The analogy between war and a health disaster is obvious when, in a situation of epidemics or endemic diseases, there is a realistic alternative to a lack of treatment or the distribution of ineffective medicines. This is primarily the case with the infectious diseases responsible for the greater part of global mortality. In this case the task of humanitarian organisations entails exposing the hidden lethality of the political order and proving through action that there are ways – if not the political will – to limit the number of deaths and reduce the suffering caused by epidemics and endemic diseases.

Opposed to power but not actively engaged in its conquest – since it rejects the logic that divides humanity into those who may live and those who must die – humanitarian action is necessarily subversive, since partisans of the established order rarely empathise with those whose elimination they tolerate or decree. In other words, the first condition for the success of humanitarian action is refusal to collaborate in this fatal selection process. This is a fundamental, non-negotiable condition; it forces us to question the violence sometimes associated with humanitarian action, violence which may arise because of the symbolic and practical importance of aid to the most powerful and violent actors on the international and local stage, or because aid agencies feel they have to defend their own institutional interests.

International reactions to crises: military intervention, political involvement and abstention

The international community of states cannot ignore contemporary armed conflicts. Their international ramifications are amplified in this period of history that is marked by the rapid growth of all kinds of international exchange – human beings, ideas and goods. International interventions are multiplying in response to these wars, and play a leading role in the regulation of conflicts and their human consequences. The end of the Cold War revived the idea of an international political system capable of anticipating wars, conducting negotiations, mediating between belligerents, and sometimes imposing peace and justice by force. In four years, from 1988 to 1992, the United Nations launched as many international military operations as it had done in the preceding four decades. This tendency, already noted in *Life, Death and Aid* (1993), has continued. International military interventions are becoming more numerous and ambitious, yet this form of international reaction to major crises still represents the exception rather than the rule. When considering the use of force by an international coalition on territory belonging to a sovereign state and its consequences for humanitarian action, three types of intervention stand out:

Intervention: the use of armed force against one of the parties to the conflict followed by international stewardship of the 'liberated' territories. It is conducted under the banner of collective security and universal morality in a context – with the exception of Iraq – of massive violence against civilian populations. These operations are accompanied by an intense humanitarian performance that legitimises the war and sidelines the crimes committed during its prosecution.

Involvement: diplomatic and humanitarian involvement, which formally addresses humanitarian concerns while subjecting aid operations to a political agenda (usually a partisan policy aimed at confining the conflict within acceptable limits).

Abstention: characterised by international indifference to the extreme brutality of certain conflicts. This equates to issuing the principal belligerents with a licence to kill.

Intervention

The post-Cold War military operations launched in Kurdistan (1991), Somalia (1992), and to a certain extent in Rwanda (Operation Turquoise, 1994) and Bosnia (1995) were manifestations of the resurgence of the concept of a 'just' war conducted by the most powerful actors on the international stage in the name of a hypothetical universal morality and collective security. The inertia of UN peacekeepers during the genocide of the Rwandan Tutsi (1994), preceded by the pitiful withdrawal from Somalia (1993) and the massacres in the former Yugoslavia (1992-5), had already demonstrated that protecting populations was not the priority in this revival of international military interventionism. Suspected since its inception of being a moral front for the defence of the interests of the most powerful, this 'right to intervene' is now being extended in the name of the 'global war on terror'. Originally intended to put a rapid end to massive violence inflicted on civilians, international involvement has veered towards 'preventive war'. Since 11 September 2001 the stated aim espoused by the British prime minister Tony Blair and American President George W. Bush is to 're-order the world' under the leadership of a 'great nation'.

The operations undertaken in Kosovo, East Timor, Sierra Leone, Afghanistan and, more recently, Iraq are typical of this new interventionism with its messianic overtones. Operations of this nature combine military, psychological, diplomatic and economic action with assistance to populations within a vast network that humanitarian organisations are expected to join if they wish to receive institutional funding. Most of these operations were mandated or approved by the United Nations. They ended with the international armed force controlling all or part of the territory of a sovereign state and led – with the exception of Iraq – to a significant reduction in the mass violence suffered by civilians. The partial success of the interventions in Kosovo, East Timor, Sierra Leone and Afghanistan derived from the limited harm inflicted on non-combatants, and the populations' support for the overthrow of the governing regimes.

In these contexts broad access to funds from major aid donors, at least in the initial phase of military intervention, is guaranteed to aid agencies ever sensitive to the preservation and growth of their budgets. Media coverage of abundant international aid being dispensed to victims of an 'evil' enemy makes it easier to forget the human cost arising from the use of force and the political repercussions of violating state sovereignty.

The American military campaign against the Taliban regime provides a particularly interesting example of the way 'just' wars are engineered, and the consequences of this illusory concept. A 'war on terror' was the rallying cry of partisans of the US offensive in Afghanistan. Reason gave way to emotion in reaction to the carnage of 11 September 2001, and all excesses were excused and criticisms quelled. Yet the misconduct of the 'armed humanitarianism' was far from negligible. The damage included the partial or total closure of the borders of Pakistan and Iran to prevent refugees escaping the war;

blockage of food aid in Uzbekistan for several weeks; use of troops disguised as humanitarian aid workers; US air strikes on the premises of humanitarian organisations; misdirected US air strikes resulting in the death of at least 1,000 civilians; US use of cluster bombs which, when unexploded, pose the same threat as anti-personnel mines; and the massacre of hundreds of prisoners of war in the north. Humanitarian organisations, encouraged by the American and British leaders to join the 'civilised' side, voiced little protest over these aspects of the military operation.

As the latest episode in a series of international military interventions that invoked humanitarian motives (although these motives are certainly secondary to the fight against 'terrorism') the war in Iraq represented the attainment by the international heavyweights of the power to do as they like by claiming their actions are dictated by security and morality. Unlike earlier interventions (Kosovo, Timor, Sierra Leone and Afghanistan), the invasion of Iraq was not decided in the context of massive violence against the population; the official reason was the need to disarm Iraq and thus prevent the possibility of Al-Qaida gaining access to 'weapons of mass destruction'. It is not the role of humanitarian actors to judge the relevance of the US-British thesis. Humanitarian action is peaceful by nature but not pacifist. Its actions are conducted within a framework of rules defined by international conventions on the use of force and the organisation of aid during armed conflict. It is the manner in which force is deployed rather than the resort to force *per se* that is of concern to humanitarian actors. To ask the military to respect the right of humanitarian organisations to deliver aid to non-combatants while denying its right to fight wars would be viewed as evidence of hostility. To refrain from judging the combatants' motives and goals can certainly be frustrating, but it is the price humanitarian organisations must pay if they are to gain access to the battlefields and assist all the victims, to whatever side they belong. There are very few exceptions to this rule but they include genocide, in which ends and means merge – the systematic and total extermination of an entire group of people who are denied the quality of being human.

Although humanitarian action remains neutral with regard to the motives that compel protagonists to kill each other, it does not remain so when they decide to attack non-combatants. The conduct of military operations in Iraq raises a number of questions in this respect. How is it possible to ensure a decisive victory and keep allied and civilian casualties to a minimum when the adversary, weakened by several defeats and more than a decade of sanctions, concentrates its troops in the largest urban centres? In other words, how do you drop vast quantities of explosives on the most densely populated zones in the shortest possible time and still spare non-combatants? To formulate the problem in this way while accepting the political necessity for a rapid victory is to face up to the impossibility of guaranteeing an outcome that totally respects the rules of war. Coalition forces had barely set foot on Iraqi territory before the American press was accusing them of entering a quagmire, and the international press was castigating American strategists for their inability to win the war in a few days.

Despite this pressure, it cannot be denied that effective measures were taken to spare the Iraqi population, but we must also stress their limitations. The

US-British offensive did not result in massive casualties or provoke a massive exodus and a major health disaster. But the preventive machine-gunning of any individual who might have posed a threat meets the criteria defining war crimes in its targeting of civilians and its disproportion to the feeble resistance offered by the enemy. Similarly, the use of cluster bombs in urban zones refutes the professed desire to spare civilian life. The reluctance of Washington and London to discuss these issues publicly is hardly surprising. But the lack of a concerted effort on the part of the anti-war camp, particularly states hostile to the US offensive, and the United Nations, to raise the issue of probable war crimes and call for an international inquiry indicates the point to which questions of the war's legitimacy override criticism of its conduct. This is one result of America's dominance of international relations: the US can enjoin the whole world to declare for or against one of its military initiatives; can sort the wheat from the chaff, punish the refractory, and impose silence regarding the limited but real crimes committed during the course of the operation itself.

The presentation becomes more sophisticated when the occupying power's responsibilities to the population (security, water, food, shelter, health care) are transformed into 'humanitarian aid' through the magic of the world's most powerful propaganda machine. Farce turns into deception when we learn that this peculiar form of 'humanitarian aid' is to be financed by Iraqi oil revenues. The ridiculous finally gives way to the sinister when bureaucratically-induced delays in the restoration of public services – essential in the aftermath of war – deprive the wounded and sick of medical care, thus aggravating the crisis in a society that is expected to feel liberated by the passage from a totalitarian regime to a foreign military dictatorship. The latest episode in the modern 'just' war saga is unfolding as this book goes to press. It seems little different from its predecessors (Kosovo, East Timor, Sierra Leone, Afghanistan): the frenzied affirmation of the right of the strongest to intervene militarily in a sovereign state overshadows the question of breaking the rules of war. The abusive employment of humanitarian aid can then offer the double advantage of justifying the war and suppressing the memory of its crimes.

Involvement

The second form of international reaction equally displays a formal preoccupation with the human cost of the crises under consideration. In 2001 North Korea, Sudan and Angola were the sites of the three largest UN assistance programs. Despite this massive humanitarian presence, the human cost of these crises remained high. In Angola, 3 million people trapped in the rebel zone received no assistance at all between 1998 and 2002, and tens of thousands died of starvation, disease or the violence directly inflicted by combatants of all sides. In Sudan and North Korea famine killed hundreds of thousands of civilians even though huge quantities of food aid were distributed.

In all three countries, international engagement took the form of a partisan involvement with the objective of containing the crisis within certain limits that would not challenge the interests of the most powerful states. The engagement benefited one camp and disadvantaged the other, but the 'international community' stopped short of offering its favoured party the critical support of military intervention. So-called humanitarian aid is so well adapted to the containment policy that it becomes its principal instrument. It matters little whether the powerful states favour an opposition party (the opposition to the Islamist regime in Khartoum), a party in power (the MPLA in Angola) or an internationally consensual political option like 'soft landing' in North Korea, the last Stalinist totalitarian regime. International aims are more concerned with containing the crisis, preferably within existing borders, than with bringing it to a rapid conclusion by a concerted military campaign against one of the protagonists.

Under these circumstances, the deployment of aid assumes greater importance and visibility because it is aimed at smoothing away the disastrous image of an international political system that is unable to prevent massacres, famines and epidemics. In many ways crisis management takes the form of a gigantic 'humanitarian' aid program organised in such a way as to primarily serve the interests of the parties favoured by the major powers. Extensive media coverage of the operation serves to allay public anxiety while civilian populations are in fact left to their executioners. In such situations aid is often abundant but inaccessible to those who most need it (as in Angola and North Korea) or becomes an important resource for local participants in the conflict through massive and institutionalised misappropriation (as in Sudan). Endangered populations are thus deprived of vital aid while their tormentors profit from it.

When an aid operation works to the advantage of a totalitarian regime, as it does in North Korea, it contributes to the maintenance of a system in which terror and extreme privation provoke the death of millions. Several million people are thought to have starved to death under the yoke of the Pyongyang regime in the late 1990s, during which time the regime was benefiting from one of the largest food aid operations ever mounted. Catherine Bertini, the former US Secretary for Agriculture and former head of the UN World Food Programme, led this operation to rescue a regime of terror, justifying it by the hollow promise to save starving Korean children. The tens of thousands of refugees driven into China by poverty and hunger attest to the slow destruction of part of the population because it was denied access to existing international aid. This did not stop Mrs Bertini from presenting the operation as an 'absolute success' that averted famine in North Korea. It is not difficult to see why the tens of thousands of refugees present along the Chinese border are ignored by the international community. They do not conform to this image of 'absolute success', and are therefore condemned to persecution by the Chinese police and forced repatriation to the Korean gulag.

Abstention

The recent revival of international activism in response to crises should not obscure the fact that the principal form of international reaction to conflicts with the most civilian casualties (Algeria, Colombia, Chechnya, Democratic Republic of Congo) is to refrain from intervention or to become involved in a marginal way. Because the violence suffered by populations is not considered an international political issue, the belligerents and local powers are free to practise every conceivable kind of cruelty and are in *de facto* possession of a veritable licence to kill. In such circumstances humanitarian action collides head-on with the mutual desire of the belligerents to wage total war that may lead to the extermination of entire groups of people. International aid is reduced or non-existent and has little impact given the prevalence and intensity of physical and social violence. The lack of international concern over the brutality of these conflicts makes it impossible to create the climate necessary for respect for non-combatants (civilians, wounded soldiers and prisoners) or ensure an effective distribution of aid. Worse still, the belligerents are often in a position to misappropriate, by violence, international aid resources which are then used to further violence.

Chechnya provides a good example of this abstention policy. In his novel *Alamut* Vladimir Bartol tells the story of Hassan Ibn Saba, chief of the Assassins sect, who – more than a thousand years before Osama bin Laden – was already offering martyrs the prospect of paradise. 'Nothing is true, everything is permitted' was the secret Hassan Ibn Saba, the Old Man of the Mountain, transmitted to his most faithful disciples. Vladimir Putin may have proclaimed his aversion to Islamism, but we should not be misled. The Russian federal army's campaign in Chechnya is the perfect illustration of the 'nothing is true, everything is permitted' doctrine conceived by an Islamist in the Middle Ages: encourage conflict by supplying arms to the adversary; stage deadly attacks on Russian soil and attribute them to terrorists; raze Grozny, the Chechen capital; bomb the country's inhabitants; rape and slaughter men and women; engage in trafficking of the living and the dead. Since 1994 at least 100,000 people are estimated to have been killed and 400,000 displaced out of a pre-war population of one million in this small republic, and all with the silent consent of the UN Security Council.

We cannot ignore the fact that there are conflicts in which mass violence is a secondary issue in negotiations between international bodies and belligerents. Some belligerents seem to benefit from a kind of limitless tolerance. The Algerian government, for instance, enjoys broad sympathy from the international powers, particularly France, in spite of its shared responsibility for the civil war that has lasted over ten years and counts 100,000 dead, 1.2 million displaced and 4,000 officially missing.

But it is probably in the Great Lakes region of Africa that the *laissez-faire* attitude to mass violence has reached the most dramatic levels since the 1990s. As the chapter on the Democratic Republic of Congo illustrates, the 'victims of no importance' in this conflict can probably be counted in millions. An American aid organisation, the International Rescue Committee, asserts – on the basis of questionable extrapolations (assuming an even distribution of events within large groups of dispersed peoples) – that 2.5 million people have died because of the war. Up to 350,000 were murdered between August 1998 and March 2001 in the eastern Congo, out of a population of about 20 million. If we add the million who died in the 1994 genocide, the hundreds of thousands killed in the Burundian civil war, and the 200,000 Rwandan refugees slaughtered in the former Zaire between 1996 and 1997, the total represents more than one tenth of the population of Burundi, Rwanda and the eastern part of the Democratic Republic of Congo.

A brief plea for an art of living

When the humanitarian spirit is stripped of the illusion that humanity is inexorably progressing toward an ideal society, it can actively resist the very human temptation to accept the death of part of our global community so that the 'common good' may prevail. The undeniable failure of the humanitarian project described in the chapters on individual countries in this book resides for many in the allegiance of humanitarian actors to institutional political authorities who have the power to condone human sacrifice, to divide the governed between those who should live and those who are expendable. The repeated failure of aid operations is due in great part to this 'alliance' – which, in reality, entails the submission of humanitarian concerns to political interests. The motor of this alienation, which each year deprives hundreds of thousands of people of aid vital to their survival, incorporates a multitude of gears. They may be economic (access to government funding for aid agencies), ideological (the attraction of a hypothetical universal morality) or bureaucratic (the aid system's defence of its own interests and sub-culture), but all contribute to aligning humanitarian action on the political axis and deflecting it from its responsibility – to save as many lives as possible. When humanitarian aid operations lose sight of their objective, they are not only ineffective for people in need, but they become embroiled in the production of political violence and exacerbate the human consequences they are supposed to relieve.

Given the power and violence of some political protagonists, the struggle is unequal and defeats are frequent for humanitarian action that is peaceful by nature. No illusion of a future ideal society will change this fact, but humanitarian action can still oppose the elimination of part of humanity by exemplifying an art of living founded on the pleasure of unconditionally offering people at risk of death the assistance that will allow them to survive. Doing so makes victories over the most lethal forms of politics possible. The 20,000 children saved from starvation by Médecins Sans Frontières in Angola in 2002 provide a shining example. Yet for world 'leaders', UN humanitarian agencies, the majority of NGOs and the media the emergency was at that time elsewhere.

SITUATIONS

PART I. INTERVENTION

1

EAST TIMOR
Better Late than Never

Gil Gonzalez-Foerster

The international management of the crisis in East Timor, the former Portuguese colony annexed by Indonesia in 1975, has been presented as an even greater success for the international community than the intervention in Kosovo. The landing of Australian Blue Helmets in Dili on 20 September 1999 resulted in the ending of the terror unleashed by anti-independence militias hostile to the prospect of a self-determination referendum. Three weeks after the wave of destruction and massacre that followed the ballot, most of the survivors were able to be protected by international forces and benefit from the humanitarian assistance dispensed by a relatively efficient cooperation between humanitarian organisations and UN troops. The operation demonstrated that an international intervention force provided with a clear mandate and the political and military means to fulfil it, and imbued with respect for the division of roles between humanitarian and military actors, could succeed in saving a great many lives.

Nonetheless, can we really talk of a 'huge success'? For over 20 years, the brutal occupation of East Timor aroused no reaction from the international community despite the Indonesian army's extermination of 35-43 percent of the island's population. The accession to independence was then driven at a forced march and ended in massive destruction, the predictable massacre of between one and two thousand people, and the deportation of several tens of thousands of Timorese to the western, Indonesian part of the island. Moreover, some humanitarian organisations (including Médecins sans Frontières) did not react to the extreme violence they witnessed in the refugee camps, where the iron discipline of former pro-Indonesia militias terrorised the 260,000 refugees and deportees held in large part against their will.

Indeed, it is difficult to share fully the optimism displayed by the UN Secretary-General when, at the very moment the Blue Helmets were landing at Dili, he opened the 54th session of the UN Assembly General by announcing a future in which 'systematic and massive violations of human rights – wherever they may take place – should not be allowed to stand.' It appears that the decisive involvement of the international community in Timor in 1999 did not symbolise a general 'revolution of moral concern' in international relations but was rather the result of a unique set of circumstances.

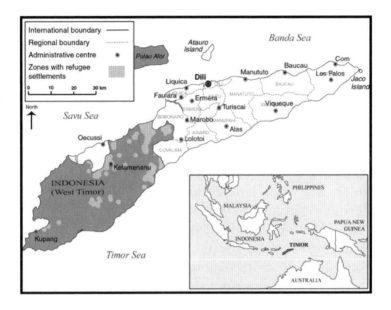

East Timor: another victim of the Cold War

After 450 years of Portuguese rule, several political movements formed in the 1970s in Dili, capital of the colony of *Timor Leste*. Led by elites of indigenous and mixed origins, they represented various forms of nationalist claims. Long neglected by its Portuguese masters, East Timor was a culturally and physically divided land that possessed barely 30 kilometres of tarred roads. The population was composed of twenty or so different ethno-linguistic groups dominated by local aristocracies. These aristocracies acted primarily as intermediaries for the colonial administration, had little contact with the urban elites, and did not share the nationalists' sentiments. Their political aspirations were chiefly limited to preserving respect for local identities and customs. When Portugal offered its colonies the possibility of exercising their right to self-determination after the 1974 revolution, immediate independence was not considered an option by any of the East Timorese political movements. A minority group advocated provisional attachment to Indonesia, which already exercised sovereignty over the western part of the island, a former Dutch colony. Other elements militated for a broader autonomy under Portuguese supervision. A third movement, the Marxist-oriented Revolutionary Front for an Independent East Timor (Frente Revolucionária do Timor-Leste Independente – FRETILIN), favoured independence after a transitional period of five to ten years. FRETILIN's ideas became popular in the more remote regions of the island and enabled the movement to win the 1975 by-elections, then consolidate its victory after a brief civil war. Taking over the administration left vacant by the precipitate departure of the Portuguese in August 1975, FRETILIN declared independence on 28 November 1975, much sooner than it had originally envisaged.

Asian communist regimes and former Portuguese colonies recognised East Timor's independence but Western powers and Indonesia refused to do so. Following the 1975 communist victory in Vietnam, the 'containment' of communism in Asia became a priority for Australia and the United States. Canberra and Washington supported the policy of General Suharto, the Indonesian leader, to annex the former colony. On 7 December 1975, Indonesian troops invaded East Timor which became, six months later, the '27th province' of Indonesia. Although the invasion of East Timor constituted a flagrant violation of international law, it only attracted subdued criticism from the United Nations whose Security Council was paralysed by the confrontation between the United States and the Soviet Union. Moreover, neither the USSR nor China had any desire to damage relations with Indonesia.

In East Timor the occupying troops faced armed resistance organised into the Armed Forces of National Liberation of East Timor (Forças Armadas de Libertação Nacional de Timor Leste – FALINTIL). The Indonesian army launched 'encircle and annihilate' operations and destroyed villages, agricultural land, and food stocks in an attempt to starve those suspected of supporting the resistance. Half the population was herded into concentration centres and suffered famine conditions described by the International Committee of the Red Cross as 'as serious as those of Biafra'. In the early 1980s, Indonesia launched two projects partially funded by the World Bank – the *transmigrasi,* which involved the settlement of thousands of Indonesian families on the island, and a family planning program designed to reduce the Timorese birth rate. Although the government failed in its military ambitions, the repression of the 1970s and 1980s left at least 180,000 dead. More realistic estimates put the figure at 250,000-300,000 or 35-43 percent of the population. In relative terms, it was the greatest ethnocide since the Second World War. The extreme violence used by Jakarta contributed to the political idea of an 'East Timorese people' ensuring the propagation of Catholicism and the Portuguese language, a feat that four centuries of domination had failed to achieve.

During the first 15 years of Indonesian occupation, the 'international community' avoided any reproof of Suharto's dictatorship, which was receiving substantial European and American economic, military, and diplomatic support. Australia officially recognised the annexation of East Timor in 1978, a decision that facilitated the resolution of a dispute over territorial waters and Jakarta's granting of oil exploitation rights in the Timor Sea eleven years later.

The East Timor question did not appear on the international agenda until the Cold War was over. As the Indonesian authorities began to allow foreign NGOs and journalists access to the officially 'pacified' province, militant separatists stepped up their actions in an attempt to internationalise the conflict. Trouble broke out in Dili when Pope John Paul II visited in 1989, and young Timorese activists organised protests in Australia and Jakarta. In November 1991 extensive media coverage of the massacre at the Santa Cruz cemetery in Dili (250 dead) finally compelled some countries to take measures against the Indonesian government. But although the Nobel Peace Prize was awarded to the Timorese separatist leaders Bishop Carlos Belo and José Ramos Horta in 1996, no effective action was taken until the Asian financial crisis of 1997 triggered the fall of Suharto in 1998.

The forced march to independence

Threatened by a popular uprising and abandoned by his American ally, President Suharto was forced to resign from office in May 1998. His successor, Bacharuddin Jusuf Habibie, inherited a bankrupt country sapped by corruption and nepotism and reeling from the Asian financial crisis. Street protests and pressure from international partners forced Habibie to initiate measures to democratise the regime and to radically alter course on the Timor question. East Timor had not been of strategic interest to the West since the end of the

Cold War, but it remained a thorny issue that continued to sour diplomatic relations with Jakarta.

Three months after Suharto's fall, Habibie opened UN-sponsored negotiations with Portugal in order to 'settle the Timor problem'. As the talks progressed, the Indonesian army revived its policy of terror in East Timor through indirect means, organising, arming and paying militias to terrorise all those in favour of independence. Witness testimony, reports and evidence have exposed murder, rape, torture, disappearances, and arbitrary arrests, and the close links between pro-integrationist militias and the Indonesian armed forces. This situation demonstrated the duality of power in Indonesia, divided between a pragmatic president pressured by the 'international community' and the armed forces determined to maintain control over the country – especially East Timor, where many officers had gained their first field experience and owned land and other assets.

Despite militia and army violence, Portugal and Indonesia signed an agreement in New York on 5 May 1999. The document provided for the organisation of a direct, secret, and universal referendum on self-determination that was to be conducted in an atmosphere 'free from intimidation, violence and interference by any party.' But it also stated that to guarantee these conditions, 'the Indonesian government will be responsible for the maintenance of peace and security in East Timor.' For the separatist leader José Ramos Horta, who was positive about the agreement even though it was not signed by any East Timorese, this was like 'asking Milosevic to guarantee the safety of the Kosovars.' In fact, the occupiers appointed themselves as guardians of the ballot and also defined the form it would take – the referendum would not address the question of independence but would allow the East Timorese to decide whether or not to accept autonomy within the Indonesian nation. At the beginning of June 1999, the UN Security Council agreed to set up a United Nations Mission in East Timor (UNAMET) to 'organise and conduct a popular consultation to take place on 8 August 1999'. Resolution 1246 stated that unarmed civil police would be deployed on the island to 'advise the Indonesian police' as well as 50 officers to liaise with the Indonesian armed forces.

The New York agreement and the arrival of the UN personnel had no effect on the behaviour of the militias or their Indonesian sponsors, and intimidation escalated in an attempt to prevent the referendum from taking place. The separatist leaders José Ramos Horta, Xanana Gusmão and Bishop Carlos Belo asked the UN to deploy an armed contingent but Jakarta immediately refused this measure. UNAMET complained to the Indonesian government that it was impossible for tens of thousands of East Timorese hidden in the mountains to register as voters, and denounced the systematic abuse of those in favour of independence. The situation continued to deteriorate in the run-up to the vote and the militias openly announced their intention of laying waste to the province should the separatists win. Nothing was done to avoid the confrontation: that would have entailed denouncing the Indonesian army and sending an international force to keep the peace, measures which would break the terms of the 5 May agreement.

Black September

Finally, on 30 August 1999, having been let down by the New York agreement and ignored when they voiced their fears about the threatened chaos, the East Timorese voted. More than 430,000 went to the 850 polling stations, some of them travelling on foot for many hours, to cast their votes in conditions of relative calm. The terror resumed the following day. In Dili, where all the ballot boxes had arrived despite the violence and intimidation, the black-clad men of the *Aitarak* militias seized control of the streets and set fire to buildings. Supported by Indonesian armed units, they harassed UNAMET personnel, humanitarian workers, and journalists with the apparent aim of driving out all foreign observers.

Kofi Annan gave the order to evacuate the territory but some UN staff refused and courageously tried to prevent the massacre of the Timorese who had taken refuge on their premises. The following day the UN proclaimed the overwhelming victory of the pro-independence vote – 98 percent of those registered had voted and 78.5 percent rejected the autonomy option. But the East Timorese did not get the chance to celebrate their liberation for they were too busy trying to save their lives. The thirteen militias supported by the Indonesian army unleashed a systematic campaign of destruction accompanied by extreme violence which, in the space of three weeks, led to between one and two thousand deaths, thousands of injuries, and many rapes. Almost all foreign nationals including staff from NGOs, humanitarian organisations, and the UN, were forced to leave the territory. Some Timorese managed to escape by sea but for tens of thousands, the only escape was into the mountains. More than 200,000 took refuge in remote jungle country, beyond the reach of the armed forces and militias, while 260,000 others fled or were deported to the Indonesian part of the island. Despite the predictability and gravity of the situation, there was no immediate reaction from the international community. The only concrete decision the Security Council took, on 8 September, was to send a mission to Jakarta in another attempt to persuade the Indonesian authorities to restore order in East Timor. The government responded by subjecting the territory to martial law and announced the despatch of another 1,400 soldiers and eight ships to help with the evacuation of refugees. The ships actually helped to accelerate the deportation of the Timorese.

On 9 September Washington suspended all military cooperation with Indonesia. The European Union declared an embargo on arms sales to the country, and the World Bank and IMF suspended their loans and froze economic cooperation for a year. Jakarta finally yielded. On 12 September President Habibie agreed to the despatch of a multinational force and, on 15 September, the Security Council passed Resolution 1264, which entrusted INTERFET (International Force for East Timor) with a mission to 'restore peace and security to East Timor, to protect and support UNAMET in carrying out its tasks and, within force capabilities, to facilitate humanitarian assistance operations.' Five days later the first Australian soldiers of INTERFET stepped onto the tarmac at Dili airport as the last Indonesian troops were leaving. The intervention force took its mandate seriously and conducted vigorous offensives against the militias still present in the territory, very much weakened by the retreat of their Indonesian sponsors.

Australia, fearing the escalation of a crisis that might lead to a massive influx of refugees, and Portugal, home to a powerful Timorese lobby, had been most active in lobbying their European and American partners to send a multinational force. But the 'international community', reluctant to send a military force without Jakarta's approval, had preferred to toy with economic sanctions while waiting for the government to yield.

Many apologists for this approach cited international legal norms prohibiting foreign intervention in sovereign states – although this had not prevented action being taken in Iraq, Somalia and the former Yugoslavia. According to the UN, however, Indonesia had no sovereignty over East Timor as its annexation in 1976 had never been ratified internationally. Australia was the only country to acknowledge Indonesia's '27th province' but this did not amount to international recognition. When the referendum took place on 30 August, East Timor was still, according to the UN, a Portuguese territory and still on its list of 'territories to be decolonised'. While Indonesia may have imposed *de facto* sovereignty over the years by force of arms, *de jure* sovereignty lay in the hands of the Portuguese.

Destruction, deportation and assistance

The INTERFET soldiers landed to find East Timor in ruins. Seventy to eighty per cent of its housing and infrastructure – administrative buildings, schools, health centres, water and electricity networks dating from the Indonesian period – had been systematically destroyed by militias bent on avenging East Timorese 'ingratitude' toward an Indonesian army that had 'generously contributed to the development' of their province. This deliberate physical destruction was accompanied by the desertion of Indonesian and pro-Indonesian civil servants in charge of public services. Many of them, particularly doctors, had begun to leave from May 1999.

Aid operations were quickly implemented and, contrary to previous experience, aid workers enjoyed relatively good relations with the international intervention forces, who had the support of the vast majority of the population. The Bosnian situation was not repeated in East Timor – the Blue Helmets did not use 'facilitate humanitarian assistance operations' as a shield to avoid their obligation to protect the East Timorese from militia threats. Unlike Somalia, they did not pay lip service to international humanitarian law and did not bomb hospitals. Unlike the American presence in Afghanistan some years later, they did not use so-called humanitarian activity to conduct a propaganda war. INTERFET lent its support to aid organisations (particularly in the transport of teams and material to crisis spots) while respecting the division of tasks and responsibilities between independent and impartial aid agencies on the one hand and armed forces inevitably involved in helping civilians on the other. Food aid from WFP, shelter from UNHCR, and rudimentary health services offered by emergency medical organisations averted a further crisis.

The situation was very different in the Indonesian part of the island, where insecurity reigned among the 260,000 East Timorese assembled there during the three weeks of 'Black September'. Only a small minority of the exiles were there because they had collaborated with the Indonesian occupiers and feared separatist reprisals.

Most had been forcibly deported by pro-Indonesian militias who then claimed that the 'flight' of tens of thousands of East Timorese invalidated the referendum result. The militias imprisoned these people in some 250 makeshift camps where they were subjected to close supervision and intense propaganda. They were constantly told that the situation in the East was uncertain; that men, women and children were separated from each other on their return; that exiles were treated as collaborators and executed; and that young girls were used as sex slaves by UN soldiers – forms of abuse that were actually the norm in militia-controlled camps. Furthermore, humanitarian aid dispensed by the Church, NGOs, the Red Cross, and the Indonesian government was usually misappropriated by the militias who used the 'humanitarian sanctuaries' of West Timor as launching pads for destabilisation operations in the eastern part of the island.

Despite restrictions that seriously hindered their independence of action and their ability to ensure the efficient distribution of aid, certain NGOs like Médecins Sans Frontières did not openly criticise the situation and came perilously close to being the health care auxiliaries to a system of terror. UNHCR on the other hand, adopted a much more forthright attitude. The UN agency went to great lengths – and even employed clandestine methods – to exfiltrate the deportees and pressured the Jakarta government to disarm the militias, exposing itself to harassment in the process. On 6 September 2000, three of its representatives were murdered in Atambua, an atrocity that forced the agency to suspend its operations and leave West Timor.

Jakarta had great difficulty restoring order in its own territory. When operating in East Timor the militias had been under the control of Indonesian forces but once across the border they were virtually autonomous. Nonetheless, 126,000 deportees had returned to East Timor by the end of 1999. The stream diminished in 2000 before surging in 2001 after the UN exerted pressure on Indonesia following the murder of the three UNHCR staff. There still remains 50,000 refugees in the western part of the island, some of whom have elected to stay there for fear of reprisals because of their past or recent collaboration with Indonesian authorities. Despite the reassurances offered by Xanana Gusmão when he addressed the refugees in April 2002, many former employees of the pro-Indonesian administration, participants in the repression campaigns of the 1970s and 80s, FRETILIN dissidents, and anti-independence militia fighters seem to feel more secure in Indonesian territory.

A World Bank protectorate

When the UN took over from the Indonesians it set up a transitional administration, UNTAET, to 'provide security and maintain law and order; establish an effective administration; assist in the development of civil and social services; ensure the coordination and delivery of humanitarian assistance, rehabilitation and development assistance; support capacity-building for self-government and assist in the establishment of conditions for sustainable development' (Security Council Resolution 1272). Although the country is of modest size – an area of 19,000 square kilometres and a population of about 750,000 – UNTAET's task is immense and involves some 8,000 peacekeeping troops, 1,350 civil police and 1,200 administrators. The mission was initially presided over by the Brazilian Sergio Vieira de Mello, a former UNHCR official and Under-Secretary-General for Humanitarian Affairs. The transitional administration is also supported by major specialised agencies including the World Bank (in partnership with the Asian Development Bank) and many NGOs. In total, more than 25,000 expatriates are participating in the reconstruction of East Timor. The transitional administration has set up parallel bodies in order to involve the East Timorese in its decisions. A National Consultative Council brings together seven members of FALINTIL's political wing, a representative of the Catholic Church, three former advocates of autonomy, and four representatives from UNTAET. Nonetheless, many Timorese are critical of the purely formal character of a consultative mechanism that seems to exist simply to ratify decisions taken by international administrators. The determination of 'priority needs' and estimates of their cost was entrusted to experts from the World Bank working with representatives from several UN agencies, the European Commission and five donor countries. The Bank actively participates in the definition of priorities, objectives, and the routes to take for reconstruction (it opposed, for example, Timorese requests to establish publicly-owned grain silos and abattoirs, arguing that any potentially profitable project should be given to the private sector), and assures respect for its directives through the control it exercises over institutional funding destined for NGOs.

Nine months after the establishment of UNTAET, the emergency phase was officially declared over. Although the public health system is still entirely dependent on international aid and WFP continues to ensure the distribution of food because of the slow resumption of agricultural activity, there is probably no further need for need for emergency humanitarian aid. A constituent assembly was elected in August 2001 and the first presidential elections were held on 14 April 2002. Xanana Gusmão was elected with 83 percent of the vote. He officially declared the independence of *Timor Loro Sa'e* on 20 May 2002.

Despite these developments, the island's administrative and economic reconstruction has been slow. Many East Timorese are resentful of the flagrant gap between the international apparatus and the funds available to it, and the amount of aid from which they effectively benefit. Apart from its political achievements, the immediate effect of the international presence has been to energise an 'aid economy' fuelled by a considerable income from expatriates (some estimates put the figure at USD 75 million a month, 15 times the budget of the East Timorese government). The hotel and restaurant sector is expanding but most import-export business is in the hands of Australian and Indonesian companies. As reconstruction continues, many projects will rely on foreign companies to the detriment of East Timorese labour and expertise. Moreover, the budding East Timorese state may find its viability threatened by the steamroller effect of massive 'development aid', which tends to impose its own agenda.

Such anxieties should not detract from the fact that INTERFET fulfilled the mission it was given. It was certainly supported by a clear mandate and firm political will. But its 'success' was chiefly due to favourable local circumstances – the vast majority of the population supported the troops sent to protect them, and the occupation forces and their militias were quick to abandon the tiny territory. This is the context that enabled soldiers and humanitarians to adhere to their respective obligations and responsibilities and actively contribute to improving the lives of the inhabitants. The reasons for international mobilisation on behalf of the East Timorese are more complex. The proximity of Australia; extensive media coverage of Indonesian repression and Timorese resistance; the disappearance of the 'communist threat'; the resurgence of human rights in diplomatic discourse; the West's intervention in Kosovo at almost the same time – all these factors certainly played a part. Moreover, the broadly shared conviction that the East Timorese had been victims of a historical wrong because Cold War priorities had denied them the right to self-determination – a right that had been granted to almost all former colonies – did much to encourage political recognition of the Timorese tragedy. Finally, the mobilisation of the 'international community' required no major sacrifices – Jakarta did not offer much resistance and abandoned a territory that Indonesians, with the exception of the military, had never regarded as part of historic 'Glorious Indonesia'. The deployment of INTERFET was, therefore, conducted in an environment that facilitated the accomplishment of its mandate. In other words, the circumstances that brought about this international commitment appear to be unique and in glaring contrast to those prevailing in Aceh and Irian Jaya, where the claims of the populations have no resonance in the 'international community'.

Bibliographical references

M. Cahen, 'Loro Sa'e, soleil levant archaïsant, ou signe de modernité à l'ère de mondialisation?', *Lusotopie* (2001), pp. 125-33.

G. Defert, *Timor Est. Le génocide oublié, droit d'un peuple et raison d'Etats*, Paris, L'Harmattan, 1992.

S. Dovert, 'Timor Loro Sa'e, un nouvel Etat à l'heure du village global?', *Lusotopie* (2001), pp. 327-45.

F. Durand, 'Timor Loro Sa'e: la destruction d'un territoire', *Lusotopie* (2001), pp. 215-32.

W. Maley, 'Australia and the East Timor Crisis: Some Critical Comments', *Australian Journal of International Affairs* 54, no.2 (2000), pp. 151-61.

W. Maley, 'The UN and East Timor', *Pacific Review* 12, no.1 (2000), pp. 63-76.

J. Taylor, *Indonesia's Forgotten War: The Hidden History of East Timor*, London, Zed Books, 1991.

2

SIERRA LEONE
Peace at any price

Fabrice Weissman

In 1991 Sierra Leonean rebels acting in the name of the Revolutionary United Front (RUF) rose up against the decaying regime in Freetown. The former British colony was then under the heel of a 'shadow state' dispossessed of its means of governing by powerful local elites engaged in the exploitation of the country's substantial mineral wealth. As the army proved incapable of repulsing the rebels, the Sierra Leonean government sought support from irregular militias and foreign mercenaries until, in 1997, the Economic Community of West African States (ECOWAS) sent a regional intervention force to Freetown with a mandate to 're-establish constitutional rule'. However, the West African troops were unable to put down a rebellion which was financed by the diamond trade and capitalized on the frustrations of a younger generation exploited by gem traffickers or denied the opportunity to participate in the urban economy.

The war was extremely brutal. The RUF practiced a policy of terror and resorted to the horrific mutilation of civilians to impose its domination, a tactic that was likewise employed by pro-government forces. The regional intervention troops were barely more respectful of international humanitarian law. Hundreds of thousands of Sierra Leoneans tried to escape the grip of the belligerents and sought refuge in the country's interior or by crossing its borders. Their efforts were in vain: the warring sides disdained the notion of territorial limits and the camps housing the internally displaced – wretched asylums – offered no protection from the violence.

After delegating the management of the crisis to ECOWAS for eight years, the United Nations was forced to take action following the disengagement of the West African troops who were exhausted by the cost of the intervention and its several military setbacks. But the 11,000 Blue Helmets who began arriving in Sierra Leone in November 1999 rapidly became bogged down. In May 2000, Britain sent 650 commandos to assist them, thus enabling a provisional end to the armed conflict. The 'ethical foreign policy' ardently defended by Tony Blair during his 1997 election campaign seemed to have found an opportunity to prove itself.

Nonetheless, this relative appeasement came at a price: in the name of the fight against the 'rebel hand choppers', tens of thousands of civilians were denied protection and access to humanitarian relief as this was judged contrary to the intervention forces' strategy for pacifying the country. A number of humanitarian organisations justified this strategy, thus trampling the very principle of impartiality on which their activity is founded. Moreover, the demonising of the RUF led to the overshadowing of the violence perpetrated by pro-government forces; it masked the social and political conflict that fuelled the rebellion. Finally, the return to peace was partly due to the expulsion of many combatants who subsequently found employment in the war that was once again raging in Liberia and which spread to Ivory Coast in 2002.

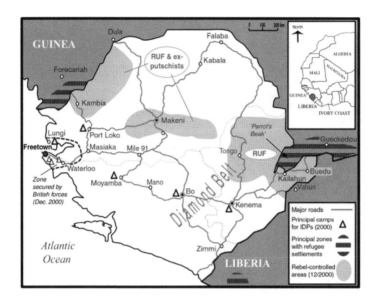

The destabilisation of a 'shadow-state'

The Sierra Leonean conflict is generally presented as an off-shoot of the Liberian civil war. It was with the help of Charles Taylor, at that time engaged in a merciless struggle to conquer Liberia by armed force, that Sierra Leonean rebels launched a revolt in eastern Sierra Leone in March 1991. The insurgents proclaimed themselves the Revolutionary United Front (RUF). For Taylor, the RUF was a means of destabilising a country he regarded as hostile due to its participation in the West African intervention force deployed in Liberia for the purpose of preventing his accession to power. The RUF was also an auxiliary force that allowed the future Liberian president to increase security along a border harbouring the rear bases of a rival faction (ULIMO) and containing large diamond deposits. The RUF rapidly seized the east of the country as well as the main mining areas.

The ease with which the rebels routed president Joseph Momoh's regular army revealed the collapse of the Sierra Leonean state. From independence to the mid-1980s, Sierra Leone's government elites had been appropriating the main natural resources (diamonds, gold, rutile, bauxite), bypassing the administration through informal alliances with foreign companies linked to the Lebanese diaspora living in the country. On his accession to power in 1985, Momoh had taken possession of a 'shadow-state', one unable to control mining profits which had passed into the hands of powerful local economic and political actors. The unjust sharing of diamond revenues had also fuelled vigorous opposition among young Sierra Leoneans, who were exploited by mine owners and excluded from government patronage.

Despite hastily boosting the regular army's strength from 3,000 to 14,000 men in 1991, the government was ill-placed to stem the rebels' advance. Under-equipped, badly paid, and poorly motivated, many government soldiers preferred to engage in pillaging and exploiting diamond deposits. The RUF, by contrast, targeted Lebanese merchants involved in gem trafficking, hence initially garnering the sympathy of some rural mineworkers and marginalised urban intellectuals. For this younger generation, which had broken with the traditional social order and been exploited by the diamond companies or marginalised in the urban economy, the rebellion was an attractive cause. Seduced by the RUF's syncretic revolutionary ideal – reinterpretation of tradition coupled with socialist notions – and its virulent denunciation of the political and economic oppression of which the young generation felt victimised, many joined of their own free will. However, the RUF grew rapidly into a socio-martial body that resorted to forced recruitment and acts of terror that differed little from the caricature promulgated in the media. Exasperated by the negligence and corruption of their superiors, a group of young officers overthrew president Momoh in April 1992. Despite enlisting young fighters on a massive scale, they proved no more able than their predecessor to repel the rebels, who reached the gates of Freetown at the beginning of 1995. The RUF's advance was halted at the last moment by the intervention of mercenaries, first Nepalese and then South African (from the company Executive Outcomes), hired in the first quarter of 1995 in exchange for mining concessions.

With the RUF driven back towards the Liberian border, the military agreed under international pressure to organise presidential elections. The poll, confined to government-controlled zones representing only some 25 percent of the electorate, was held in a climate of extreme violence. The RUF responded to candidate Ahmad Tejan Kabbah's slogan, 'The future is in your hands', with a campaign of mutilation, amputating the arms or forearms of dozens of civilians. The maiming was imitated by government soldiers, nicknamed 'sobels' by the population due to their proclivity for passing themselves off as rebels when looting or carrying out violent acts. Kabbah, a former United Nations official and the favoured candidate of the international community, won the elections of 15 March 1996 and was installed as the 'democratically elected president of Sierra Leone'.

Kabbah consolidated his economic and political positions in Freetown by entrusting the administration of reconquered areas to mining companies operating under the protection of Sierra Leonean branches of Executive Outcomes. Some of the firms created local NGOs to develop social services in the areas where they mined. Claiming to represent 'civil society', some of these NGOs managed to obtain donor government funding by subscribing to slogans popular among them such as 'building self-sustaining local capacity', 'micro-projects for peace', and 'encouraging women's empowerment'.

In January 1997 President Kabbah was forced to part company with Executive Outcomes, who were too expensive and regarded as undesirable associates by the World Bank. Distrustful of a regular army that had been extensively 'sobelised', Kabbah replaced the mercenaries with village militias – the *Kamajor* (traditional hunters) self-defence groups that had started in 1991-2 to resist acts of violence from all quarters. The presidential support they received was to the detriment of the army, and the military seized power in a coup on 25 May 1997. Having been allied with the RUF in the fight against Kabbah and his associates, the army reached an agreement with the rebels, and members of the RUF were named to ministerial posts.

Internationalisation of the conflict

This new turn of events led the 'international community' to become increasingly involved in the conflict. The coup was firmly condemned by the Economic Community of West African States (ECOWAS), which imposed an embargo on the junta and entrusted ECOMOG – its armed wing deployed in Liberia – with the mission to 'restore the constitutional order' of Sierra Leone. The end, albeit temporary, of the Liberian conflict in 1996 allowed the Nigerian-led West African intervention force to shift its military presence to Sierra Leone. The regional organisation's entry into the fray provoked an ambiguous reaction from the United Nations. In October 1997 the Security Council affirmed its 'unreserved' support for the ECOWAS initiative, but without formally authorising recourse to force by the West African troops. Moreover, it imposed a series of sanctions against Freetown, including a ban on the supply of arms to any of the parties to the conflict, including ECOMOG. In violation of the ban, Britain employed the services of a private security firm to equip Kabbah's partisans and the West African force. Unfortunately humanitarian action was not helped by special efforts of this kind; the international embargo affected food and medical shipments to the country, touching the whole population of Sierra Leone.

Assisted by British diplomatic and military support, ECOMOG launched an offensive against Freetown in February 1998. The rebels, accompanied by the military putschists, were driven back to their strongholds in the north-east, perpetrating countless acts of violence against civilians and humanitarian organisations along the way. Kabbah resumed his place at the head of the mining concessions archipelago that served him in lieu of territorial administration. In the absence of foreign mercenaries, defence of the government zones was assured by the *Kamajors* and ECOMOG. The Security Council congratulated itself after the event on the West African troops' success. But western states balked at financing ECOMOG directly, fearing that it would support the Nigerian military regime and be linked to an intervention force whose disregard for international humanitarian law was common knowledge.

In a final effort to put an end to the conflict and seize the diamond-rich areas, ECOMOG attacked the rebel strongholds in the north-east of the country in December 1998. But they met a violent counter-offensive by the RUF and former military putschists, who occupied Freetown for a few days at the beginning of 1999. The devastating battles left between 3,000 and 5,000 dead. To the violence and cruelty of the rebels was added the brutality of ECOMOG forces, who massacred prisoners of war and suspected rebels after bombarding the suburbs of the capital with heavy artillery.

This episode, together with the mounting human and financial cost of the intervention, led the civilian Nigerian government that took power in 1999 to consider withdrawing from ECOMOG. This prospect compelled Kabbah to sign a new peace agreement with the RUF in Lomé on 7 July 1999. It provided for the disarmament and demobilisation of the troops, the establishment of a new national army, and the formation of a coalition government that would bestow honours and emoluments on some rebel officers.

The United Nations, which had hitherto contented itself with an observer's role, decided in October 1999 to dispatch a peacekeeping force to Sierra Leone. They entrusted UNAMSIL (United Nations Mission in Sierra Leone) with the task of supporting the coalition government to ensure that the peace process unfolded smoothly. Its mandate referred to Chapter VII of the United Nations charter authorising the use of force, in particular for 'the protection of civilians under imminent threat of physical violence'. When the first contingent of

11,000 Blue Helmets disembarked in Freetown in November 1999, ECOMOG started to withdraw.

The peace process soon bogged down. Only the government forces agreed to be demobilised and reincorporated into the new national army. In a tense atmosphere UNAMSIL, despite insufficient operational resources, set about deploying in May 2000 in the diamond-rich areas held by the RUF and the former military junta. This operation provoked new rebel offensives. Seven peacekeepers were killed and five hundred others taken hostage. Alarmed by rumours of an imminent rebel attack on Freetown, the United Nations urged the humanitarian organisations to evacuate the capital. Faced with a wave of panic and the rout of UNAMSIL, the United Kingdom dispatched an expeditionary force of 650 men to support the new governmental army (on a bilateral basis). The British commandos secured Freetown and helped the peacekeepers free their captured colleagues and continue their mission.

Confronted with this new military situation and growing internal divisions, the RUF adopted a more peaceful stance. This change was also influenced by the international condemnation directed towards Charles Taylor for his continuous support of the rebels since 1991. In July 2000 the Security Council ordered an embargo on the export of Sierra Leonean diamonds, before blacklisting Liberia the following year. A final ceasefire agreement between the government and the rebels was signed in November 2000. At the end of 2001, the government army, still supported by British soldiers and followed by UNAMSIL (which now numbered 17,500 men), deployed throughout the country. Despite frequent skirmishes between the

Kamajors and the RUF, UNAMSIL announced the demobilisation of some 45,000 combatants in January 2002, which allowed Kabbah to declare the war officially over.

The return of peace was, however, only relative. While most of Sierra Leone's territory was now safer, the areas bordering Guinea and Liberia remained subject to incursions by armed groups in Kailahun district that looted and forcibly recruited combatants. Above all, the conflict continued in Liberia. Anti-Taylor factions, supported by Guinea and Britain, made forays into the Lofa region, and RUF soldiers joined Taylor's men in its defence. In fact, the pacification of Sierra Leone was made possible by the transfer of the most implacable combatants to Liberia and the rest of the region: the RUF, former military putschists, and *Kamajors* who had not been incorporated into the new army found places on one side or the other of the front lines of the Liberian conflict or in the Ivorian conflict from 2002.

The Special Court for Sierra Leone

In 1999 the United States and Britain advocated an amnesty for Sierra Leonean war criminals in order to facilitate the signing of new peace agreements. For Susan Rice, then American Assistant Secretary of State for Africa, 'peace is more important than justice'. The Lomé Agreements of July 1999 included a general amnesty for crimes committed since March 1991. This clause, totally at odds with international law and growing initiatives to crack down on international crimes, was not recognised by the United Nations.

The United States and Britain had a change of heart following the rupture of the peace agreement and the RUF's capture of 500 peacekeepers in May 2000. The judicial weapon then served in a strategy to politically eliminate the RUF's leader and induce the emergence of alternative, more conciliatory, rebel representatives. On 14 August 2000, the Security Council called for the creation of a special court responsible for punishing crimes against humanity, war crimes, and some common law crimes as defined by Sierra Leonean legislation (UN Resolution 1315).

Officially established on 16 January 2002 by an agreement between the Freetown government and the United Nations, the special court for Sierra Leone serves on an ad hoc basis like the international courts for the former Yugoslavia and Rwanda. It differs from them in being made up of both national and international judges. Furthermore, it was not imposed, but rather negotiated with the government. Its competence covers crimes committed in Sierra Leone since 30 November 1996, the date of the first peace agreement between the Freetown government and the RUF.

Highly political in origin and uncertain in practice due to a shaky financial and organisational basis, the court will have a hard time establishing its credibility and proving its independence from the US and Britain. At present, its chief prosecutor, David Crane, former Pentagon National Security Director, has not attempted to do so. Considering that he is charged with investigating an 'international criminal affair' having as its 'principal stake' the diamond traffic, he charged Charles Taylor on 5 June, obliging him to abandon peace negotiations that he had started that day with his principal opponents. 'The negotiations can continue, but without the presence of the accused' declared David Crane to the press, while Monrovia plunged anew into chaos.

The logic of terror

Contrary to a widely held view, the RUF was not a conglomeration of drunken, drugged fighters giving free rein to their morbid impulses. Their chain of command was far better structured than that of their Liberian (and even governmental) counterparts. It was controlled by two or three commanders-in-chief (such as Sam Bockarie) who, at various times, controlled the arms supply networks and channels for marketing diamonds (i.e. who were connected in some degree or other to Charles Taylor).

Backed by mining revenues and resources furnished by the Liberian president, the RUF's war economy was able to dispense with any popular support. Terror played a central role in organising the rebel zones. These were inhabited by villagers who had been unable to flee the RUF's advance, by the extended families of combatants (whose wives had often been abducted or forced into marriage), and by prisoners captured in government-held zones during armed raids. The latter constituted a servile workforce, exploited as slaves in the mining areas or as domestic, or even technical, staff at the rebel bases. The RUF lacked competent people capable – as was required in Kailahun district – of running its mechanical maintenance workshop, the officers' clinic, or the several schools it made a point of maintaining. Doctors, nurses, teachers, and qualified mechanics, all abducted from government zones, enjoyed a markedly higher status than other captives or residents, who were subject to the whims of the combatants. The latter could prove extremely cruel. Many soldiers had been forcibly recruited at a very young age and subjected to a brutal process of socialisation as fighters that tested both their endurance and their capacity to administer death and suffering.

The RUF lived in a situation of near autarchy, content to pillage from the government zones those resources it could not obtain from Taylor. Curiously, public infrastructure in rebel territory was not dismantled with a view to possible resale, but subjected to meticulous, almost psychotic, destruction. As if to demonstrate the combatants' resentment of the symbols of a modernity that excluded them, water towers were pulverised with rocket launchers, administration buildings and health facilities wrecked in a fury, and electric distribution networks methodically demolished. Civilians and combatants alike lived in a landscape of total devastation strewn with military debris, where food shortages and a lack of medical care were the norm. Health conditions were deplorable, including those for wounded or sick soldiers. Only officers could enjoy a modicum of care.

The RUF's behaviour towards populations living in government-held zones was every bit as violent, but different in nature: looting and burning villages, attacking displaced persons' camps, amputating, raping, and abducting or killing men, women and children. The aim of these practices was to drive away rural populations living on the fringes of rebel strongholds in order to create a protective no-man's-land. Further into government areas they sought to sap the confidence of Sierra Leoneans in a government that was unable to ensure their safety.

Yet the RUF did not have a monopoly on terror, far from it. The 'sobels' who, following the 1997 putsch, had turned into a faction allied to the rebels, adopted a markedly similar mode of operation. The *Kamajors* also recruited child soldiers and used the same techniques as their opponents. They burnt villages, killed, wounded, and mutilated civilians suspected of links to the RUF. With less of a foothold in the diamond economy than the other factions, the *Kamajors* had a greater tendency to engage in extortion and pillage, especially of displaced persons. Although the mutilations were habitually ascribed to the RUF, a significant number of them were the work of pro-government forces. Lastly, following its bitter defeat of 1999, ECOMOG displayed extreme violence towards non-combatants during the recapture of Freetown: wounded rebels were executed in their hospital beds, young adolescents – invariably suspected of being insurgents – were tortured and murdered, and civilian neighbourhoods were bombarded indiscriminately. As in Liberia, ECOMOG was also involved in diamond trafficking.

Encircled by violence

Nearly half a million inhabitants left their homes during the war, taking refuge mainly in Guinea and Liberia, or moving elsewhere within the country. Most of them came from rebel-controlled territory or the combat zones. In February 2002 the United Nations counted 140,000 displaced persons sheltering in camps. Several thousand more remained hiding in the forests to escape the combatants, or found refuge in villages in the governmental zone. OCHA, which was theoretically mandated to safeguard the displaced persons' right to protection and assistance, left that task to a state body, the NCRRR (National Commission for Reconstruction, Resettlement and Rehabilitation). This commission in turn entrusted the running of the camps to humanitarian organisations whose professionalism was sometimes debatable. The growing bureaucratisation of humanitarian work tended to confine foreign aid workers to supervisory tasks that kept them at a distance from the populations they were supposed to be helping. Their only link with the displaced people often came down to more or less regular contacts with a camp's 'chairman' or 'committee', who were appointed under unclear circumstances and whose representation was questionable. Responsible for registering displaced persons and allocating distribution cards that entitled them to food and non-food items (such as shelter materials, kitchen utensils, and blankets), the committees and their chairmen regularly behaved like local potentates, cheerfully diverting humanitarian aid towards their own supporters. Hence, although figures for the number of beneficiaries were systematically inflated, many did not receive the aid to which they were entitled unless they obtained a distribution card by yielding to the various demands of the 'big men'. The granting of sexual favours and submission to all sorts of forced labour proved to be, for the poorest, a common means of buying their survival.

Exposed to social violence in the camps, the displaced also suffered physical violence from combatants. On several occasions, displaced camps were targeted by rebel offensives, and they remained open to infiltration by armed men (such as *Kamajors*, or 'sobels') who engaged in all sorts of extortion and brutality. Flight abroad then became the last way out.

In August 2000 UNHCR estimated that 330,000 Sierra Leonean refugees were living in Guinea, mainly in the districts of Guékédou and Forecariah. Settled near the border, they were regularly harassed by the RUF. Moreover, the support provided by the Guinean authorities to groups hostile to Liberia's president (such as LURD, discussed in the Liberia chapter) transformed the region into a battle zone. From 1998 onwards, armed elements coming from Sierra Leone and Liberia launched several offensives against the camps and the Guinean forces. The confrontations culminated in September 2000 with an attack on Macenta by a coalition comprising Guinean rebels, members of the RUF, and Liberian fighters. Guinea's president, Lansana Conté, then accused the refugees of causing the insecurity, as well as smuggling and spreading AIDS. He encouraged his fellow citizens and the police to flush out the 'criminals' hiding among them. Militias attacked the camps (several of which were burned and abandoned by their inhabitants), violently confronting the Sierra Leoneans and accusing them of sympathising with the RUF which they had, in fact, spent their last energies escaping.

From September 2000 to mid-2001, the 100,000 to 250,000 refugees in the 'Parrot's Beak' (see map) were largely inaccessible to humanitarian organisations. In addition to obstacles posed by Guinean forces engaged in anti-insurgency operations in Liberia and Sierra Leone, pro-Taylor factions targeted UNHCR and NGOs for their indirect support for LURD dissidents who were using the Liberian refugee camps as sanctuaries, rendering it too dangerous for aid workers. The refugees who settled in towns such as Conakry or Nzérékoré were not spared the fate of their compatriots, falling victim to systematic search operations that turned into pogroms.

UNHCR's attitude in Guinea reflected the priorities of its government donors: to prevent the conflict spreading to Guinea and to strengthen President Conté's regime. Faced with enormous funding problems, UNHCR delegated the bulk of its assistance mandate to local NGOs. These were not only less expensive than international agencies, but were also supposed to ensure the 'sustainability' of UNHCR's investments by strengthening the capabilities of its local partners ('capacity building'). This policy had two consequences: it distanced international NGOs from the context, and produced a system of patronage that engendered corruption because most of the Guinean NGOs were sponsored by local politicians looking for funds. Like in the displaced camps, the poorest resorted to forced labour and prostitution to obtain the basics to survive. UNHCR's failure was even greater with regard to its mandate to protect refugees. Insufficient funding and international pressure on the Guinean government left UNHCR unable to transfer refugees to camps a safe distance from the border until the end of 2001. The only option seriously considered for ensuring their safety was to send them back to Sierra Leone.

Yet UNHCR's repatriation policy was dictated less by the evolution of security conditions in Sierra Leone than by the pacification policy envisaged by the various foreign intervening parties. In 1998 UNHCR encouraged the return of 'qualified Sierra Leoneans' to support the Kabbah government's reinstatement following the ousting of the junta. One year later, UNHCR interrupted the first large-scale attempt to move the refugees from the border shortly after the signing of the Lomé agreements in July 1999. Despite the serious instability that continued in the country, UNHCR launched a repatriation program whose timetable replicated that of the peace process. In UNHCR's eyes, 'the return of the refugees constitutes a vital part of the peace process' and therefore deserved to be encouraged. It seemed to matter little if the refugees were sent into the arms of the RUF or near the front lines where they would have to suffer the final convulsions of the conflict.

Programs for the repatriation and resettlement of displaced persons and refugees initiated after the signing of the last peace agreements in November 2000 also conformed to this logic. Carried out in haste to ensure their completion in time for the elections planned for 2002, they failed to provide advance information to the people concerned on the physical and security conditions awaiting them at their places of origin. The displaced persons and refugees were sent back to destroyed villages lacking health facilities and access to drinking water and sometimes exposed to residual insecurity. They were 'encouraged' to return by suspensions of food distributions and the sudden closure of some camps. Moreover, the people were transported in appalling conditions before being deposited, sometimes at a distance of several days' walk from their final destination.

The bias of the international community

International management of the displaced persons and refugees was emblematic of the way in which humanitarian considerations were set aside by the 'peacemakers' in the name of the moral superiority of their aim: the fight against rebel 'barbarity'. In 1997-8 the embargo aimed at ostracising the military junta extended in practice to humanitarian aid, thus depriving the Sierra Leonean people of vital food distribution for a period of several months. Similarly, the provision of emergency aid in the rebel strongholds was used as a negotiating tool by the United Nations from the end of 1998 onwards. Donors and UN agencies pressured the

RUF to conform to the various peace agreements by making the implementation of vital aid programs subject to the disarmament of the rebel fighters. The very few organisations providing basic aid inside RUF territory after 1998 had to circumvent the vindictive manoeuvres of the 'humanitarian community', which opposed their intervention in the name of 'ensuring that the peace process proceeds smoothly'.

It was, of course, legitimate to question the sense of operating an aid program in rebel areas subjected to a reign of terror. Aid organisations had to ask themselves whether it was possible to help populations in RUF zones without significantly strengthening the system of domination oppressing them. It was imperative that it be discussed in light of successes and failures encountered in negotiating humanitarian space with the rebels. But this was a completely different train of thought from one that refused *a priori* to assist populations in RUF zones for fear of compromising an uncertain peace process. Peace was certainly a highly defensible project from a political point of view. But this did not make it one that could oblige aid organisations to discriminate between 'good' and 'bad' victims – between Sierra Leoneans who deserved to be saved and others whom it was permissible, indeed desirable, to sacrifice in the hope of attaining peace in the future. Humanitarian aid cannot submit to such political judgments without calling into question the basic principle of impartiality underpinning its very *raison d'être*.

The aid bodies were drawn into the political settlement on a massive scale. This was facilitated by their adoption of the binary interpretation of the crisis promoted by Kabbah and all the foreign intervening parties. The international community considered that the former United Nations official, elected by 25 percent of the electorate in the midst of a civil war – and whose territorial administration was based on an archipelago of mining concessions and his coercive power over the goodwill of his foreign partners – represented the 'democratic and legitimate government' of Sierra Leone, and as such deserved to be supported. The continued violence allegedly stemmed from the 'barbarity' of the RUF, which was just a pack of psychopathic bandits subservient to Taylor and with which negotiation was impossible. Seen in this way, the violence was exclusively attributable to the rebels, as was suggested by the staging of 'RUF atrocities' in the Murray Town displaced camp in Freetown. Containing several hundred amputees – not all of whom were victims of the RUF – this camp was an obligatory site on the itinerary of all international journalists and diplomatic delegations. This organised display of suffering provokes a feeling of malaise at its use as propaganda.

The fact nonetheless remains that the wide media coverage given to this Manichean interpretation of the conflict had two positive consequences. First, it impelled the United Nations to abandon the pusillanimity that had led it to delegate management of the crisis to a regional intervention force without even providing it with logistical or financial resources or a legal framework for intervention. The international indignation aroused by the violent battles around Freetown in January 1999 forced the United Nations to contemplate ECOMOG's retreat. The Security Council could not abandon the 'democratically elected government of Sierra Leone' to the RUF's 'barbarity' without inflicting a fresh blow on its own credibility. The UN's failures in Somalia and Angola, and its passivity during the Rwandan genocide, had pushed the Security Council to look for an opportunity to reaffirm its commitment to Africa, hence the deployment of UNAMSIL, the United Nations' biggest peacekeeping operation up until then. Second, the media coverage of 'RUF atrocities' had encouraged Britain to become decisively involved in its former colony. On assuming power in 1997, the Labour government vowed to break with its predecessor's foreign policy by endowing its international action with what the then foreign secretary, Robin Cook, termed an 'ethical dimension'. Diplomatic expression of the 'third way' promoted by New Labour did not involve difficult issues such as cutting back on arms exports, radically changing Britain's attitude towards China or Russia, or abandoning the neoliberal credo of its development aid. Instead, defence of the 'democratically elected government' of Sierra Leone against the 'barbarian hordes of the RUF' provided a golden opportunity to translate this 'ethical foreign policy' into action. By dispatching an expeditionary force to support the Kabbah government at a time when UNAMSIL was dangerously bogged down, British diplomacy killed two birds with one stone: it gave substance to the 'ethical dimension' of New Labour's foreign policy, while simultaneously allowing the United Nations to save face and carry its mission through to a successful conclusion.

There is no question that the marked improvement in security conditions in Sierra Leone was made possible by the decisive action of the British government and the deployment of UNAMSIL. Today, order reigns in most of the country and nearly all the camps for internally displaced persons have been closed. Many Sierra Leoneans have returned to their places of origin. Those

who remain away include 50,000-70,000 refugees in
Guinea, internally displaced persons who settled and
rebuild their lives in host villages, and some inhabitants
of Guinean and Liberian border areas who are afraid to
return due to continued cross-border incursions.
Substantial international aid had allowed the civilian
government to gradually take charge of the country,
supported by UNAMSIL specialists who are present in
every ministry.

But the Sierra Leonean security forces are still highly
dependent on foreign assistance: a British officer
oversees the police force, and the new national army
that was trained by Great Britain is proving unable on its
own to offer any resistance to the armed men who cross
the border in the district of Kailahun. The announced
withdrawal of the UNAMSIL Blue Helmets, whose
numbers are to be reduced from 16,000 to 2,000
between now and the end of 2003, gives grounds for
fearing a marked deterioration in security conditions.
The dominance of Kabbah and his party in the new
administration has provoked anger among other Sierra
Leonean political figures, some of whom could rearm in
order to reassert their demands for inclusion in the
political process.

Lastly, however justified the British and UN
interventions may have been, it is regrettable that the
'just war' declared against the RUF led to silence over
the violent abuses committed by the various pro-
government forces. It is equally regrettable that the 'just
war' entailed the subordination of aid operations to the
international strategy for settling the conflict. The fate
reserved for the Sierra Leonean refugees in Guinea, the
displaced persons, and the populations of the RUF
zones was appalling. Lastly, it is pertinent to ask whether

the international community's 'success' in Sierra Leone was not achieved at the expense of the destabilisation of neighbouring countries, like Ivory Coast and Liberia, which have become an arena where civilians are at the mercy of West Africa's most implacable combatants.

Bibliographical references

R. Abrahmsen & P. Williams, 'Ethics and Foreign Policy: the Antinomies of New Labour's "Third Way" in Sub-Saharan Africa', *Political Studies*, 49 (2001), pp. 249-64.

W. Reno, *Corruption and State Politics in Sierra Leone*, Cambridge University Press, 1995.

P. Richards, *Fighting for the Rain Forest: War, Youth and Resources in Sierra Leone*, Oxford, James Currey, 1996.

P. Williams, 'Fighting for Freetown: British Military Intervention in Sierra Leone', *Contemporary Security Policy*, 22-3 (2001), pp. 140-67.

3

AFGHANISTAN

From 'Militant Monks' to Crusaders

François Calas & Pierre Salignon

Twelve years elapsed in Afghanistan between the departure of Soviet troops and the arrival of American forces, a period during which conflict continued to rage. The disinterest of the international community for a region that lost its strategic interest with the end of Soviet occupation in 1989 left the field open to regional powers. Playing on rivalries among local 'warlords', these powers fuelled a civil war that took a large toll on civilians.

The arrival of the Taliban in Kabul in September 1996 brought the population a semblance of respite. But the re-establishment of public order by the 'militant monks' was accompanied by the imposition of an ultra-religious moral order that was particularly oppressive for women. Furthermore, the conflict gradually became reorganised along political, ethnic and religious lines, leading to a resurgence of identity-related violence. Combined with the effects of several years of drought, the violence created serious food shortages and contributed to the massive displacement of several million Afghans both within the country and across its borders.

It was not until after the attacks of 11 September 2001 that intervention in Afghanistan by Western powers went beyond a token condemnation of the mullahs' 'obscurantism' that implicitly avowed Western 'moral superiority'. A vast 'coalition for good' was assembled to support the American riposte to the terrorist attacks and the overthrow of the repressive regime. The coalition called upon humanitarian organisations to join its side – without, however, itself showing any great respect for the laws of war. The downfall of the Taliban regime may have brought fresh hope to the great majority of Afghans but the international dimensions of the new war meant that the local conflict was sidelined rather than resolved. Beyond Kabul the political void created by the eviction of the Taliban was soon filled by the 'warlords' who regained their old fiefdoms and revived their predatory rivalries.

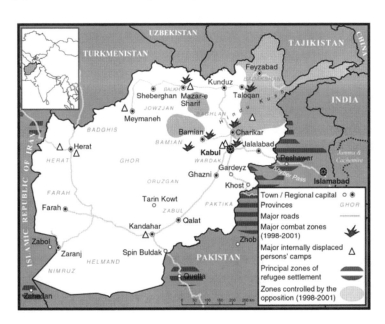

From warlords to the Taliban

In February 1989, after 11 years of war, the last Soviet units left Afghanistan. A million Afghans had lost their lives, a third of the population had fled abroad (mainly to Pakistan and Iran) and hundreds of thousands of rural inhabitants had left their villages to find refuge on the outskirts of the towns. The Red Army left behind it a country in ruins and a disintegrated society. In this devastated landscape, radical Islamism took root and rapidly gained ground. A product of the Soviet war's inordinate violence, Islamic fundamentalism obtained sufficient resources from Pakistan, Saudi Arabia and the United States to assert itself as a major political force.

Far from leading to a cessation of hostilities, the Soviets' departure intensified competition among local factions and commanders, as well as the struggle for influence among regional powers. Decimated by the communist regime, traditional notables (*ulemas*, landowners, tribal aristocracies) saw their authority challenged by young commanders whose power rested on their weapons and their skill at establishing links abroad. Heading politico-military solidarity networks, they engaged in endless battles aimed not so much at conquering the state but at maintaining and extending their power at the local level.

Exploiting the divisions between factions, Mohammad Najibullah's communist regime managed to hold on to power until March 1992, when it was overthrown by a coalition of Tajik, Uzbek and Hazara resistance fighters who seized Kabul. The Pashtun leaders thus found themselves excluded from central government, which they had monopolised almost continuously for nearly three hundred years. Some of them allied themselves with Gulbuddin Hekmatyar's predominantly Pashtun Hezb-e Islami party which was trying to dislodge the new Tajik-based government of Burhanuddin Rabbani and Ahmad Shah Massoud. Rashid Dostum's Uzbek troops and the Hazara factions took part in the battles according to the dictates of their shifting alliances, which were as complex as they were volatile. From 1992 to 1995, Kabul and its surroundings were the scene of violent confrontations that claimed more than 30,000 civilian victims in the capital, which had hitherto been spared by the war. The conflict was fuelled by neighbouring states. Taking advantage of the West's disinterest in a country that in 1989 had lost much of its strategic interest, Pakistan, Iran and Uzbekistan sought to extend their influence there via local intermediary factions (Pashtun for Islamabad, Shiite Hazara for Tehran, and Uzbek for Tashkent). While Iran and Uzbekistan were content to support their protégés in Kabul and their regions of origin, Pakistan got more directly involved on the side of Hezb-e Islami. Nevertheless, Hekmatyar's faction proved unable to seize Herat or Kabul, and in the mid-1990s, Islamabad switched its support to the emerging Taliban movement. The Taliban were uprooted young Afghans, many of them orphans, who had grown up in the Pakistani refugee camps and been educated in fundamentalist Koranic schools (hence the name, which is derived from the Arabic word 'Talib' meaning religious student). They were assembled and trained by Pashtun mullah-commanders, formerly resistance fighters or members of the pro-communist Khalq faction.

The Taliban seized the Pashtun areas with relative ease (Kandahar fell on 5 November 1994) and then made progress in the rest of the country due to decisive support from the Pakistani secret service and members of the Pakistani military. Herat fell on 5 September 1995 and Kabul followed one year later. Expelled from the capital, the former masters of Kabul regrouped in the north of the country, forming the Northern Alliance. The Tajik, Hazara and Uzbek factions, long at loggerheads, had to learn how to fight together once more. Rivalries and misalliances prevented them from stemming the advance of the Taliban, who by 1998 controlled 90 percent of the country. Only parts of Hazarajat, Panjshir and Badakhshan held out, against a background of worsening identity-related violence.

Worsening identity-related violence

As the conflict continued and fighting spread to non-Pashtun areas, the belligerents' predatory ways mutated into mass violence against whole populations, stigmatised by virtue of their ethnicity or religious practices. By choice or by force, large components of Afghan society were sucked into the war effort of one armed faction or another and exposed to collective reprisals by the opposing side.

During the winter following the retreat of Massoud's forces from Kabul in 1996, the inhabitants of the Shamali plain, one of the most fertile and densely populated in Afghanistan, were the targets of a Taliban scorched-earth policy. This involved violence against civilians, the destruction of irrigation systems and villages, the mining of houses and, lastly, the forcible removal of tens of thousands of villagers to the capital.

The Taliban's first major defeat, at Mazar-e Sharif in May 1997, marked a further stage in ethnicising the violence. A few days after the town fell to Taliban troops, the local Hazara and Uzbek forces, who had been bribed by the authorities in Kabul, suddenly rebelled. Several hundred Taliban were killed in the town's streets and 2,000 prisoners of war were executed. During the summer of 1998, the Taliban launched a fresh offensive in the north of the country, supported by thousands of Pakistani fighters. The recapture of Mazar-e Sharif on 8 August was accompanied by large-scale massacres; several thousand civilians, mostly Shiite Hazaras, were killed in the course of a few days. This exterminatory fury was reminiscent of the methods used a century earlier by the Pashtun emir Abdur Rahman in subduing the Hazara populations, and echoed the expressions of sectarian hatred for Shiite Muslims regularly espoused in some fundamentalist Pakistani mosques.

The battles of Hazarajat displayed the same pattern of violence. Bamyan fell into Taliban hands for the first time in October 1998, forcing the Hazara resistance to take refuge in the isolated valleys of Yakaolang to the west, from where they continued to harass the mullahs' forces. The resistance implanted itself among the population, using it as a source of provisions and fighters. The Taliban, unable to consolidate their positions, increased their violence against civilians. From 1999, the district of Bamyan, with a population of nearly 80,000, was emptied several times of its inhabitants. Those villagers who escaped the carnage fled to the mountains on a massive scale, sometimes in the depths of winter, finding refuge in makeshift shelters or isolated villages. They remained confined there for months on end, despite the lack of food and health care. In the provinces extending to the north between Herat and

Taloqan, whole communities – Uzbeks or Pashtuns, depending on the invaders of the moment – experienced similar violence.

The rule of hunger and the whip

Outside the resistance zones the Taliban's capability of putting an end to the warlords' arbitrary violence and of restoring a modicum of order initially endowed them with an almost messianic aura. But this gradually faded: by seeking to impose an ultra-rigid moral order, the Taliban alienated a growing portion of the population. Afghans were subjected to the rigours of a 'department for the promotion of virtue and the suppression of vice' that kept watch over public and private practices. Moral codes were firmly circumscribed by decrees inspired by a rereading of the Koran and of certain local, mainly Pashtun, traditions. Among other measures, women were obliged to wear the famous *burqa* and deprived of the right to work or to leave their home unless accompanied by a male relative.

While the Taliban's sharia was applied strictly in Kabul – regarded as a 'depraved Babylon' that needed to be 'purified' – it was imposed in a more lax fashion in the rural areas. Unlike towns that had experienced the communist revolution, the new moral order in rural areas did not, as a rule, drastically alter the status of women or the pre-existing social rules. Nonetheless, most Afghans regarded as humiliating the state's intrusion into the private sphere that was traditionally governed by the family or immediate community. This sentiment was exacerbated by the government's lack of interest in the increasing hardships suffered by the population as a result of the continuing conflict.

Taking the view that 'the fate of men rests above all in the hands of God', the regime showed little concern for the population's material living conditions. International aid agencies struggled to keep the health system going and food availability was precarious. Numerous food shortages arose as the result of food levies systematically imposed by all factions; the destruction of goods and food reserves; forced recruitment of men of working age; the mining of fields; the destruction of irrigation systems, as well as blockades of 'enemy' villages or regions. Many families lived all year on bread and tea, and chronic malnutrition became widespread among children. The situation was aggravated by a drought that commenced in 1998 and lasted for three years, leading to a scurvy epidemic among displaced populations in northern Afghanistan in 2001. At the time, the World Food Programme (WFP) estimated that 5.5 million Afghans were in need of emergency food aid.

Border closures

Hunger and violence drove hundreds of thousands of Afghans to move to large towns such as Herat, Kabul, Kandahar and Mazar-e Sharif. In 2001, some 800,000 people were internally displaced within the country, with millions more having sought refuge across the border. According to UNHCR, there were 2.2 million Afghans in Pakistan in 2001, and a further 1.4 million in Iran. Although underestimates of the real number, these figures make Afghans the world's largest refugee population.

However, Islamabad and Tehran became progressively less tolerant of the presence of these undesirables, who were accused – as in the West – of fuelling crime and swamping the labour market. From the mid-1990s, 'encouraging' returns to Afghanistan became a priority. Borders were closed to new arrivals, deportations commenced, aid operations were cut back, and the right to asylum was increasingly contested. In 2000, a repatriation program was launched with the support of UNHCR despite the deteriorating security and food situation in Afghanistan. Reports depicting the terrible conditions under which the returns took place, including the arrest of men on arrival, the lack of resources of repatriating families, ethnic and religious persecution, and fresh population displacements, failed to alter the course of this policy.

UNHCR was caught between its legal obligation to guarantee the Afghans' right to seek asylum, and the host states' refusal to receive them – a refusal supported by UNHCR's donors, who favoured turning back the asylum seekers. At the end of the 1990s, Afghans were the leading nationality among applicants for asylum in Europe. OECD countries, too, had no hesitation in turning them away, refusing to respect the right to asylum, or packing them into detention camps under military supervision, as was done in Australia. Hence, it would have been hypocritical for western powers to ask the central Asian countries to accept new arrivals, particularly when donor governments refused to respond to Pakistan's and Iran's appeals for financial assistance to assist the refugees. The 'fatigue' of donor governments, whose contribution was reduced to emergency aid inside Afghanistan, and the absence of any envisaged alternative to the Taliban regime were both arguments for directing the fleeing Afghans to camps inside their war-torn country. Faced with stricter border controls, Afghans were reduced to entrusting their lives to clandestine people smugglers who would get them abroad in exchange for what little money remained to them, even if it meant leaving a family member as hostage pending payment of the contracted debt.

Humanitarian action and totalitarian aspirations

The refugee *refoulement* was all the more worrying because aid organisations had found it impossible to provide Afghan populations with material assistance commensurate with their needs throughout the Taliban period. To be sure, it was relatively easy for aid agencies to help the conflict's victims in zones held by the Northern Alliance, but in the 90 percent of the country controlled by the Taliban, they experienced great difficulties assisting populations near the front lines or under intense repression, such as in Hazarajat, on which a blockade of food and medical supplies was imposed. In addition to repeated official refusals to authorise aid teams to travel, the Taliban maintained an atmosphere of insecurity in these areas – particularly via foreign fighters trained by bin Laden's networks – that regularly forced the humanitarian organisations to evacuate them.

In the rest of the country the Taliban constantly pressured aid agencies to integrate their activities into the 'purifying' project for Afghan society. Discriminatory measures against women were already hindering their access to health care when, in September 1997, the regime tried to prohibit medical agencies from receiving women in mixed-gender health facilities. Strong mobilisation by ICRC and medical NGOs persuaded the authorities to retract this decision that, had it been implemented, would have deprived almost all Afghan women in Kabul of access to medical assistance.

The regime also sought to isolate humanitarian volunteers from all contact with Afghans. Kabul's inhabitants risked punishment if they ventured to have relations, other then strictly professional ones, with foreigners. Although the authorities succeeded in curbing exchanges between the population and humanitarian volunteers, most NGO doctors and nurses nonetheless managed to maintain close contact with patients, both male and female, who consulted them. In the hospitals and clinics supported by medical organisations, female Afghan staff worked alongside international staff and female patients outnumbered male ones.

In fact, the mullahs lacked the means to achieve their totalitarian ambitions. Contrary to their wishes, they were unable to oust the Western aid organisations in favour of Islamic NGOs which, although closer to their conception of solidarity, were poorly endowed with resources. By exploiting the regime's weaknesses, the humanitarian organisations managed to preserve a minimum of freedom to work in a way that more or less respected the principle of impartiality, although this was constantly challenged by shifting conditions. This allowed WFP to distribute vital food aid, albeit with considerable difficulty, to hundreds of thousands of Afghans.

The moral stance of the international community

The work of humanitarian organisations proved all the more difficult because the Taliban classed them together with the 'international community', with whom relations rapidly deteriorated. Although at the end of 1996 the American administration stated that it 'finds nothing objectionable in the policy statements of the new government, including its move to impose Islamic law' (VOA, 27 September 1996), it soon backtracked. Like other Western governments, it was confronted with a mobilisation of public opinion and feminist lobbies outraged by the zeal of the Taliban who executed, stoned, mutilated and whipped both men and women who infringed sharia law. The Taliban sought recognition of their regime but found that the main representatives of the international community refused to admit into their midst a government whose 'obscurantism' and 'medieval practices' with respect to women they openly condemned. Only Pakistan, the United Arab Emirates and Saudi Arabia recognised the Islamic Emirate of Afghanistan, while the rest of the international community demanded that it display greater respect for human rights.

These admonitions – devoid of any tangible consequences, notably in terms of aiding refugees fleeing the regime so vehemently decried – met with incomprehension from the authorities in Kabul. An underclass spawned by the war and refugee camps, the Taliban had little mastery of the codes prevalent on the diplomatic scene. They would not accept any compromise with laws and international opinion at odds with their interpretation of Islam. Raised in a strictly masculine society, where the oppression of women was regarded as a sign of manliness and of commitment to 'jihad', the Taliban had made the status of women a matter of principle, the cornerstone of their Islamic radicalism, and an expression of their determination to 'purify' Afghan society.

The United Nations mission despatched to Kabul –
with no real resources – 'to advance the peace'
immediately came up against the Taliban's irritation at
the ritual condemnations to which they were subjected,
and their determination to see their government
recognised internationally. Lacking any political strategy
to advance their mission, the UN then sought to
strengthen its control over the humanitarian
organisations. Confronted with the mullahs'
intransigence, it hoped to use aid as a bargaining chip to
open space for dialogue, even if it meant accepting their
discriminatory demands with respect to the distribution
of aid. Thus in April 1998, the UN's Office for the
Coordination of Humanitarian Affairs signed a
memorandum with the government accepting its
apartheid policy with respect to women, and
strengthening the authorities' grip on the NGOs. The
United Nations' tutelage proved all the more deleterious
to the humanitarian agencies because the UN was
perceived by the Taliban as highly biased both for
having protected Najibullah, the former communist
president, and for passing unilateral sanctions against
them in 1999 and 2000.

The Taliban's radicalisation and fall from power

Prisoners of their defiance towards Western states that
refused to recognise their government, or even to enter
into economic relations (including for the construction
of a gas pipeline linking the Turkmen gas deposits to
Pakistan's Indian Ocean coast), the Taliban drew
progressively closer to Osama bin Laden. Following his
expulsion from Sudan in 1996, he found refuge in
Afghanistan through the good offices of the Pakistani

secret service. The Taliban allowed him to establish training camps in the south for his young 'jihadist' recruits who came from all over the world, but particularly from Pakistan, central Asia and the Middle East. The 'international Islamist brigades' took part in offensives against the Northern Alliance and lent a hand to the Kashmiri separatists.

It was the implication of bin Laden's networks in the August 1998 attacks in Nairobi and Dar es Salaam that sealed the Western powers' break with the Taliban regime. Faced with the mullahs' refusal to hand over the CIA's former protégé, the United States bombed southwest Afghanistan in 1998. It imposed a trade and financial embargo on the regime in July 1999, and froze Taliban assets in the US. In November 1999 and December 2000, the UN Security Council generalised and strengthened these sanctions, including an embargo on weapons destined for the authorities in Kabul. The latter were enjoined to extradite bin Laden and to observe various international obligations ranging from respect for human rights to reducing opium production.

In August 2000, the Taliban presented a conciliatory face by banning poppy cultivation, which had nearly doubled between 1995 and 1999, making Afghanistan the world's leading opium producer. But this measure neither dried up the opium market (due to existing stocks) nor brought recognition to the regime. The influence of bin Laden's networks thereupon became stronger. The government forged recklessly ahead with a series of repressive measures and provocations against the 'infidels': the destruction of the giant Buddhas of Bamyan in February 2001, the requirement, imposed in March, that members of the Hindu religious community wear an identifying yellow patch, and the imprisonment in August of a Western NGO's staff accused of Christian proselytism. Islamabad's efforts to exercise a moderating influence on the regime proved futile, indicating that the mullahs had cut loose from their former supporters.

With the assassination of Commander Massoud on 9 September 2001, it looked as if the last bastion against Taliban ascendancy over the entire country had been breached. But two days later, the murderous attacks in New York and Washington radically changed the situation. The Security Council unanimously condemned the terrorist attacks and declared the United States entitled to exercise its right of self-defence. Responsibility for the attacks was quickly ascribed to the Al Qaida network. In a final gesture of defiance, the Taliban refused to hand over their guests, making American military action inevitable.

Humanitarian organisations were forced to leave the country because the Taliban proclaimed itself unable to guarantee their safety from the foreign fighters of bin Laden's networks. Supply convoys continued and Afghan staff managed to maintain food and medical aid operations, although at a reduced level. Fearing the worst, UNHCR increased its fundraising appeals in anticipation of a flood of refugees. Yet nothing was done to ensure that Afghans already massing at the borders could cross them, and some who tried to do so were shot on sight.

The aerial bombardments of operation 'Enduring Freedom' that started on 7 October 2001, together with the offensives conducted by Northern Alliance fighters with support from their new western partners, overcame the Taliban regime in little more than a month. Kabul was taken on 13 November, but fighting continued in the south-east of the country even after the fall of

Kandahar on 7 December. The Taliban forces broke up and found refuge in the mountainous regions of the south-east, which provided access to the tribal areas of Pakistan, where a social base and protection allowed them to regroup.

Bread and bombs

From the beginning, operation 'Enduring Freedom' introduced a pernicious confusion between the exercise of the United States' right to legitimate self-defence and the independent and impartial humanitarian action of aid organisations. The first American bombardments were accompanied by high-altitude drops of individual food rations accompanied by leaflets offering a reward to anyone who made possible the capture of bin Laden, and asking the Afghans not to leave the area ('Stay where you are, we will feed you'). According to President George W. Bush, it was a matter of letting 'the oppressed people of Afghanistan… know the generosity of America and our allies. As we strike military targets, we'll also drop food, medicine and supplies to the starving and suffering men and women and children of Afghanistan.' (Presidential Address to the Nation October 7, 2001.) American strategists added that the aim of this psychological operation was to avoid a massive influx of refugees into Pakistan and to convince the population – as well as Muslims all over the world – that the war was not directed against them but only against the Taliban and their terrorist guests.

These air-drops, however, were presented as an enormous 'humanitarian' operation intended, according to statements by the director of the US Government's aid agency (USAID), 'to prevent as many people from dying as possible' in a situation 'well beyond pre-famine stage'. Yet not only was the impartial provision of aid to the Afghan population not their primary intention – simultaneously, ICRC's clearly identified food warehouses in Kabul were twice bombed immediately prior to food distributions, and road convoys transporting aid were suspended – their impact on the food situation in Afghanistan was also extremely marginal. In the course of one month, the American air force dropped enough food to sustain one million people... for one day. Many of the parcels fell onto mined land and their shape and colour were similar to those of the fragmentation bombs being dropped at the same time, leading to a number of lethal mistakes. Furthermore, the humanitarian organisations were called on to abandon all neutrality and to join with the Western forces to form what the British Prime Minister called a 'military-humanitarian coalition'. The American Secretary of State was equally explicit, asking humanitarian NGOs to convey a message about American values to the rest of the world and considering them to be a 'force multiplier for us, such an important part of our combat team.'

Already regarded by many Afghan military actors, particularly the Taliban, as political auxiliaries of Western powers, the humanitarian organisations were now called upon to become military auxiliaries as well, thereby further compromising their ability to assert their impartiality and, consequently, their capacity to provide assistance to all victims of the conflict. This confusion continued with the deployment of ground troops: some American special forces operated in civilian clothes, and introduced themselves as 'humanitarian volunteers'. They dispensed direct help to the local authorities –

security, military support, restoration of public buildings, assistance to populations – and, as the humanitarian organisations gradually returned, displayed some desire to control the latter's operations. The aim was to justify the international military presence by endowing it with a friendlier image; to practise community policing and avoid being perceived simply as an occupying force. For all that, the coalition forces did not always bother to observe international law. Following the fall of Kunduz on 24 November 2001, the transfer of prisoners of war to the Uzbek jails at Shebergan, which was supervised by American special forces, was carried out under appalling conditions that resulted in the death of several thousand prisoners. To date, no international investigation has been launched to identify those responsible for these war crimes. Similarly, a revolt by Taliban prisoners in the Qalai Janghi fort near Mazar-e Sharif a few days later was put down by aerial bombardments that left hundreds of the encircled prisoners dead. Lastly, those prisoners selected by the United States for their special links to the Taliban or Al Qaida networks were extradited to the American military base at Guantanamo in Cuba. Washington refused them prisoners of war status, and their incarceration at Guantanamo puts them beyond the jurisdiction of American criminal law that would guarantee their right to a fair trial. Hence the prisoners are subjected to special regulations affording them no rights beyond those granted in discretionary fashion by the American administration.

Waiting for peace

The collapse of the Taliban regime was an immense relief to the great majority of Afghans. In Kabul and other towns around the country, women gradually started working again. In health care facilities, nurses rejoiced at being able to work freely with their male colleagues once more and to receive female patients without fear. Over 1.7 million Afghan refugees spontaneously returned to their country before the end of October 2002, surpassing UN predictions. But many of them headed for urban areas where general living conditions deteriorated. A shifting population, many of them destitute, set up makeshift shelters on the outskirts of the capital. Lacking any prospects of integration into the city's economy or of return to their places of origin, these uprooted people fuelled an unplanned urban growth that generated social tensions. The concentration of international aid in towns attracted more settlers, so aid agencies made strenuous efforts to penetrate the countryside, where the lack of resources was flagrant and insecurity once more a nagging problem.

The authority of Hamid Karzai's interim government, set up with the international community's support following the convening of a 'traditional tribal assembly' in June 2002, was confined to Kabul and its outskirts, where 4,000 soldiers of the International Security Assistance Force (ISAF) were deployed. Hundreds of international and Afghan NGOs are concentrated there, limiting their movement outside Kabul and other major urban centres due to security concerns. The frustration of the population is at its height, and criticisms of the lack of assistance available become stronger each day. The promises of reconstruction made in Tokyo in

January 2002 have not been honoured, and the 500 million dollars of emergency aid was only a palliative. In the rest of the country, the vacuum left by the Taliban government was swiftly reoccupied by the former 'warlords'. They regained their regional fiefdoms and resumed their predatory rivalries, barely held in check by the subsidies and dissuasion of their new Western allies. Each of them played the game of participation in a central government whose legitimacy and future were still uncertain, all the while ferociously defending the prerogatives accruing from their local autonomy. The identity-related violence fanned by the confrontation with the Taliban was directed at some Pashtun populations, casting a shadow over future inter-communal relations.

Furthermore, contrary to the claims of the American Secretary of Defense in Kabul on 1 May 2003 that Afghanistan had 'moved from major combat activity to a period of stability and stabilization and reconstruction activities', the war against the Taliban and Al Qaida is not yet over. Two years since their arrival, the coalition forces continue to hunt down armed fighters in the south-east region of Afghanistan bordering the Pakistani tribal areas and in regions around Kandahar.

The foreign military presence fuels in turn the radicalisation of armed Islamist groups and growing insecurity in the south of the country as well as Kabul. This insecurity has spared neither the population nor the aid agencies trying to assist them. In the first half of 2003, attacks against humanitarian personnel have multiplied, forcing the majority of NGOs to evacuate the south of the country. On 27 March 2003 an ICRC delegate was executed in cold blood in Oruzgan Province by a 'non-identified' group who consciously targeted a humanitarian aid worker and not an American soldier. Afghan personnel working with 'Westerners' have received death threats from some extremist combatants who deliberately associate humanitarian staff with soldiers of the anti-Taliban coalition. The deteriorating security conditions prompted the UN to suspend all activities in the south of Afghanistan, where the only Western presence is now a military one.

After having been abandoned for over twelve years, the Afghan populations received renewed international attention as a result of the attacks of 11 September. To be sure, Afghanistan had not been entirely forgotten, the oppression of women under the Taliban regime having been abundantly described and denounced in Western nations from 1996 onwards. But the ritual condemnation of 'the mullahs' obscurantism' mainly took the form of self-congratulation on the 'moral superiority' of the West, accompanied by symbolic acts (such as 'a flower for the women of Kabul', an initiative by Emma Bonino, former European Commissioner for Humanitarian Affairs) devoid of any tangible impact. While the 'international community' waxed indignant over the destruction of the Buddhas of Bamyan and the obligatory wearing of the *burqa*, it accepted the mass violence perpetrated, without distinction of gender, against some ethnic communities, the *refoulement* of refugees, and the closure of the country's Western borders to Afghans fleeing hunger, war and oppression.

The Western intervention launched in response to the attacks of 11 September marked a further stage in the erosion of a space for humanitarian action independent of political and military players. Increasingly identified with Western armed forces, aid actors are today victims of the resurgent attacks and bombings directed towards the international presence. The shrinking space for humanitarian action is of even greater concern given that the war is far from over. Today, the hope awakened in Afghanistan by the overthrow of the Taliban regime has been dimmed by the return of the 'warlords' with their destructive rivalries. Nonetheless, it is on the latter that the international community has chosen to rely in attempting to 'construct' a state in this segmentary society, profoundly destabilised by more than twenty years of war. Having enlisted some Afghan factions in the 'war on terror', the foreign forces risk being caught up in turn in a civil and regional war whose dynamics have not been broken by the overthrow of the Taliban. Order and security seem to depend today on the presence of foreign troops, whose longer-term implantation is itself a factor of insecurity.

Bibliographical references

W. Maley, *The Foreign Policy of the Taliban*, New York, Council on Foreign Relations, 2000.

W. Maley (ed.), *Fundamentalism Reborn? Afghanistan and the Taliban*, London, Hurst, 1998.

Médecins Sans Frontières, *Report on New Afghan Refugees' Situation in Gulshar Town, Iran, October 2000 – January 2001*, Paris, MSF, 2001.

A. Rashid, *Taliban : Militant Islam, Oil and Fundamentalism in Central Asia*, New Haven, CT, Yale University Press, 2001.

O. Roy, 'L'humanitaire en Afghanistan: entre illusions, grands desseins politiques et bricolage', *CEMOTI*, 29, January-June 2000, pp. 21-30.

PART II. INVOLVEMENT

4

NORTH KOREA
Feeding Totalitarianism

Fiona Terry

Half a century since an armistice ended the Korean War (1950-3), the Korean Peninsula remains the site of the last Cold War confrontation. Some 37,000 American troops are stationed in South Korea to deter any new attempt to reunify the Peninsula by force, and North Korea keeps its 1.1 million-strong army permanently mobilised against the 'imperialist aggressors'. The citizens of North Korea, the last bastion of Stalinism on the planet, are among the world's most deprived and oppressed peoples, lacking even the most basic freedoms in a country controlled by the grotesque personality cult of its dead yet eternal leader, Kim Il-Sung and his son, Kim Jong-il. Between 150,000 and 200,000 people are believed to be languishing in North Korea's gulag for having committed a 'state crime', which any act of defiance or disrespect, however small, can be labelled.

Over the last decade, famine has exacerbated the suffering of the North Korean people. North Korean refugees in China suggest that up to three million of their compatriots died from starvation and related illness between 1995 and 1998 alone. Aid organisations responded to the crisis, but reached the limits of humanitarian action in this totalitarian state. North Koreans continue to suffer and to die in spite of the largest food aid program in the UN's history.

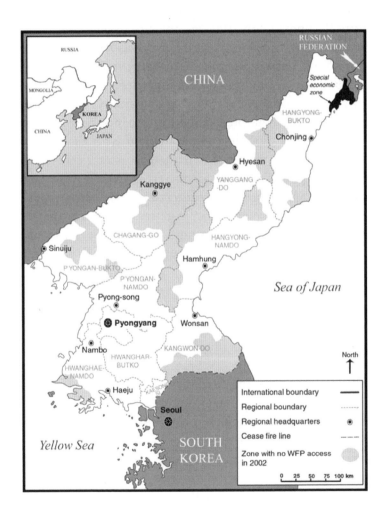

The origins of the crisis

Although no outsiders know with any certainty what goes on inside the borders of this reclusive state, food shortages are thought to have begun in North Korea in the early 1990s, reaching famine proportions within a few years. Refugees in China tend to mark the death of Kim Il-Sung in July 1994 as the time when starvation began, and official Chinese sources also spoke of 'the worst food crisis in history' in North Korea in mid-1994. Yet it was not until heavy flooding devastated the rice-growing regions of North Korea in mid-1995 that the regime made an unprecedented international appeal for assistance. The flooding was in many ways a blessing for the regime as it provided a 'natural disaster' pretext that not only deflected blame for the crisis from government mismanagement to the weather, but also shielded the regime from opening the country to more than a minimum of outside scrutiny. Dependent upon the extreme personality cult surrounding Kim Il-Sung and Kim Jong-il for its survival, the regime could not countenance any suggestion that the system they created was at fault. Despite all indications that natural disasters only exacerbated an already crippled agricultural sector, it has taken a decade for the first concrete reforms to appear in North Korea.

Rather than having 'natural' causes, the famine and continuing food shortages are the result of a severe economic crisis afflicting the country, provoked by a combination of internal policies pursued by the regime and international events. Ironically, it was the country's rigid pursuit of self-sufficiency, while remaining dependent on foreign aid and trade with former Eastern-bloc countries that precipitated the economic crisis and left the country unable to feed its people. In the pursuit of self-sufficiency, the cornerstone of the guiding *Juche* philosophy of Kim Il-Sung, the North Korean government embarked upon ambitious agricultural reforms in the 1960s to maximise agricultural output in this harsh and mountainous land. Agriculture was collectivised; production quotas were set; crops were sown further up mountain slopes; and people and resources were mobilised in a technological revolution that emphasised irrigation, mechanisation, electrification, and chemicalisation of the agricultural sector. While faltering agricultural production in the 1960s gave way to steady production increases in the 1970s and 1980s, the reliance of the agricultural sector on manufactured inputs and power, and the environmental degradation that resulted from these agricultural policies, set the scene for the food crisis of the 1990s.

Despite the rhetoric about self-reliance, North Korea was heavily dependent upon highly concessionary trade with the Soviet Union to provide oil and coking coal to run its industries. Concessions ceased in 1991 after the collapse of the Soviet Union, and North Korea was asked to pay standard international prices in hard currency. Having defaulted on international loans in the 1970s, North Korea had no access to international finance, and the country's lack of hard currency led to a drop in trade with the Soviet Union from $3.2 billion in 1990 to $360 million in 1991. Oil imports fell from 506,000 tonnes per year in 1989 to 30,000 tonnes in 1992[1]. The ensuing energy crisis ground industry to a

---

[1] Cf. Hy-Sang Lee, 'Supply and Demand Grains in North Korea', *Korea and World Affairs*, vol. 18, no. 3 (1994), pp. 509-52.

standstill or sharply reduced its functioning capacity, and North Korea found itself in a vicious circle where a lack of foreign currency restricted the purchase of fuel and other imports that were needed to manufacture exports to generate foreign currency.

The lack of fuel, fertiliser, chemicals and spare parts undermined the entire agricultural plan, and food production rapidly declined. Food shortages were exacerbated by a massive reduction in 'friendship grain' from China in 1994 after poor harvests of its own. Thus by the mid-1990s North Korea was facing a large food deficit and people were beginning to starve.

But like in every famine, not all segments of the population were equally affected by food shortages, and starvation had more to do with entitlement to food than an overall shortage *per se*, to which continuing reports of starvation despite the massive international food aid operation attests. North Korean citizens are treated in accordance with their perceived loyalty to the regime – based primarily on their family history – with those in the 'core' class holding government posts and living a privileged life in Pyongyang and elsewhere, and those of the 'hostile' class destined to a hard life of manual labour in poorer areas outside Pyongyang. Kim Jong-il's response to food shortages in the mid-1990s was simply to jettison the 'hostile' elements of society by sharply reducing or stopping the fortnightly rations of basic foods distributed through the Public Distribution System (PDS) in certain regions. Refugees, who are predominantly from North Hamkyong Province, say that the only rations they received after 1994 were a few kilos of corn on important dates such as the birthdays of Kim Il-Sung and Kim Jong-il. They say that workers in 'useful' factories like those producing fertiliser received food periodically, but the vast majority of people were left to fend for themselves.

Those who managed to survive the famine did so by foraging for wild foods, scavenging and stealing in markets that sprang up in the parallel economy, or crossing into China where they clandestinely worked or begged for money and food to take back to their families. Extrapolations from refugee testimonies suggest that some three million people died during the worst famine years[2]. Malnutrition, exacerbated by a lack of heating and medicines, continues to claim many more lives each year.

Contrary to claims by international aid organisations that conditions have significantly improved in North Korea over the past five years, refugees continue to risk their lives crossing the border into China for help. The risk they are willing to take attests to their desperation. Those who make it past border guards are vulnerable to many hazards in China, including being sold by Chinese smugglers for sex or slavery. And Beijing's crackdown on what it considers are 'illegal immigrants' that began in early 2001 has intensified the danger the refugees face: those who are arrested, as thousands have been, are delivered into the hands of North Korean security forces. Considered as traitors by the regime for having left the country, refugees face interrogation, 're-

[2] Cf. Korean Buddhist Sharing Movement, *The Food Crisis of North Korea witnessed by 472 Food Refugees*, Seoul, KBSM, 18 February 1998; W. Courtland Robinson, Myung Ken Lee, Kenneth Hill, Gilbert M. Burnham, 'Mortality in North Korean migrant households: a retrospective study', *The Lancet* 345, July 1999, pp. 291-5; and W. Courtland Robinson & Gilbert Burnham, *Famine, Mortality and Migration: A Study of North Korean Migrants in China*, Washington, DC, Workshop on Mortality Patterns in Complex Emergencies, National Research Council, 18 November 1999.

education', imprisonment and hard labour in North Korea's infamous prison system.

The crackdown has also targeted underground networks of predominantly religious people who offer food, shelter and employment to the refugees, with the local population, in posters and banners reminiscent of China's Cultural Revolution, urged to denounce anyone sheltering these 'criminal elements'. House-to-house searches and road checkpoints have closed the net on thousands of refugees, leading to the increasingly desperate measures seen in recent months of refugees climbing into the compounds of foreign embassies and consulates, demanding asylum. Some one hundred refugees have managed to reach South Korea using this method in 2002, due in large part to the media exposure the escapees received. But for every successful bid, there are dozens of unsuccessful attempts to escape the hardships of North Korea that do not make the international news. And even the success stories have a bitter twist: the extended families of those who have escaped will pay the price for the public humiliation their actions have brought to the North Korean regime.

When caring is a crime

The Chinese Government's crackdown along the Sino-North Korean border has drastically reduced the already limited possibilities to offer assistance to North Koreans fleeing hunger and persecution. The target expanded in 2002 from refugees to the people helping them: caring has been declared a crime. Strict enforcement measures have led to the closure of many underground networks of missionaries and lay aid workers who provided vital food and shelter to refugees. Many Chinese volunteers have been arrested and forced to pay fines equivalent to several months' salary. In May, border police, led by an informer, raided a school and arrested six North Korean orphans who had resettled in China, some as long as five years ago. They were deported across the border the following day. Mr. Choi, the aid worker who had raised them was forced into hiding.

International aid workers have also been arrested. Hiroshi Kato, leader of the Japanese NGO Life Fund for North Korean Refugees, disappeared on 30 October as he was delivering money, food and clothes to local volunteers on the Sino-Korean border. The security police released him after a week of physically straining interrogation, during which they threatened to send him to North Korea if he was not cooperative. Mr. Kato was fortunate that his case generated concern from the Japanese public, prompting the Ministry of Foreign Affairs to confront Chinese authorities over his disappearance. Other aid workers have not received such support from their home governments. Kim Hee Tae, a South Korean aid worker, was arrested on 31 August in Jilin province with 12 North Korean refugees en route to request asylum in Beijing. He is facing a seven-year gaol sentence. Choi Bong Il, also South Korean, was arrested in April and kept in-communicado for months. He had been providing assistance to refugees sheltering in the Yanbian Autonomous region. John Choi, a US citizen, has been in gaol for more than six months for running a small orphanage for North Korean children.

It seems that most governments prefer to ignore the fate of North Korean refugees and those who assist them rather than compromise their relations with China. National interests coupled with the need to ensure a stable peninsula do not leave space for a refugee crisis. Diplomats from various countries are eager to obtain information on the border situation from aid workers but are not ready to actively question China's policy. Moreover, the organisation responsible for refugee protection, UNHCR, has failed to engage in constructive dialogue with the Chinese authorities to remind them of their obligations to refugees under international law.

Optimism at North Korea's recent decision to initiate reforms in the economy seems premature, at least in the short-term for the poorer segments of society. The abolition of the Public Distribution System in July 2002 has ended one of the most oppressive tools in the hands of the government, but the sudden change to a command system to regulate the flow of goods has generated massive inflation: the price of rice is reportedly 30 times more expensive than previously, when it was already too expensive for most people to afford. Wages – for those fortunate enough to have jobs – have not risen at the same pace as the price of commodities, and for those attached to factories that remain closed due to power shortages, no amount of wage increase is going to improve their access to food. On the contrary, what little they were able to barter in the past will now be beyond their means.

The aid business

That up to three million people starved to death in complete obscurity during the last years of the twentieth century is tragic enough. But that this occurred while the UN was mounting the largest food aid operation in its history – but was unable to reach those at greatest risk of dying – is nothing short of scandalous. Yet no scandal has been declared by the UN, and no changes have been implemented in the food aid operation that will ensure that food is going to those who need it most rather than those who the regime decides are worthy of it. Aid organisations even engage in a deceptive discourse that conceals their inability to reach the starving. North Korea is the site of the most manipulated aid program in the world today, and the manipulation is carried out with the active participation of humanitarian organisations.

The former Executive Director of the UN World Food Programme (WFP), Catherine Bertini, claims that the food aid operation in North Korea averted famine and has been 'an absolute success'.[3] Refugees in China, however, say they have never received food aid, despite being from the hard-hit northern provinces where WFP concentrates its aid. Some have heard of it, and others have seen it for sale on the black market, but none have ever tasted it, even children. WFP's assertions disguise the fact that they have no way of knowing whether their food reaches the hungry or even who and where the hungry are. Despite operating in North Korea for seven years, providing up to one million tons of food per year, WFP is unable to determine the real extent of the food crisis and its impact on the population. The North Korean regime tightly controls the movement of foreigners inside the country, and does not allow aid organisations to undertake an independent assessment of the needs of the population. All assessments are carried out in conjunction with the government at predetermined destinations, and aid workers are accompanied by government-appointed translators and 'minders' to ensure that they have no unmonitored contact with ordinary North Koreans. The UN is not even allowed to bring Korean speakers to the country.

WFP claims that it is delivering food to 'the most vulnerable' members of society. But in the absence of an independent assessment, WFP cannot determine who is the most vulnerable and instead uses the standard

---

[3] Cf. D. Struck, 'UN Says Aid Averted N. Korean Famine', *Washington Post*, 24 August 2001.

formula of 'children, pregnant and lactating women and the elderly'. But in a system that discriminates between classes of people, vulnerability has more to do with social standing than with age or gender. As the profiles of the refugees demonstrate, men from the 'hostile' class destined to a life of coal mining in North Hamkyong Province have more need of food aid than a child from the 'core' class.

Even if WFP were able to identify those most in need of food aid, it has no guarantees that its food reaches the intended recipients because WFP neither controls the distribution of its food nor is permitted to satisfactorily monitor its use, or measure its impact. All food is channelled through government structures. The authorities take possession of WFP food the moment it arrives in the country, and are responsible for all handling, warehousing and internal transport. The food is then supposedly distributed through the government Public Distribution Centres (even after the abolition of the PDS according to WFP's monthly update from September 2002), either to individuals 'targeted' for special attention by WFP such as 'vulnerable' categories and food-for-work participants, or to institutions such as paediatric hospitals, nurseries, kindergartens and schools for onward distribution to children. WFP employees do not accompany the food aid to its final destination but rely on transport waybills and monitoring visits to 'verify' where the food has gone. But the monitoring visits are also tightly controlled by the regime, requiring approval four to seven days in advance, and only to specified locations. WFP has never received a full list of institutions to which its food allegedly goes, and is not permitted to conduct a spontaneous visit to a school or a food-for-work participant's house to ensure that food is distributed as intended. Nevertheless, UN representatives claim that they 'monitor, have access and know where the aid is going'. Citing an impressive array of statistics, technical jargon, and anecdotes about the 'deplorable' or 'vastly improved' health of orphans and school children, the UN both warns of impending famine when appeals for money and food are launched, and shows that food aid has averted famine whenever donors or the public require reassurance. Even top WFP officials return from guided visits of state institutions claiming to know aid is distributed correctly because the health of children had visibly improved. But even if visual impressions were an acceptable nutritional measure, refugees say that much is staged by the regime for the benefit of international monitors. One man from Musan in North Hamkyong Province told of how he carried sacks of food from a military warehouse to a kindergarten prior to a UN monitoring visit, while another explained how he and others were mobilised to exacerbate 'flood damage' before an assessment team arrived. Staff of Médecins Sans Frontières (MSF) and Action Contre la Faim (ACF) cite similar experiences: sick children in spotless rooms with new blankets wrapped around their shoulders for the foreigners to see, and unused kitchens that supposedly produced meals for dozens of children.[4]

---

[4] Cf. Action contre la Faim, 'The Inadequacies of Food Aid in North Korea', Paris, February 2000 and S. Brunel, 'Corée du Nord : L'absence d'espace humanitaire, un famine masquée' in Sylvie Brunel (ed.), *Géopolitique de la Faim*, Paris, Action Contre la Faim & PUF, 2000, pp. 131-69.

MSF and ACF left North Korea in the late 1990s when it became apparent that in spite of their efforts to forge acceptable operating conditions to ensure they were assisting the populations most at risk, they were not permitted to do so. Malnutrition rates in the nutritional programs they operated were lower than expected in a country suffering famine, and they often spotted malnourished, filthy children dressed in rags scavenging for grain along the railway tracks, or hidden away in state orphanages in deplorable conditions. Requests to the authorities to assist these outcasts were met with the claim that they did not exist. Thus rather than collaborate with Kim Jong-il in his triage between those worthy of food and those who were not, MSF and ACF withdrew from the country. Such discrimination runs counter to the very idea underpinning humanitarian action, that all people are entitled to certain standards by virtue of their membership in humanity.

Other aid organisations, however, accept to work in North Korea despite the wanton disrespect for the very values they profess to uphold. Unable to obtain the minimum conditions necessary to ensure the humanitarian nature of their work, they justify their continued presence as necessary to influence the political scene in the pursuit of peace. The view expressed by Erich Weingartner, a veteran of the aid program, at a conference on humanitarian assistance to North Korea in Tokyo in 2000, is exemplary: 'The challenge for NGOs is not to withdraw for fear of getting our hands dirty, but rather to help shape the outcome of geopolitical relationships. In other words, to ease tensions, increase confidence, enable rational discussion, and influence governments to make decisions to advance our humanitarian aims.' Thus he advocates continuing aid to North Korea 'without setting conditions which threaten or undermine the DPRK's political system'. Similarly, the Federation of Red Cross and Red Crescent Societies considers that humanitarian dialogue helps to mitigate a major political upheaval in North Korea that might have disastrous humanitarian consequences. In the Federation's *World Disasters Report* of 2000, Margareta Wahlström, under-secretary general for disaster response and operational coordination stated:

> The [aid] system might be utilized but I must say I think it is for a good purpose because you cannot create stability in this part of the world without creating a bridge. The humanitarian agencies, be it the UN, the Red Cross or NGOs… have made an incredible contribution to creating that bridge because they have been there in an almost unconditional manner. The conditions we have imposed are the conditions that belong to the humanitarian agenda. But we have not said that in order to give food we need something else from you. I believe our presence has greatly assisted in making possible the continuation of a dialogue.[5]

Hence these aid officials accept to forgo the conditions necessary to ensure that they are assisting the most at risk in the hope that their collaboration with the regime assists dialogue between North Korea and the outside world which might eventually lead to peace and hence improve the humanitarian situation. Meanwhile,

---

[5] IFRCRC, *World Disaster Report 2000*, p. 85.

and for the last seven years, those excluded by the
regime suffer and die. It is not the role of humanitarian
organisations to facilitate peace on the Korean
peninsula, even if this might – but will not necessarily –
improve the lives of the North Korean people. In
choosing to pursue this objective, aid organisations are
abrogating their real responsibilities to help North
Koreans who are dying from a lack of food and medical
assistance.

For such a controversial aid program, there is
surprisingly little discussion or debate within the aid
community: clearly it is not welcome by those
organisations operating in North Korea. Suggestions
that the aid program might not be the 'absolute success'
that Bertini states it is, are met with acrimonious
rebuttals. When the UN's special rapporteur for food
rights, Jean Ziegler, wrote in a report that food aid sent
to the DPRK was not reaching its intended recipients,
Bertini demanded that the paragraphs be removed. In a
letter to Ziegler she explained that she was concerned
that 'this erroneous information will undermine the
political will of our donors. This will is essential to feed
the over eight million hungry women, children and men
in DPRK.'[6] But donor governments are not quite as
naïve as Bertini suggests. They are well aware of the
monitoring restrictions placed on aid agencies, and the
absence of guarantees that aid is feeding famine victims.
Yet their 'political will' is not undermined because the
primary objective of food aid donations from the three
largest donor nations, the United States, Japan and
South Korea, is not to alleviate the suffering of North

---

[6] Cf. 'World Food Programme Official Denies Report on North Korean
Aid', Agence France-Presse, Geneva, 6 July 2001.

Koreans, but to gain progress on political issues with Pyongyang. Food aid donations follow a political, not a humanitarian, agenda.

Humanitarian diplomacy

The overriding concern of donor governments is not that North Korea is beset by famine *per se* but the possible consequences this could have on the stability of the Korean peninsula. Internal political upheaval and a flood of refugees into China or, worse still, across the demilitarised zone with South Korea could unleash a whole host of frightening scenarios involving North Korea's highly-strung army and its weapons of mass destruction. Claiming to have a nuclear arms program and possessing the missile technology to launch an attack on its neighbours, North Korea is viewed as a major potential threat to the US and its regional allies, especially given the unpredictability of its leadership. Hence donor governments use food aid as part of a 'soft-landing' strategy to diminish the possibility of a sudden collapse of the regime, and to pave the way for diplomatic negotiations aimed at eventual peace.

In addition to the shared overall objective of preventing instability on the peninsula, Japan, South Korea and the United States have specific interests that the provision of food aid serves. For South Korea, donations of food and fertiliser have been an important part of President Kim Dae-Jung's 'sunshine policy' of constructive engagement, providing incentives to the North to hold discussions between the two countries on reducing military tensions; reuniting family members separated after the war; the abduction of South Korean citizens; returning prisoners of war; relinking the cross-border railway; and trade and economic ties. Not surprisingly, aiding the North is a highly political domestic issue, with pressure from some quarters to placate Pyongyang in order to secure more reunions of aging families before it is too late, and pressure from other quarters to cut all aid unless real advances are made in diplomatic relations.

Japan has also closely linked food aid to domestic political issues. Tokyo is keen to normalise relations with Pyongyang to improve its security, but this depends on the resolution of several tricky issues including the negotiation of a final reparation settlement for Japan's colonial past on the Korean peninsula (1905-45). Pyongyang's surprise confession in September 2002 that it had indeed kidnapped eleven Japanese citizens in the 1970s and 1980s lifted a long standing impediment to normalisation talks, but its subsequent bellicose behaviour concerning its nuclear and missile development programs put a stop to such talks before they began.

Tokyo has used food aid as both a carrot and a stick to encourage Pyongyang to the negotiating table. All food aid was suspended after North Korea fired a missile over Japan in August 1998, with a resumption dependent upon 'constructive measures' between the two countries. The suspension was lifted in December 1999, two days before talks began in Beijing on reestablishing diplomatic relations. In March 2000 the Japanese Government donated 100,000 tonnes of rice to North Korea but stated that no more would be given until the issue of abducted Japanese citizens was resolved. The threat did not work, so in October 2000 the government offered an enormous carrot in the form of 500,000 tonnes of rice, a quantity that vastly exceeded the 195,000 tonnes of grain required by WFP to fulfil allocations until the end of 2000. The failure of this generous gift to attain any diplomatic progress pushed Tokyo to reach for the stick once more, and food aid was again suspended in December 2001 after the sinking of a suspected North Korean spy ship. Despite pleas from WFP that shortfalls in aid necessitates drastic reductions in its feeding program, Japan has held firm on its demands for political concessions in return for its 'humanitarian' aid.

In the past the timing of food aid allocations from the United States was also strongly linked to North Korean agreement to participate in talks over issues of concern to America. Such issues include improved relations with South Korea and Japan; international inspection of nuclear sites and facilities; and the export of missile technology to countries like Iran. Food has been a diplomatic currency in relations between Washington and Pyongyang: in response to a North Korean demand to pay $3 billion in compensation for lost revenue if it froze development of its long-range missile program and halted exports, the US ruled out cash payment but was willing 'to discuss direct or indirect humanitarian aid'. More recently, Washington's inclusion of North Korea in the 'axis of evil' lead to a significant reduction in US food donations: 250,000 tons in 2001 dropped to 150,000 in 2002 and no pledges have been announced for 2003. North Korea's decision to resume its nuclear arms program – expelling inspectors from the International Atomic Energy Agency and withdrawing from the nuclear non-proliferation treaty – appears to have pushed Washington resolutely away from the soft-landing strategy in favour of a policy of isolation aimed at asphyxiating the regime and ending the reign of Kim

Jong-il. Today George W. Bush affirms that the North Korean leader 'starves his people', yet he does not suggest doing anything to force Pyongyang to permit aid agencies to reach the starving. On the contrary, he suggests that Washington might recommence deliveries of food (and fuel) to the government if it is prepared to abandon its nuclear development program.

By definition, any aid given to induce political, religious or economic compliance is not humanitarian aid: the only compliance that should be sought for humanitarian aid is with conditions that will ensure that aid is given to those most in need. But the 'humanitarian' label is useful to donors due to the moral weight the term possesses. Domestic opposition to aiding an enemy state, particularly one as pugnacious as North Korea, is strong in each of the donor countries, but is subdued when the public is confronted with a moral argument in favour of feeding starving civilians. In the US the 'humanitarian' label also exempts the food aid from legislative restrictions imposed on states designated a 'sponsor of terrorism'. Imbued with a neutral image, humanitarian action is portrayed to be above politics, and by definition 'good'. Hence when Kim Dae-Jung publicly announced plans to provide 600,000 tons of grain to North Korea in September 2000 he invoked a humanitarian rationale: 'As long as North Korea suffers from food shortages and it asks for help, from either [a] humanitarian or brethren perspective, South Korea will continue its food aid... We help North Korea develop its economy on the principle of reciprocity but helping North Koreans suffering from food shortages is not reciprocity, but humanity'. [7]

---

[7] Cf. *Chosen Ilbo*, Seoul, 30 September 2000.

All three major donors have important political and diplomatic issues to resolve with North Korea which necessitate some form of engagement with Pyongyang. As political processes, South Korea's 'sunshine policy' and the more global 'soft-landing' strategy employed by Western governments are arguably sensible approaches to lure Pyongyang out of its isolation and ease it on a path to reform for the benefit of North Koreans and their neighbours. But to use food as a bargaining chip in a country beset by famine is reprehensible, all the more so as governments use the prospect of starving civilians to justify their aid and then do nothing to ensure that this aid actually gets to those who suffer. The purpose of humanitarian action is to save lives, but by being channelled through the government responsible for perpetuating the suffering, it has become part of the system of oppression.

Bibliographical references

J. Becker, *La famine en Corée du Nord. Aujourd'hui, un peuple meurt*, Paris, Esprit Frappeur, 1998.

F. Jean, 'Corée du Nord : un régime de famine', *Esprit*, February 1999, pp. 5-27.

'Corée du Nord : L'absence d'espace humanitaire, une famine masquée', in S. Brunel (dir.) *Géopolitique de la Faim*, Paris, Action Contre la Faim and PUF, 2000, pp. 131-169.

N. Eberstadt, *The End of North Korea*, Washington, DC, AEI Press, 1999.

International Federation of Red Cross and Red Crescent Societies, *World Disasters Report: Focus on Public Health*, Geneva, IFRCRC, 2000.

M. Noland, *Avoiding the Apocalypse: the Future of the Two Koreas*, Washington, DC, Institute of International Economics, 2000.

H. Smith, 'The Food Economy: Catalyst for collapse?', in M. Noland (dir.), *Economic Integration of the Korean Peninsula*, Washington, Institute for International Economics, 1998.

E. Weingartner, 'Appropriateness vs. Inevitability', paper presented to International NGO Conference on Humanitarian Assistance to the Democratic People's Republic of Korea, Toyko, June 30-July 1, 2000.

5

ANGOLA
Woe to the Vanquished

Christine Messiant

The war in Angola is over. With the exception of the Cabinda enclave, the agreement signed on 4 April 2002 between UNITA rebels and the MPLA government has put an end to the long cycle of conflicts that started before independence in 1975. This peace is precious for a ravaged country whose infrastructure has been destroyed, its population brutalised and its society disintegrated. The dead have never been counted – the meter stopped sometime during the 1992-4 war at 'over 500,000'. When the peace accord was signed, a third of the population (4 million people) was displaced and half a million Angolans had fled the country. Mine victims numbered in the tens of thousands and innumerable people were suffering from disease and malnutrition.

During the final episode of this war (1998-2002), neither side gave any quarter to civilians. Yet Angola is not some isolated land far from the gaze of the 'international community' but the second largest oil power in Africa, deeply immersed in international relations. The Angolan conflict was not 'forgotten' or ignored:

peace was sought since the end of the Cold War, and the UN played a major role in providing humanitarian aid to Angola aid during the ups and downs of the peace process. But this aid was always insufficient, and the human cost of the conflict tragically 'excessive', due in part to the singular nature of the UN's commitment to what it referred to as 'peace efforts'. In practice, these consisted of direct and indirect support for the government's military option, coupled with limited and selective repair of damage caused by the increasingly murderous practices of both sides.

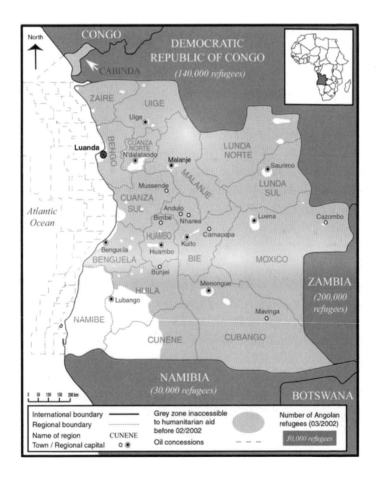

The roots of the conflict and slide into the 1998 war

The origins of the 1998 war can be traced to the split within Angolan nationalism which, fed by Cold War rivalries, exploded at independence into a civil and international conflict. The strategic regional and international stakes and Angola's oil wealth fuelled the confrontation which pitted UNITA (National Union for the Total Independence of Angola) against the MPLA (Popular Movement for the Liberation of Angola) to the end of the 1980s. By then UNITA was a powerful, totalitarian guerrilla movement supported by Washington, and the MPLA, allied to Cuba and the Soviet Union was a repressive Marxist-Leninist party-state which soon began to misappropriate public property on a massive scale. Both wealthy due to outside support, the two camps depended little on their exhausted population, which longed for peace.

A peace accord was signed in 1991 at the instigation of the Cold War patrons – the USSR and the USA – and of the former colonial power, Portugal. The UN played only a peripheral role. The peace process reflected the balance of power in favour of the rebels and their American allies, and was principally designed to accompany UNITA's assumption of power via the ballot box.[1] The bias of the agreement and its implementation set off a logic of confrontation. The rejection by many Angolans of UNITA's leader, Jonas Savimbi, and the strength bestowed on the MPLA by its continuing control of the state, allowed the party in power to win the legislative elections, and Savimbi was

---

[1] Cf. C. Messiant, 'Angola : le retour à la guerre ou l'inavouable faillite d'une intervention internationale', *L'Afrique politique 1994,* Paris, Karthala, 1994: 199-229.

surpassed in the first round of the presidential election. The agreement thereupon exploded into a war of unparalleled violence; UNITA refused to accept its defeat and the MPLA refused to share 'all the power' which the elections had just given back to it.

The transition to a multiparty system under the continued ascendancy of the former single party led to a realignment of Angola's international partners. As strategic confrontations ebbed, the government's new legitimacy merged with a growing interest in oil, which multinational companies and the Luanda government had long been exploiting in offshore oilfields shielded from the war. The turnaround by UNITA's former allies, initiated by the United States, induced the UN in 1993 to vote for sanctions against the rebels. Isolated and with considerable military inferiority, UNITA signed the 'Lusaka Protocol' in November 1994. This required the unilateral demilitarisation of UNITA and the handover of territories under its control as a prelude to its participation in government. As an additional inducement towards peace, the sanctions aimed at bringing UNITA to the negotiation table remained in place.

Despite the deployment of significant international peacekeeping forces, implementation of the protocol suffered from a structural impasse: the rebels did not want to disarm without having access to power that the government had no intention of sharing except in a purely formal manner. The UN (represented first by UNAVEM III, then by MONUA) once again failed in its role: it let the two sides violate both the agreement

('UNITA by day, the government by night'[2]) and citizens' rights with impunity. Preferring to 'see nothing, say nothing', it proceeded with a 'peace process' that was undermined by the fictitious character of the 'progress' being made: UNITA did not demilitarise and the 'Government of Unity and National Reconciliation' (GURN) remained so only in name. Secure in its legitimacy, the government rearmed massively, almost openly, while UNITA did so secretly from the illicit sale of diamonds mined in the zones under its control.

The impasse that crystallised in 1997-8 could only be resolved by reviewing the implementation of the agreements or by force of arms. The UN clearly chose to side with the government in its choice to pursue the latter option, a choice which was to have a devastating effect on civilians in UNITA zones, described further below. The UN did not condemn the government's military operations in the Democratic Republic of Congo and in Congo-Brazzaville which aimed to deprive UNITA of its rear bases, and the Security Council passed new sanctions – extended in June 1998 to the diamond trade – against the rebels, who were continuing to delay the handover of their territory. This led the government to believe it had sufficient strength and support to launch a 'war to put an end to the war'. UN member states considered that UNITA had 'tried the patience of the international community', and they acquiesced in a military weakening of the rebels in order to force them to disarm. Thus recommended a war between an 'illegitimate' rebellion that used diamonds to fund the military imposition of its political demands, and

---

[2] According to the Special Representative of UN Secretary in Angola, Issa Diallo.

a 'legal' government which chose to impose forcibly the disarmament agreed in a political process.

But this was also a government whose hegemonic control and drift towards political racketeering had increased since the war of 1992-4, causing misery and social discontent which was contained only with difficulty by the existence of the 'enemy', UNITA. The regime had other ambitions than disarming its main political opponent: Angolan President José Eduardo dos Santos stated publicly that his government was aiming for the 'military *and political* annihilation' of the rebels. He ruled out 'forever' any negotiations with 'the warmongering UNITA'. For the MPLA what mattered was assuring its own continued hegemony and impunity by means of a military victory. This meant that the UN would have to give up trying to resolve the conflict peacefully and relinquish its role as mediator.

Governmental intransigence and international concessions

The government prepared the political ground for its offensive by creating in September 1999 a so-called 'reformed' UNITA, as well as by increasing the number of *faits accomplis* and stepping up pressure on the UN. Constantly denouncing MONUA's passivity vis-à-vis UNITA, it barred Kofi Annan's Special Representative from establishing contact with Savimbi, and forbade all UN flights, even humanitarian ones, to enter rebel territory. On 5 December 1998 Angola's president declared war and demanded that MONUA leave as soon as its mandate expired. The Angolan Armed Forces (FAA) launched an offensive that was immediately followed by a UNITA counter-offensive.

Banking on their considerable superiority in military resources (including a powerful air force), the authorities anticipated a short war. But the first two offensives (end of 1998, beginning of 1999) failed to dislodge the rebels from their strongholds. In order to ensure continuing international support, the government reformulated its war aims in terms that accorded with the Lusaka Protocol. But it still ruled out negotiations with 'the warmongering UNITA' – recognising only its 'reformed' dissidents – and told MONUA to leave the country.

After withdrawing in February 1999, the UN tried to get the government to readmit it in the hope of not having to acknowledge final failure in Angola. It deployed all means at its disposal to assuage the hostility of the government and, eventually, to support it. To be sure, it could not declare Luanda's war to be 'just', nor recognise the 'reformed UNITA' upheld by the government. But neither was the UN in a position to set limits to its commitment, if only with regard to international law. It had neither the authority nor the political will to do so.

Almost all the most powerful states within the UN were henceforth on the 'good' side of the 'legal' government, and more precisely that of the president who, with the oil profits under his control, made all the decisions. Many states supported Luanda almost unconditionally (Russia and the former 'socialist bloc', Brazil, Portugal, Israel, Spain, and African allies in the regional wars). Others favoured *a priori* a political solution to the conflict. But, like the United States – which saw Angola, from which it obtained 7 percent (soon to be twice as much) of its oil supplies, as a 'strategic partner' – they knew that competition was harsh, even for great powers. After all, the Angolan president had been able to threaten retaliation against French oil interests following the judicial explosion of 'Angolagate' in February 2001, and the government issued a warning to any oil companies who considered making public the payments they had made to 'Angola'. In support of their multinationals and in defence of their influence in the region, most powerful governments were ready to give their support, if not directly to the war, then at least to the 'legal' government that had opted for it. The latter obtained economic and even military resources for the war from a number of its partners.

Influenced by the interests of its members and anxious to be involved at all cost in any future peace process, the UN confined its support to the legal government side, reinforced by the vote in favour of sanctions against the rebels. The UN chose not to understand the government's war aim, to conceal the regime's categorical refusal to negotiate with UNITA, and to designate the rebels as the 'party mainly to blame for the failure of the peace process'. It referred to the resumption of the conflict as if it were a phenomenon with no cause. When the government repeatedly predicted an imminent end to the conflict – which it reduced to 'UNITA's atrocities' – especially following its victorious offensives in the autumn of 1999 and in 2000, it was soon only the rebels' crimes and 'acts of war' that the UN mentioned.

True to the government's expectations, the UN devoted all its efforts to strengthening application of the sanctions decreed against UNITA. It was encouraged in this by an international climate favourable to the 'moralisation of international relations'. In fact, numerous NGOs mobilised against the 'conflict

diamonds' which enabled the rebels to finance their war
effort (a mobilisation unlikely to displease De Beers'
competitors, who at the time were engaged in major
manoeuvres to try and break the South African
company's near-monopoly of the diamond market). The
UN's Sanctions Committee had support and was active.
It did not worry about the illicit pillage of diamonds by
the government side, nor did it make use of exemptions,
though these were explicitly provided for in its mandate,
in order to assist civilian populations in rebel areas. On
the contrary, the UN and its member states referred to
the sanctions to justify their refusal to enter into contact
with UNITA, even for the purpose of negotiating the
transit of humanitarian aid. Seen in this way, the
sanctions did not just contribute considerably to the
government's legitimacy, but were also an essential
element in its strategy of isolating its enemy politically.
Together with the discreet aid provided by a number of
countries, the sanctions had a direct effect on the
military outcome: applied for the first time to a rebellion
(rather than a state), they were exceptionally effective to
the point of progressively cutting off UNITA's external
provisions. The denial of aid to the populations under
rebel control, populations that had become UNITA's
only 'resource', also weakened its ability to conduct the
war and even to survive.

    In return for these outstanding efforts, the
government finally (in September 2000) authorised the
UN to return within the framework of a mission,
ONUA, but only on the government's terms: with 30
members and without any mandate for mediation or
power. Thus, the UN let itself be sucked into
unwavering support for the authorities to the point of

violating its own legality, to the detriment of the civilians caught up in the war.

In the 'grey zones': a war without witnesses, without limits

The UN's abdication of its humanitarian obligations left populations in battle zones and rebel areas without assistance or protection. Without witnesses, the war could unfold at leisure with all the violence 'required' or authorised by the two sides. Some 80-90 percent of the territory situated outside the 'security perimeters' drawn between 5 and 30 km around government-controlled towns and villages remained beyond the reach of humanitarian organisations. In addition to numerous practical obstacles (battles, mines, destroyed bridges, impassable roads), aid agencies were confined to the more secure zones for two reasons: the government's determination to enforce the UNITA blockade, and the consent of the UN. After ceasing negotiations with UNITA over 'humanitarian corridors' in October 1999, the United Nations stopped asking government authorisation for access to populations in the 'grey zones', without, however, envisaging any alternatives (an air bridge or operations from neighbouring countries). The Security Council diplomatically ceased issuing reminders that the belligerents had a duty to facilitate access by humanitarian organisations to all populations affected by the conflict. Having abandoned those Angolans declared 'inaccessible', it no longer spoke of their existence except in veiled terms, minimising their number and their needs.

UNITA, for its part, did not pursue contacts with the very few organisations – ICRC and Médecins Sans

Frontières – which had tried to provide help to 'its' populations, either. Until the FAA's first victorious offensives in September 1999, this *de facto* refusal revealed UNITA's subordination of humanitarian concerns to its goal of political recognition. This recognition could only come from the UN. With the subsequent deterioration of its military strength, it is hard to know to what point in time UNITA would have been able to guarantee the safety of relief operations which had become vital, even to persons close to the rebel leaders. The fact remains, however, that this refusal played no part in the UN's renunciation of negotiations for humanitarian access outside the governmental zones.

For over three years (from the end of 1998 to the beginning of 2002), hundreds of thousands of Angolans were unable to request or receive assistance: more than 3 million were estimated to be beyond reach in 1999, with an additional million at the time of the ceasefire. The war was conducted without witnesses, but first-hand accounts of it exist. Collected from all sorts of survivors, they do not provide a complete picture of the situation in the main war zones, the war having assumed different forms, rhythms and dimensions in the numerous provinces it ravaged. But wherever the survivors came from, they allow us to discern both common traits and differences in the practices of the two armies. They also show a clear intensification of the violence during the last two years of the conflict.

UNITA had always had recourse to terror as a means of domination, and increasingly 'relied on its own forces', i.e. on the populations it controlled, to wage war. Its methods became increasingly radical: it stepped up forced recruitment of men and children, extortion and pillage, and the exploitation of those who accompanied it willingly or unwillingly (such as soldiers, porters, servants, labourers, and women forced into marriage). Its violence worsened. Although UNITA soldiers had always dealt out beatings and humiliations and even killed in order to impose obedience, they had not, as a rule, cut off ears or arms. From this point on, first-hand accounts report such practices and, more generally, a worsening of the combatants' cruelty.

The government army did not have the same traditions, nor was it in the same position. But throughout the war, its aircraft and artillery remained deadly to civilians. Men and adolescents were forcibly recruited in battle zones. With some exceptions, the troops – the FAA, but also the Civil Defence and police that were sometimes involved – were poorly paid and poorly supplied. Enjoying almost total impunity, they too paid themselves at the expense of the population, whom they plundered through *batidas*, a common practice consisting of stripping a village of its goods and forcing its inhabitants to carry them to the base. While rapes had not been a common practice in this war, they henceforth became frequent. The greatest violence, however, was not that marked by cruelty or humiliation, but that linked to the anti-guerrilla strategy which, from 2000 onwards, aimed to 'drain the pond' (the population) which allowed the 'fish' (the guerrillas) to survive. This policy gave rise to massive forced transfers of tens of thousands of people. Their villages burnt and their means of subsistence gone, they left under the threat of execution should they refuse to obey, or sometimes even submitted voluntarily, in the hope of finding aid. Civil and military authorities periodically announced to humanitarian organisations the arrival of new 'displaced persons', produced not by fighting but by 'cleansings' (*limpezas*), and sometimes brought by truck or even helicopter.

From these first-hand accounts it emerges that occasionally from 2000 onwards, and especially from 2001, a second phase of the war – one which they recall with the words 'too much suffering' – gave rise to three types of existence in the 'grey zones'.

The first concerns civilians living in areas that were not under permanent control by either side and were the object of incessant attacks and counter-attacks. These were increasingly accompanied by the pillage of goods (down to kitchen utensils and clothes) and by reprisals, if only for having remained there – both by UNITA, as it found itself increasingly hard-pressed, and by the FAA, determined to 'cleanse' (*limpar*) the area of civilians in order to tighten the noose around UNITA. In these areas, where the people often spoke of *'a tropa'* (soldiers) – referring to those of either side who plunder, kill, rape and burn villages, indistinguishable in their violence – they paint a picture of a flight, initially meant to be temporary but prolonged due to the impossibility of returning to their villages to farm, the arrival of famine and sickness, and 'many dead'.

The second type of existence concerned the populations accompanying UNITA units, often by force, that faced ever more frequent moves from base to base, sometimes leaving everything behind. They suffered long deprivation of salt, medicines and clothes, and a regime of fear and harsh repression of those who tried to flee or who, wounded or sick, might simply 'provide information to the enemy'. In some regions where FAA's encirclement tightened, they faced months of reduced subsistence on honey, mushrooms and roots, provoking the death of the weakest and increasing the fragility of all (including senior UNITA leaders).

The final months of the war saw the creation of a third type of grey zone which, though shielded from the battles, remained inaccessible to humanitarian organisations but not to the FAA. Tens of thousands of Angolans remained 'stored', without any assistance, in places where the army had assembled them and which it forbade them to leave. Initially, these 'displaced persons' were able to find food and were somewhat relieved to finally have some 'quiet', but soon there was nothing left. Then, the survivors recount, 'we started to die' (see Box below). Tens of thousands of Angolans perished silently in these death camps, without the army raising the alarm and without the UN, which was aware of the situation, showing any public concern about it.

Bunjei, a cemetery town

At the end of 2001, the Médecins Sans Frontières teams based at Caala in Huambo Province began to receive an increasing number of severely malnourished children, brought from the advanced military post of Bunjei by government forces. Situated 4 hours away by road and the site of an FAA encampment, the village was considered to be in a 'grey zone', i.e. inaccessible to relief organisations.

Two weeks after the government declared a unilateral ceasefire, the Caala military authorities authorised MSF to conduct an exploratory mission to Bunjei on 29 March 2002. MSF found a horrifying situation. The former village had been transformed into a vast displaced persons' camp where, crammed together, hundreds of huts made of branches and leaves stretched as far as the eye could see. 'When we arrived, the people were seated in front of their straw houses, so weak that some of them could no longer move; they were waiting for death,' explained an MSF doctor. A rapid assessment estimated that 30 percent of the children were suffering from acute malnutrition and that 14 people were dying daily. Three new cemeteries containing over 1,050 newly dug graves had been created at the entrance to the village.

The 14,000 displaced persons at Bunjei were among those Angolans 'cleansed' by the government forces in the course of their offensive against UNITA. Some had been there since September 2001. The FAA had forbidden them to leave the village. Only small groups escorted by soldiers could leave to look for wild berries or a few cassava roots.

MSF took charge of the severely malnourished children in its Caala therapeutic feeding centre and launched a nutrition program for children under five years old. General food distributions only began 6 weeks later, after the World Food Programme received authorisation from the UN Office of Humanitarian Affairs (OCHA), i.e. from the government.

A retrospective mortality study estimated that between 1 January and 22 June 2002, the mortality rate among children under five years old rose to 9.9 deaths per 10,000 persons per day. This is ten times higher than the alert threshold characterising extreme emergency situations.

Assistance to accessible populations

From the time fighting began, salvation lay in flight abroad or towards the 'security perimeters' around towns. The war produced enormous numbers of displaced people: there were 1.6 million displaced before the conflict resumed, and there were a million more in June 2000, at the end of the FAA's victorious offensives. Throughout almost the entire country, they continued to arrive every month by the thousands or tens of thousands; survivors who, individually or in groups, had managed to slip away from the 'grey zones', UNITA, or the death camps, or who were picked up by the FAA from 'cleansed' areas. From mid-2001 on, the United Nations estimated that 4 million people were displaced – one third of the population.

Yet it was not until over one year later, when the conflict ended for good, that the Security Council met to consider the humanitarian issues. UN relief agencies and national and international NGOs – some 300 in number, almost all of which operated under OCHA's coordination – worked within the limits established by the UN's political branch. Hence they ignored the populations in the 'grey zones', concentrating their activity and their appeals instead on those that were politically and physically accessible in and around government-held towns.

The humanitarian response was substantial (in 2001, the Angolan crisis received the third largest volume of aid after North Korea and Sudan) but insufficient. This was partly due to the cost of air transport that was necessary for most operations due to the insecurity on the roads. But it was also due to the fact that it was not only war victims that received aid: humanitarian aid was used to compensate for failures of the MPLA's 'governance'. Accustomed to allocating any state revenue that was not already embezzled to the war effort and privileges of the elite, the government provided only minuscule health and education budgets and derisory salaries to state employees. The government had long since abandoned the care of marginalised and destitute Angolans to the churches and international aid organisations, and gave humanitarian aid the least importance in its 'integrated' politico-military strategy. Thus international assistance was welcomed by the regime to address the serious food and health crisis affecting hundreds of thousands of displaced persons assembled in camps, those who had flocked to the towns, and a growing number of 'residents'. The leaders' indifference to their people made humanitarian aid vital to the survival of a large percentage of the Angolan population. Yet, under such conditions, help for the victims inevitably remained inadequate.

Given its weak position, the UN was not even able to ensure that civilians' minimum rights were respected in government-held zones. 'Rapid assessments' carried out in April 2000 revealed the generally appalling conditions in which displaced persons had been assembled, often without access to cultivable land, in camps lacking water or shelter, and sometimes on mined land outside the security perimeters. OCHA tried to get the government to put an end to this state of affairs and apply minimal standards for camp facilities. Seven months later, a report found that very little had been done, save for the elimination of the most intolerable situations. Nonetheless, the UN highlighted 'undeniable positive developments'. It likewise praised the government for having finally accepted the standards discussed, even if they were not being adhered to in practice. Indeed, until the end of the war, minimum standards were not generally respected in either the camps of origin or in the places where the authorities 'resettled' displaced persons from mid-2000 onwards.

Although the 'war for peace' was intensifying, the government tried to say and show that 'normalisation' was underway by eliminating the 'problem of displaced persons.' This was done via a process of resettlement in areas other than the IDPs areas of origin, sometimes by force or with the lure of false promises. The vast majority of relief agencies collaborated in this further 'positive development', arguing that it was better for the populations to be out of the squalid camps. While it had not been party to these decisions, OCHA backed the policy, which accorded with the line promulgated by the government and the UN to downplay the war and its ravages.

Confronted with the 'fatigue' of donors increasingly reluctant to finance seemingly endless humanitarian assistance in a country with a rich government, the regime took some steps to demonstrate a more resolute concern for its population. Out of an annual budget of between 3 and 5 billion dollars, it ended up at the end of 2000 devoting some 50 million to aid work. It then laid claim to the position of 'biggest donor of humanitarian aid in Angola', which suffices to indicate how it saw its relationship with its people.

Disquiet and intensification of the war: towards victory

As the war continued and the incessant arrival of displaced persons made it difficult to ignore the scorched earth policy underway in the grey zones, the United Nations' position became uncomfortable. This discomfort was exacerbated by the formation in 2001, for the first time, of a movement in opposition to the war. Speaking through the Catholic Church, which was respected and to which the majority of the population belonged, the movement denounced the war as 'criminal' and 'unjust' on both sides. Assembled around an Inter-Church Committee for Peace (Coiepa), this movement called for the opening of humanitarian corridors and for negotiations with UNITA and Savimbi in order to achieve a genuine political solution to the conflict, with the involvement of civilian parties.

This coincided with mounting revelations from abroad regarding the embezzlement of oil revenues by the presidential 'oiligarchy' and of the misappropriation of public funds, estimated at nearly a billion dollars a year. This undermined the image of a government which was demanding political support in the name of its democratic legitimacy, and requesting humanitarian assistance on the basis of a lack of funds. Other, more prosaic factors caused some of the regime's props to wobble: some states wondered whether a political solution to the conflict might ensure a more favourable climate for greater investment. The UN and several states had recently become involved in the DRC's peace initiatives by routes involving more dialogue than in Angola, and considered that the indefinite continuation of the conflict might compromise their initiatives. Some states began to question the relevance of sanctions.

Faced with the risk that the international community might distance itself from the regime's military radicalism, the FAA intensified their offensive in the hope of eliminating Savimbi and dealing the rebels a final blow. A weakened UNITA was seeking to open negotiations, the Sant' Egidio Community was working towards the same end, and Coiepa's voice was finally being heard abroad (in December 2001, the European Parliament awarded its president the Sakharov peace prize). The Security Council took a long time to 'welcome' Coiepa's activity and remained deaf to its appeals. This mobilisation, however, had emerged from 'civil society', whose 'vibrant development' the UN claimed to be supporting and which was campaigning for a 'just and lasting peace' – precisely the one that the 'international community' claimed to be seeking. The UN, who could only note (unofficially) that the government did not want to negotiate, undertook no initiatives at the political or humanitarian level that might displease Luanda. The Secretary-General's report of October 2001 showed that the UN knew the situation in the 'inaccessible' areas was desperate, yet it makes no mention of 'humanitarian corridors', the necessity for which was henceforth defended by some governments and the European Parliament. Under pressure from countries friendly to Luanda, the UN called for... the strengthening of sanctions against the rebels.

When, in mid-December 2001, victory seemed well and truly 'around the corner', Angola's president gave the UN 'authorisation' to contact UNITA and called for the mobilisation of humanitarian relief. The UN then reacted, but without any great haste: Savimbi's death on 22 February occurred before the authorisation by President dos Santos had had any political consequences. Moreover, the human tragedy of the war's final months was not in the least mitigated in the still 'inaccessible' areas.

The ensuing tragedy

Having achieved peace by force of arms, the government was in a position to dictate terms to UNITA's surviving leaders. They accepted the agreement that Luanda put to them out in the bush, which essentially came down to the disarmament of the rebels. In barely two months UNITA sent more than 80,000 soldiers and their families (over 250,000 people) to demobilisation camps. In this respect the ability of a greatly weakened rebel leadership to get its troops to march, and its willingness to adopt this course, invalidated the prevailing discourse about UNITA's disarray.

The victory enabled UNITA's surrender to be registered under the Lusaka Protocol. This re-labelling was highly desirable for the UN – in order to reinstate this 'exemplary' peace (exemplary because it was 'the work of Angolans alone') among 'UN successes', it was desirable to reactivate the protocol and for the UN to regain its place in it. At the end of a war whose aim had been to avoid negotiating the country's future with anyone, the government, however, did not intend to allow any interference in its peace plan or impediments to its political objectives.

Although the war was over, the Angolans continued to pay the price for the subordinate relationship between the UN and the Angolan government. While the end of hostilities was celebrated with great pomp in Luanda, nothing was said about civilians in the grey zones or those herded together by the army and lacking assistance, who continued to die en masse. It took an independent humanitarian organisation, MSF, to listen to the haggard survivors of the high plateau, and to venture beyond the security perimeters to publicly raise the alarm. In the death centres it found in Bunjei, Chilembo, Chitendo and Chipindo, MSF discovered that 10 percent of children under five suffered from severe acute malnutrition, while mortality rates were three to six times greater than the threshold characterising extreme emergency situations (see Box pp. 123-4). Suddenly the catastrophe which had been sensed but piously concealed was glimpsed in its full gravity and magnitude: these survivors in grey zones were soon estimated at some 500,000.

It took appeals by individual administrators and FAA soldiers, as well as open denunciations, before people began to talk publicly about the catastrophic state of soldiers and civilians assembled in the UNITA demobilisation camps, where malnutrition and mortality rates sometimes reached those observed in the civilian death centres. The authorities, of course, did not want a food crisis to jeopardise the rebels' demobilisation, so appealed for international assistance. But they also wanted to marginalise the UN from a peace process that had yet to be defined and which they planned to reduce to its simplest terms. They had no intention of allowing the UN to interfere in the running of the demobilisation areas, which they entrusted to the FAA. They preferred to allow the UN to mobilise aid which the government would distribute. Nor was Luanda inclined to forgo the profits associated with delivering relief supplies: one of the President's companies was assigned to do so and dealt with favoured partners in Brazil, despite the delays this would cause in reacting to the emergency.

The glaring insufficiency of aid in the newly accessible demobilisation areas and displaced camps led MSF to publicly denounce the 'scandalous' inertia of the government and UN on 11 June 2002 in Luanda. This denunciation was important in bringing about some change in the situation, directed as it was against both the government and UN. After having worked in contravention of international humanitarian law for a long time, OCHA had thought that it could enter into a covert trial of strength with the government – without, however, distancing itself publicly from the Angolan authorities. When the authorities themselves failed to respond to the crisis, OCHA demanded that they henceforth allow the United Nations relief agencies to operate according to their own norms within the UNITA demobilisation areas. Simultaneous public denunciations and discreet but persistent pressures lasting for over two months were needed before Luanda finally accepted that OCHA and the NGOs working under its wing could access the soldiers' families and areas of forced assembly. The government benefited from the UN's silence and abdication of responsibility by publicly attributing to it a responsibility which was, in the first instance, its own. OCHA meanwhile defended itself vigorously against MSF's accusations of inertia, first by playing down the crisis, and then by claiming it had insufficient aid to react to this 'sudden' emergency. The government seized on the dispute to launch a solemn and dramatic appeal for international aid, and criticised the 'international community' for having not provided Angolans with the help it owed them.

The fate of forcibly displaced populations and combatants and their families held in camps hung on the politico-military negotiations underway between the UN and the government. Almost all Angolan and foreign NGOs, which since the start of the conflict had been working mainly as 'operating partners' of the UN, refrained from taking relief directly to the grey zones until the UN gave permission. For two and a half months following the ceasefire, the UN's humanitarian agencies and their partner NGOs responded only to the needs of populations already accessible to them, while seeking to assess the situation in the new areas. They took time to identify the groups in distress and to organise a response. Swamped by an emergency whose dimensions it had not allowed itself to gauge, the 'humanitarian community' was then forced to juggle its resources, taking from some people in order to deal with the most pressing crises. At the end of 2002 some isolated pockets of people had still not received help. Seriously undernourished, sick people continued to emerge from the bush, leaving numerous dead behind them.

OCHA and its 'non-governmental' operational partners once more found themselves tagging along behind decisions taken unilaterally by the authorities for the return of the displaced persons and the demobilisation of combatants (see Box). At the start of 2003 over a million people were still in an emergency situation. Unable to meet their own needs, hundreds of thousands of Angolans were at risk of once more needing assistance. When the rains came, many would be beyond the reach of the aid organisations – for technical reasons this time, or because of mines.

Reintegration or dispersal?

Just when the humanitarian community had organised itself to provide rudimentary assistance in the demobilisation areas, the government decided to change its announced plan to reintegrate UNITA soldiers into 'civil society and the labour market' and instead to organise their 'evacuation' and 'dispersal'. At the end of 2002, OCHA's role was once again reduced to attempting to 'regulate', delay and humanise a 'dispersal' which cared little about conditions in the areas of return and which would once again render inaccessible these people who had almost nothing with which to 'start over'.

Much of the resettlement of displaced persons and refugees occurred spontaneously: out of over 4 million internally displaced persons, about a million returned home before the end of 2002, as did a quarter of the 500,000 refugees. This return illustrated the enormous relief the population felt about a peace in which, at last, they believed. But this spontaneous return also meant that the great majority were returning home without any assistance, and invariably to places lacking even minimal living conditions and security to enable them to resettle. The government was also engaged in 'evacuating' displaced persons from overpopulated camps or towns. It forced the pace of returns by playing on the miserable conditions under which the displaced were living, and promising better conditions elsewhere. The UN was again forced to try and repair the damage caused by unilateral official decisions taken without consideration for their human consequences.

In November 2002, the head of OCHA remarked publicly that only 15 percent of returns had been organised. Of these, barely 30 percent were carried out in conditions meeting minimal acceptable standards (food security, de-mining, access, means of production).

The human and political costs of an abdication of responsibility

Taking refuge in a legalistic argument, Angola's international partners and the UN gave the government political support while the basic principles of neutrality and impartiality of humanitarian assistance were violated. In this sense, they collaborated in 'the peace' won by a military victory that was not decided only on the battlefield. They had also created conditions that allowed a war to be fought without limits by both sides, and a total war in the final months. Hence peace was achieved at considerable cost to human beings. The UN and the 'international community' had without doubt provided invaluable assistance to hundreds of thousands of victims. But they had also contributed to producing victims, and to preventing help from reaching them.

The human cost of the conflict was excessively high, and remained so following the ceasefire due to the tragedy the UN and government allowed to unfold, and which they jointly concealed. It might have remained hidden because the government's victory left it in a position of strength not only in relation to UNITA but also to 'all the others' (notably the UN and the peace movement). The marginalisation of the UN in an ad hoc 'peace process', and its general discredit in Angola (in the eyes of all) meant that no real political solution was found to the Angolan crisis. The peace fulfilled the government's promises of a return to 'normality', but did not involve 'reconciliation' or 'transition'. It was also achieved without the UN, except for technical and humanitarian assistance, hence leaving the regime in a position of strengthened hegemony. From now on, if 'all went well', it would be in a position to exercise even greater control over political life until elections would legitimise its power, ensure its hegemony and guarantee its impunity.

To be sure, Angola's international partners henceforth maintained a greater distance vis-à-vis the authorities. They called on them to account for public funds and to 'do more for their people'. In July 2002 Britain's ambassador to the UN remarked that some 150 million dollars requested from the international community to finance relief operations were equivalent to 3 weeks' worth of oil revenues. But the international community was not able to use aid to blackmail the government any more than it had been during the war, because of both the magnitude of the needs and the risk that a botched demobilisation would pose to peace. Furthermore, given the closeness of the ties forged with the highest level of Angola's government by so many businesses and foreign governments, it was feared that the 'battles' undertaken by the international community for the democratisation of Angola would be waged in other areas (such as privatisations and the 'governance' needed for security of contracts) than that of 'answering the people's needs'. Moreover, President dos Santos announced a few days after Savimbi's death that Angola would oppose any 'interference' and 'police demands'. Nevertheless, there remains an Angolan civic, social and political movement that mobilised during the war without international help and for that movement peace – even this one – is something precious.

Bibliographical references

C. Messiant, 'La Fondation Eduardo dos Santos (FESA): à propos de l'investissement' de la société civile par le pouvoir angolais', *Politique Africaine* 73, March 1999, pp. 82-102.

C. Messiant, 'Angola, une 'victoire' sans fin? Une 'petite guerre' dans 'l'endroit le plus excitant du monde'', *Politique Africaine* 81, March 2001, pp. 143-61; and 'Fin de la guerre en Angola. Vers quelle paix?', *Politique Africaine* 86, June 2002, pp. 183-95.

C. Messiant, 'Angola: des alliances de la guerre froide à la juridisation du conflit', in P. Hassner and R. Marchal (eds), *La guerre entre le global et le local*, Paris, L'Harmattan, 2003.

A. Richardson, *Negotiating humanitarian access in Angola: 1990-2000*, Geneva, UNHCR Working Paper 18, June 2000 ; and *Angola: civil war and humanitarian crisis – developments from mid 1999 to end 2001*, Geneva, UNHCR, January 2002.

Global Witness, *A Rough Trade: The Role of Companies and Governments in the Angolan Conflict*, London, Global Witness, 1998; and *All the President's Men: The Devastating Story of Oil and Banking in Angola's Privatised War*, London, Global Witness, 2002.

Human Rights Watch, *Angola Unravels: The Rise and Fall of the Lusaka Peace Process*, New York: HRW, 1999; and *The War is Over: The Crisis of Angola's Internally Displaced Continues*, New York, HRW, June 2002.

Médecins Sans Frontières, *Derrière les faux-semblant de 'normalisation', manipulation et violences, une population abandonnée*, Luanda, MSF, November 2000; *Angola, une population sacrificiée*, Paris, MSF, October 2002; and *Angola, après la guerre, l'abandon*, Geneva, MSF, August 2002.

6

SUDAN
Who Benefits from
Humanitarian Aid?

Marc Lavergne & Fabrice Weissman

Since 1983, the war in Sudan has led to hundreds of thousands of deaths, triggered several famines and forced millions of Sudanese into internal exile or refuge abroad. Operation Lifeline Sudan, the huge multi-NGO aid operation launched by the United Nations in 1998, was not the success it should have been. Belligerents have acquired great expertise in capturing or controlling humanitarian resources which then become vital to the political economy of the conflict while Western states seem more concerned with using aid as an instrument of political pressure than with the fate of the victims of war. Consequently, aid operations are of limited benefit to civilian populations who are often sacrificed to the political and military objectives of the different actors in the conflict. As most aid organisations are preoccupied with maintaining a presence at almost any price, they bear a heavy responsibility for this state of affairs.

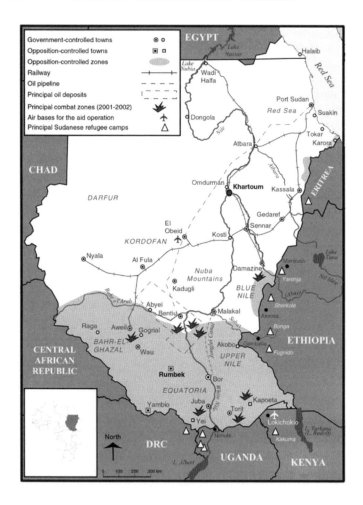

The Cold War and tribal militias

Sudan has barely experienced ten years of peace since it gained independence in 1956. The duration of the conflict illustrates the difficulties involved in transforming the former Anglo-Egyptian condominium into a state capable of according equal rights to all its ethnic and religious components. Africa's largest country in land area, Sudan has 31 million inhabitants and more than 500 ethnicities and 100 languages. It is also distinguished by great religious diversity and a plurality of practices within each religion (Islam, Christianity, and Animism). Arab-Muslim culture is the predominant component of this mosaic. Its supremacy is both numeric – 70 percent of the population has Arabic as its mother tongue or Islam as its religion – and symbolic, the Christian-Animist populations of the South being objects of contempt for the dominant culture.

Even before independence, the keys to central power were given to tribes north of the Nile Valley who considered themselves the country's legitimate masters. Northern Sudan has benefited from the lion's share of public and private investment over the last fifty years although most of the country's natural resources (notably oil) are located in the South. The ostracism suffered by the southern Sudanese – and to a lesser extent by the Muslim populations furthest from central power (the Fur in the west, the Beja in the northeast, the Funj in the east) – fuels a conflict that, in various forms and with varying intensity, has been a fixture of the country's history since 1955.

In May 1983 the central government reneged on a peace agreement signed with the leaders of an early southern independence rebellion, provoking a new insurrection in the Upper Nile basin, a region populated mainly by Nilotic peoples (Nuer, Dinka, Shiballah). John Garang, a former colonel in the government army, organised the rebels into the Sudan Peoples' Liberation Army and Movement (SPLA/M). Its stated aim was not the secession of the South but the establishment of an equitable power-sharing structure in a united and secular 'new Sudan', that would ensure the equality of all citizens. From the beginning, the conflict was shaped by Cold War considerations. The SPLA enjoyed the military support of Ethiopia's Dergue regime, a Soviet ally, while the Gulf kingdoms and Western powers, seeking to 'contain communism' in the Horn of Africa, backed the Sudanese government.

Over the next few years the SPLA seized most of the territory in the South with the exception of the major urban centres. The government proved incapable of controlling the rebel threat and, from 1984-7, armed tribal militias recruited from the Arabised and Islamised nomadic tribes of the west. These *Murahilin*, hordes of horsemen equipped with automatic weapons, were unleashed on the civilian populations of the South. They razed villages and stole livestock, causing major population displacements and a terrible famine that killed over 500,000 people, mostly Dinka. In military terms, the use of tribal militias did not yield the expected results while a poorly equipped and disorganised army did little to hinder the SPLA's pursuit of its goals. The government was about to initiate peace talks when it was deposed by a military coup that brought the National Islamic Front (NIF) to power on 30 June 1989.

A 'rogue state' and its 'civilising project'

The NIF, with its mixture of local traditions and Islamist modernity, intended to 're-Islamise' Sudanese society (particularly by the imposition of *sharia* law throughout the country) and establish Sudan as the leader of a new, independent, and popular international Islamic order. The new regime could envisage no end to the conflict other than military victory and the country's submission to its 'civilising project'. War was henceforth glorified with the title of *jihad* ('struggle for the faith').

Yet government troops met with little success until 1991 when Tigrayan and Eritrean guerrillas backed by Khartoum toppled the Ethiopian Dergue. The SPLA was forced to abandon its rear bases in Ethiopia, and the loss of this external aid, vital to John Garang's control of the movement, triggered a series of splits. Several SPLA generals denounced their leader's authoritarianism and his tendency to favour officers from his own clan (Dinka-Bor), and defected, taking their weapons and troops with them. The SSIM (South Sudan Independence Movement, mostly Nuer) rapidly emerged as the most powerful of the breakaway factions. The SSIM and other dissident groups accepted military and financial support from Khartoum in order to combat SPLA loyalists and effectively became proxy forces for the Sudanese army. The war between the SPLA and the regime was thus exacerbated by internal conflict between southern factions, a situation fully exploited by the central power.

In 1992, while the government was re-equipping its troops with Iranian financial support, John Garang was rapidly acquiring new international sponsors. Khartoum, eager to promote the NIF political agenda at the international level, backed guerrilla movements hostile to the Eritrean, Ethiopian and Ugandan regimes which were all regarded as obstacles to the spread of Islamist revolution in Africa. The three countries severed diplomatic relations with Sudan in the mid-1990s and provided the SPLA with active support, a policy that was encouraged by the new American administration that took office in January 1993.

For Bill Clinton and his team, Sudan was no longer a Cold War ally but a 'rogue state', a perpetrator of human rights violations against the 'Christian populations of the South' and a 'Mecca for international terrorism'. Sudan supported Saddam Hussein during the first Gulf War and played host to a stream of international political and sometimes terrorist organisations, all fiercely hostile to the 'new world order' promoted by the US (particularly in the Arab sphere). 'Carlos the Jackal', Osama bin Laden and Sheik Omar Abd el-Rahman (later convicted of the 1993 attack on the World Trade Centre), as well as officials of Hamas and the Palestinian Islamic Jihad, all enjoyed the hospitality of the Sudanese government.

In addition to backing neighbouring states supportive of the SPLA, the US urged the United Nations to vote for sanctions in 1996 against Khartoum after the regime refused to extradite suspects implicated in an assassination attempt on the Egyptian President, Hosni Mubarak, in Addis Ababa in June 1995. Following the lethal attacks on its embassies in Nairobi and Dar es Salaam in 1998, the US bombed a pharmaceutical factory located in a suburb of Khartoum which it claimed – mistakenly, as it turned out – was manufacturing chemical weapons. Washington regarded the NIF's Sudan and the Taliban's Afghanistan as Osama bin Laden's principal international strongholds. France was the only Western state to maintain cordial relations with Khartoum, which had offered to hand over 'Carlos' and facilitate communication with Algerian Islamists in exchange for military, diplomatic and economic support.

The oil factor

Increasingly isolated on the international stage, the Sudanese government signed a peace protocol ('peace from within') in 1998 with the SSIM and five other SPLA dissident factions, mainly active in the Upper Nile region. Although it was supposed to demonstrate Khartoum's desire for peace, the agreement made it easier to enhance security in a region where important oil reserves were discovered in the 1970s. Several Western and Asian (particularly Chinese) companies resumed production on concessions in the Bentiu region that had been abandoned since 1983. By 1999 the construction of a pipeline linking the oilfields to the terminal at Port Sudan had been completed. Oil revenues allowed the government to build up its cash reserves and double its defence budget. Khartoum was thus in a position to intensify its war effort and offer more resistance to Western economic pressure designed to obstruct the regime's consolidation.

These developments encouraged the European Union to distance itself from the US position and turn towards a policy of 'constructive engagement' with the Sudanese government. Washington found itself in an awkward position - while ultra-conservative lobbies, the 'Black Caucus', and human rights activists were insisting that Sudan was a 'rogue state' that supported terrorism and 'genocidal' action against Christians as well as other violations of human rights, the business lobby was trying to shift the State Department towards a more conciliatory stance. Many in the US, particularly the oil industry, regarded Sudan as a major field of commercial opportunity which was being seized by Asian, European and Canadian companies. The US government was increasingly divided between those advocating greater pressure on Sudan and those who believed that the 'Sudanese threat' had been exaggerated. The latter took the view that the lack of a credible alternative to the current regime meant that it was better to renew dialogue with Khartoum before the regime consolidated economic and diplomatic ties with China and other Asian countries like Indonesia and Malaysia, and further strengthened its position.

Against this background the war in the Upper Nile region intensified as the SPLA concentrated on disrupting oil production. The sharing out of oil revenues also provoked rivalries among pro-government factions, some of which rejoined the SPLA following bloody internecine fighting that took a heavy toll on the civilian population.

Meanwhile, the government pursued its charm offensive on the international stage. In 1999 Hassan al-Turabi, founder of the NIF and alleged ideologue of Islamist terrorism, was ousted from his position as Assembly President and, two years later, placed under house arrest. Although the government could still count on fervent militants of the Islamist Revolution (like Vice President Ali Osman Mohamed Taha), its 'civilising project' was gradually relegated to the status of a simple slogan for internal political use. The regime increased its gestures of goodwill towards the international community in the hope of attracting funding and investment that would enable it to enhance its grip on power.

Although political repression eased in the northern cities, the war in the South gathered pace. In 2000, the conflict in the Bentiu region began to go the government's way despite the U-turn by the SSIM alliance (renamed SPDF), which returned to the SPLA fold at the end of 2001. The 1998-2000 war between Ethiopia and Eritrea also caused a setback for the armed opposition. Seeking to limit the number of fronts on which they were engaged, Addis Ababa and Asmara resumed more or less cordial relations with Khartoum and became increasingly cautious in their support for the Sudanese rebels although the latter still maintained a large strike force in their traditional strongholds in the South.

The arrival of George W. Bush in the White House on 3 January 2001 was good news for Khartoum: the new administration had close links with the business world and offered the possibility of a less hostile attitude towards it. Although it continued with public denunciations of America, the Sudanese government sought to capitalise from the change in leadership by giving the CIA access to its security files on terrorists wanted by the US. Following the attacks of 11 September 2001, Sudan proclaimed its innocence and denied any contact with Osama bin Laden since his departure from the country in 1996. Despite pressure from rightwing lobbies, President Bush became more involved in the search for a peaceful solution to a conflict that was judged to be a major cause of regional instability. The priority had shifted from isolating a regime guilty of 'genocidal' actions against Christians to the fight against terrorism in which Khartoum offered support. The White House remained distrustful of the NIF but nonetheless named John Danforth as special envoy to the region. Senator Danforth was charged with gauging the sincerity of the Sudanese government by submitting it to a number of 'tests' on the question of the war in southern Sudan. The efforts of the American administration and the EU led to a cease-fire in the highly symbolic central region of the Nuba Mountains (see Box), and the opening of new and more promising peace talks at Machakos in Kenya.

Peace in the Nuba Mountains?

The Nuba Mountains are a group of hills located in central Sudan, a predominantly Arab-Muslim region. The population is composed of some fifty linguistically and culturally diverse ethnic groups of African origin. Islam, introduced at a very early date, is widespread despite the work of Christian missionaries and the resistance of groups attached to animist cults.

Victims of racial discrimination and economic marginalisation, young Nuban intellectuals took up arms in the mid-1980s and joined the SPLA. The Nuba Mountains were excluded from Operation Lifeline Sudan and blockaded by Khartoum while remaining of marginal importance to SPLA strategy. The region was devastated by government repression as regular army and local militias wiped dozens of villages off the map, massacred the inhabitants or forced them into the towns of the North or the Dar es Salaams ('peace villages') below the hills.

This situation received a great deal of media attention in the West, where it was perceived as emblematic of Khartoum's persecution of 'Christian populations'. The American senator John Danforth insisted that negotiations between the government and the SPLA should include a renewable six-month cease-fire for the region.

Terms were agreed in January 2002 and provided for the disengagement of ground forces, an end to violence, freedom of movement between rebel-held mountain zones and plains controlled by the government, and the opening of the region to international aid. A military commission composed of representatives from the two camps and international observers would ensure that these conditions were respected. One year later, troops had been withdrawn but tribal militias had not disarmed. Food aid was reaching rebel zones but because of the conflict between the legitimacy claimed by the SPLA and the sovereignty affirmed by Khartoum, the measles epidemic that broke out in the summer of 2002 was allowed to run its course unhindered and claimed many lives.

The SPLA regarded the ceasefire as a feeble goodwill gesture designed to impress the international community, not as a prelude to the settlement of the problem in the Nuba Mountains. Despite the wishes of the exhausted civilian population, this remained secondary to a general settlement of the conflict.

The destruction of society in the South

The war has claimed many victims. The SPLA forces are equipped with armoured vehicles and heavy artillery and are organised on semi-conventional lines. They conduct a war of territorial conquest punctuated by guerrilla activity. The government deploys devastating attack helicopters (piloted by former-Soviet mercenaries), largely inaccurate bombers, and large mechanised units. Although military operations are relatively localised in space and time (they are usually conducted in the dry season in and around the northern part of the Bahr-el-Ghazal region, the garrison towns of Equatoria, the southern part of the Blue Nile region, and the oil-rich province of western Upper Nile), the threat the combatants pose to daily life is omnipresent. Khartoum controls the skies and bombs the whole territory with impunity. Militias continually form and disband and their attacks are as brutal as they are unpredictable.

All factions engage in massive reprisals against the inhabitants of 'enemy' villages conquered after violent battles. Summary executions, rape, abductions, the burning of houses, the theft of livestock, the destruction or pillage of food stocks, and forced recruitment follow every victory. A retrospective mortality study conducted by Médecins Sans Frontières in a village in Bahr-el-Ghazal revealed that more than one quarter of the villagers were executed (13 percent of the initial population) or abducted (9 percent) during a *murahilin* raid on 21 June 2001. Symbolic destruction and direct violence are employed to force populations into flight and thus deprive the opposition of popular support and the opportunity to replenish supplies. As for the government, it prioritises the protection of strategic installations like the railway to Wau, the oil pipeline to the Red Sea, and the oil concessions in western Upper Nile. It is also active securing land for Arabised pastoralists, allies of Khartoum, and large agricultural companies backed by Arab-Muslim capital in regions such as south of Damazin in the Blue Nile region and South Kordofan.

In addition to the violence employed to further strategic goals, the war encompasses a multitude of confrontations linked to the proliferation of militias. The intertribal strife between southern pastoralists and Islamic pastoralists belonging to the *murahilin*, and the fighting between southern militias are very different in their scope and significance from traditional conflicts over grazing rights or water. The massive distribution of firearms, inter-clan divisions fostered by the government, and the establishment of a predatory economy which unites northern livestock merchants and faction leaders have shattered the institutions that once regulated the use of force. As traditional conflicts are transformed into merciless wars, the spread of modern weapons erodes the social and political hierarchies within the various societies, rendering more difficult an eventual return to peace on the basis of the old social order.

> ## Soldier and victim
>
> At the end of July 2001, about 40 soldiers belonging to the SSUM (South Sudan United Movment, a pro-Khartoum militia) were hospitalised in a clinic run by Médecins Sans Frontières at Bentiu in the Upper Nile. They all had been forcibly recruited five or six months previously. Simon, the youngest, was twelve years old, and weighed 32 kilos for a height of 1.72 metres. All displayed signs of severe malnutrition aggravated by anaemia, diarrhoeal diseases, oedemas or tuberculosis. Most were unable to walk and were confined to their beds all day.
>
> On 21 August five of the combatants fled the clinic during the night. The SSUM reaction was immediate and brutal – armed men with orders to remove the remaining 34 soldiers surrounded the clinic. MSF negotiated a compromise: the SSUM officer would accompany the MSF doctor to judge whether or not the patients were fit to leave. The selection on a case-by-case basis was difficult and cruel. The officer decided that 24 soldiers were 'fit' and immediately took them away. One of them was incapable of walking. After several attempts to climb into the pick-up, he collapsed on the ground. Nine combatants were left in the clinic and seemed surprised that they had not been removed. The look of resignation in their eyes was heart-rending. Despite their condition, two of them managed to escape the following night.
>
> Fighters for the pro-government militias are forcibly recruited from the local Nuer populations or immigrants in the large towns of the North. Their resistance is broken by a regime of extreme brutality based on corporal punishment, intense training and underfeeding. Some attempt to flee, knowing they face death if they are caught. Others ensure that the population suffers as much as they do – at nightfall, the displaced persons of Bentiu lie low,

fearful of encountering soldiers drunk on home-brew who are liable to beat them, steal their meagre possessions, rape them, or press them into militia service. Recruitment intensified during the 2002-3 period. Although MSF managed to free members of its local staff and demand that sick soldiers should not be forced back to duty until they had recovered, the organisation is often forced to return these young Nuers to their tormentors. This is the terrible price that must be paid for continuing to feed and care for the 50,000 civilians who flocked to Bentiu in the hope of escaping the fighting and militias.

War is demolishing the institutions that provide balance to rural societies. Shepherds are particularly affected – their flocks might escape the raids but face difficulty obtaining access to pasture. Seasonal livestock migration is disrupted and grasslands are sometimes mined. Lack of animal vaccines has led to a resurgence of epizootic diseases. Farming has become an extremely hazardous occupation in a country where front lines are constantly shifting, especially as cultivated fields are prime targets at harvest time. In spite of what most humanitarian workers claim, the recurrent famines that afflict the South are due more to military operations, livestock and harvest theft, forced recruitment, and population displacement than to the vagaries of the climate.

When villages are subjected to repeated attacks, flight becomes the only option. Almost half a million Sudanese refugees have crossed the border into Uganda, Kenya, Ethiopia and the Central African Republic. Many of the refugee camps serve as SPLA rear bases and have been attacked as such in northern Uganda by the Lord's Resistance Army. Sudanese also flee to the larger towns of the North and South and are frequently subjected to the rough justice of pro-government militias who brutalise and rob the southern populations with impunity.

According to the UN, over 2 million displaced people have flocked to Khartoum and the northern cities where they are crammed into vast and squalid urban extensions, clusters of makeshift shelters that are gradually transformed into permanent shacks. Several thousand were forcibly transferred to 'peace villages' installed several kilometres from the capital at the edge of the desert. The government is torn between two attitudes towards the displaced: retain the maximum number of southerners far from their land and subject them to processes of Arabisation and Islamisation, or expel this population which is difficult to assimilate and represents a potential 'fifth column' introducing ways of life contrary to those imposed on the populations in the North. Having tried in vain to push back the displaced, the government opted to keep them under strict control. Yet the southerners' areas around Khartoum remain zones of poverty, massive unemployment and repression. The disintegration of southern societies is nevertheless giving way to attempts at reconstitution: conversions to Christianity are on the rise and new forms of solidarity that transcend ethnic divisions are addressing the prospect of a common future.

Conditions of life in SPLA zones are extremely variable. The Dinka dominate the movement and their clan system operates to the detriment of other ethnicities. In Equatoria, for example, Toposa pastoralists and warriors from the east, Didinga mountain people from the centre, and the Zandé farmers of the west all suffer from the predatory conduct of Dinka troops and frequently rebel against the insurgents' control. Despite a 'national convention' held Chukudum in 1994 with the intention of introducing a semblance of democratic transparency, the SPLA is still a strictly military movement overseen by a ruthless security apparatus. Its civil wing, the SPLM, is merely an appendix, as is the SRRA (Sudan Relief and Rehabilitation Association), the movement's 'humanitarian' branch, which exists to exercise control over the population and to secure international aid. The SPLA was influenced by its contacts with Mengistu's Ethiopia and its cadres have been trained in the Soviet style: the liberation struggle is conducted on authoritarian, Marxist-Leninist lines and civil society is at the disposal of the combatants. In this respect, John Garang's approach is little different from the modernising and authoritarian methods favoured by the Islamist leaders.

Humanitarian organisations in the service of diplomacy

Sudan has been the special focus of humanitarian attention since the 1985 famine that struck the Sahel regions and even more so since the 1987-8 famine that claimed 500,000 victims. Its image as a 'cursed country' is a 'selling point', with Western concerns about the desertification of the Sahel in the early 1990s replaced by sensitivity to the Christian/Muslim problem, which regularly takes the form of a one-sided condemnation of the North Sudanese regime. Sudan is also the site of Operation Lifeline Sudan (OLS), a vast, UN-sponsored international aid effort. Launched in the latter part of 1988, OLS is based on a tripartite agreement between UNICEF, the Sudanese government, and the SPLA.

The agreement was later extended to other southern factions (including the SSIM) and is intended to ensure the impartial provision of humanitarian aid in all the conflict zones.

The UN agencies and the forty-odd NGOs who chose to benefit from the operation's legal framework and logistical facilities (airlifts, a rear base at Lokichokio in northern Kenya, security guarantees) are strictly bound by the rules of the OLS charter. Two of these rules, however, directly contravene the basic principles that govern all humanitarian action. First, the Sudanese government retains a veto on where aid can be delivered: it can arbitrarily forbid humanitarian flights to populations affected by food shortages or violence and thus shield entire zones from the eyes of foreign witnesses. Second, in 1995 OLS signed an agreement with the SPLA that formally recognised its humanitarian wing, the SRRA, and gave it a key role in the organisation of aid and the control of its distribution. Although it is a branch of an insurrectionist movement dominated by a ruthless martial culture, the SRRA is regarded as an exceptional partner and humanitarian actor and has been given responsibility for guaranteeing that aid is distributed 'in all neutrality' and without regard for any 'political, military or strategic interest'.

In practice OLS has virtually no presence in the government-controlled zones, where humanitarian operations are strictly monitored by the regime. Khartoum believes NGOs are troublesome witnesses, tools in the pay of foreign powers, and purveyors of an ideology that is contrary to its 'civilising project'. The priority is therefore to exclude NGOs by operating a strict selection procedure ostensibly conducted in the name of efficiency and professionalism. Government-approved organisations have to abide by strict rules; access to populations is severely restricted (they are not allowed into theatres of armed operations like the Red Sea coast and the Blue Nile region) and their presence must be useful to the state or local institutions (as in Bentiu, where they help to resettle displaced populations on designated sites and where the presence of humanitarian organisations is used to deter attacks on strategic positions). Aid agencies are therefore engaged in a permanent and exhausting trial of strength with their 'partner' government institutions as they attempt to reach the populations most at risk. They struggle to avoid being manipulated into contributing to goals that are contrary to their humanitarian objectives.

The regime often accuses Western NGOs of seeking to evangelise southerners or convert Muslims to Christianity, and favours the new form of Islamic charitable work carried out by NGOs like Al-Da'wa al-Islamiya, the Islamic African Relief Agency, and Al-Muaffaq which all have close links to the government. These favoured organisations (whose operations extend from the former Yugoslavia to Kashmir) combine aid provision with Islamisation and subject the southern populations to coercive and sometimes brutal supervision and ideological training.

In the SPLA zone humanitarian aid represents a greater resource for the rebel movement than for the civilian population. The central role that OLS accords the SRRA in evaluating needs and distributing aid permits it to divert a significant part of the aid to the rebel army and local elites. This is achieved in various ways: simulated attacks force humanitarian workers to evacuate an area and food stocks are then pillaged; the SRRA massively inflates the number of people requiring food; supplies are systematically misappropriated before distribution takes place; and civilians are compelled to transport rations they have just been issued to SPLA warehouses. In addition, the SRRA obliges aid organisations to hand over part of their budgets. This system of taxation is formalised in an official 'memorandum of understanding' and finances the apparatus dedicated to the seizure and control of aid (such as SRRA radio operators and 'visa' departments). The SPLA 'humanitarian' wing also benefits from direct funding through so-called 'capacity building' projects theoretically designed to improve its efficiency and thus contribute to the greater good.

The SRRA has further responsibilities: it selects NGOs on the basis of their adherence to its policies and does not hesitate to expel those who criticise its methods. It authorises access to regions according to political and military priorities and demonstrates acute paranoia when dealing with French humanitarian organisations whom it suspects of sympathy for Khartoum because of the ambiguous relations between the French and Sudanese governments. Freedom of movement in the rebel zone is extremely restricted. Humanitarian workers are assigned permanent escorts known as 'liaison officers' who prevent any direct contact with local populations, supposedly in order to minimise the risk of espionage.

Finally, the SPLA uses humanitarian organisations as tools for controlling populations and protecting strategic positions. Aid agencies are pressured into setting up operations near rebel bases and contribute to the movement's propaganda by regularly denouncing government bombardments of civilians while ignoring that the SPLA deliberately assembled civilians around their military installations. Although not all SRRA employees share the SPLA's military ethos, their room for manoeuvre is limited by heavy supervision. SPLA methods are instructive: each war chief has founded his own aid organisation and strives to have it officially recognised by donors. A major consequence of the manipulation of aid operations is that it increases the logistical capacity of rebel movements, particularly when road access to zones suffering from chronic food shortages is difficult or impossible and food is dropped by air. Not only does this lead Khartoum to often forbid the transport of aid to crisis-hit areas to prevent it ending up in rebel warehouses, but the institutionalisation of misappropriation by the rebels deprives civilian populations of the chance of survival that humanitarian aid would offer if it did get through to them. Although sufficient food was delivered to Ajiep in the Bahr-el-Ghazal region from July 1998 onwards, 10 percent of children afflicted by famine died in the space of three months because they did not receive the aid intended for them (see Box). At the same time, the SPLA, then in the middle of a military offensive, was able to restock its warehouses, and certain groups and individuals enjoying privileged relations with the SRRA, the SPLA and their local agents became notably more prosperous.

The 1998 famine in the Bahr-el-Ghazal region

In December 1997, Kerubino Kwanin Bol, a founding member of the SPLA who had defected to the government camp in the late 1980s, decided to rejoin the rebels. Originally from the Bahr-el-Ghazal and renowned for his brutality, he attempted to capture Wau, the provincial capital, and several neighbouring towns. Victorious at first, he was eventually dislodged by a violent government counter-offensive that compelled tens of thousands of Dinka to flee their homes. The fighting gradually encroached on the surrounding regions and forced the populations to flee. About 20,000 displaced people congregated at Ajiep, a small, SPLA-controlled community of 1,500 inhabitants several kilometres from the front line.

The townspeople had few resources, the displaced people even less and by the spring of 1998, there was a serious food crisis. The Sudanese government then decided to forbid food deliveries. The embargo lasted a month but its partial lifting at the end of February did not allow sufficient aid to get through because of security concerns, a situation which prevailed until late April. OLS, loyal to the conventions that linked it to Khartoum, agreed to what amounted to a death sentence for thousands of civilians.

At the end of April, a lull in the fighting allowed humanitarian organisations greater access to the zone. From May to October 1998, 2,500 tons of food were dropped by air on Ajiep and the town was visited by several hundred journalists and aid workers. Yet this did little to alleviate the famine: five months after the beginning of the aid operation, half of Ajiep's children were still suffering from malnutrition. Retrospective mortality studies estimate that an additional 3,000 people died between 3 June and 28 September 1998.

In conformity with the agreements signed by OLS and the SRRA, the rebel 'humanitarian' wing distributes aid through the intermediary of 'local committees' composed of traditional chiefs supervised by the SRRA. Displaced people who are not from the region received only a tiny part of the aid intended for them and died in great numbers. The Bahr-el-Ghazal famine killed tens of thousands of people while the leaders of powerful clans and the SPLA replenished their food stocks.

Government and SPLA practices have an equally devastating effect on the civilian population. In a situation of severe food shortages it is enough for the government to forbid aid agencies to deliver emergency food aid (by exercising its veto on OLS flights) or for the SPLA to misappropriate it (through the SRRA) to trigger a famine like the one that afflicted Bahr-el-Ghazal in 1998. This is a well-documented situation that has been widely acknowledged since the latter half of the 1990s, yet it persists. OLS, which directly finances the SRRA (in contravention of the principle of neutrality although this seems to pose no problem), has never offered any seriously protest. Hence in 1998 the NGO Action Contre la Faim (ACF) was expelled from the SPLA zones for 'espionage' when it asked why, despite substantial food deliveries, it had proved impossible to reduce malnutrition rates in the Labone displaced persons camps (whose residents described themselves as 'John Garang's cash cows'). The OLS ratified the rebel authority's decision without the least sign of disapproval.

It is not difficult to understand why the principal aid donor to South Sudan, the United States, prefers this situation to continue. Operation Lifeline Sudan offers an easy way of indirectly supporting a rebellion against a regime it regards as hostile or at least extremely unreliable. By supporting the SPLA in its war of attrition against Khartoum but without giving it the means to victory – which would antagonise other US allies such as Egypt – Washington is subjecting a 'rogue state' to a classic containment policy. The recourse to so-called humanitarian aid allows it to avoid directly arming or financing the SPLA, an approach more difficult to justify to Congress (which in 2000 refused to authorise direct food aid to the insurgents) and which could be taken up as a *casus belli* by Khartoum. The option of a 'humanitarian whitewash', moreover, turns out to be a cheap way of reconciling the conflicting interests of the business and ultra-conservative lobbies that influence American foreign policy. The European Community maintained a similar position before denouncing the SPLA's treatment of NGOs, a change of direction that happened to occur at a time when it was engaging in 'constructive dialogue' with Khartoum, shortly after the resumption of oil production.

The diplomatic goals of Western powers do not fully explain the persistence of such a perverse system. Humanitarian actors, UN agencies and NGOs are also responsible. The Sudanese crisis represents a significant source of income for many organisations who would not be able to balance their budgets without the large cash injections destined to fund their operations in South Sudan. Furthermore, many humanitarian organisations tend to sympathise with the SPLA view that it is 'immoral to remain neutral in the face of the brutality of a North Sudanese regime that seeks to forcibly Islamise the Christian populations of the South.' They thus relinquish their neutrality and become partisans in the south Sudan liberation struggle while their mission to assist civilian populations is relegated to a secondary consideration. The most extreme examples of this tendency are found in evangelising organisations like Christian Fellowship International and Christian Solidarity International – virtual counterparts of the Islamist NGOs operating in the North – who champion the SPLA cause in the name of defending Christianity against the encroachment of Islam.

Other organisations justify the diversion of aid to the rebels by claiming that the aid distribution is managed by 'local committees' that represent 'civil society': to dispute the decisions of these committees would be a mark of neo-colonialism. 'South Sudanese civil society' therefore presumably has the right to sacrifice part of its own people in order to liberate the majority from the yoke of Islamist oppression. But to our knowledge, no representatives of the 3,000 people who died of starvation between July and October at Ajiep consented to the death of their families so that the SPLA could pursue its war. Finally, the bureaucratic drift of most aid organisations, particularly those run by the UN, provides a final clue to the problem. By maintaining that misappropriation is simply due to poor management practices in the SPLA's 'humanitarian' branch and that, given a little good will, they can 'resolve the problem', these organisations actually strengthen the very institution – the SRRA – which is responsible.

The international community is involved in the Sudan problem at several levels: regional powers are fighting a regime that seeks to destabilise them; oil companies strive to further interests that do not necessarily coincide with the policies of their governments; Western states seek to contain a 'rogue state' which has ambitions to become the leader of a new international Islamic order and humanitarian agencies have ambiguous agendas. All these forms of intervention complicate the resolution of a conflict in which violence is fed by the contempt of the Sudanese political elites – from both the North and the South – for the civilian populations they claim to represent. The central stake remains the construction of a state capable of integrating the social, cultural and political plurality of the old Anglo-Egyptian condominium. Although the various forms of foreign involvement are the product of the classic 'great game' of international relations being played out in an era of globalisation, the 'humanitarian whitewash' aspect of several Western states' foreign policy towards Sudan is exceptionally perverse. As long as aid operations are designed as an indirect means of mollifying the Sudanese authorities or of supporting the insurgents, they will be incapable of saving thousands of Sudanese from certain death. The same is true if humanitarian action is used as a means to pressure or lure warring parties to the peace negotiations table, as seems to be currently occurring. Humanitarian actors are heavily implicated in the abuse of humanitarian action. It is their duty to ensure that their actions conform to the principles they claim to uphold.

Bibliographical references

African Rights, *Food and Power in Sudan: A Critique of Humanitarianism*, London, African Rights, 1997.

V. Brown *et al.*, 'Violence in Southern Sudan', *The Lancet*, 359, 12 January 2002, p. 161.

H. Creusvaux *et al.*, 'Famine in Southern Sudan', *The Lancet*, 354, 4 September 1999, p. 832.

S. Jaspar, *Targeting and Distribution of Food Aid in SPLA Controlled Areas of South Sudan*, Nairobi, WFP, 1999.

M. Lavergne and R. Marchal (eds), 'Le Soudan contemporain, l'échec d'une experience islamiste?', *Politique Africaine*, 66, June 1997.

M. Lavergne (ed), *Le Soudan Contemporain*, Paris, Karthala, 1989.

R. Marchal, 'Le Facteur soudanaise, avant et après', *Critique Internationale*, 17, October 2002, pp. 44-51.

Médecins Sans Frontières, 'La Famine au Sud-Soudan et le fonctionnement du système de l'aide: un premier bilan', Paris, MSF, 1999.

PART III. ABSTENTION

7

LIBERIA
Orchestrated Chaos

Jean-Hervé Jézéquel

In 1999 Liberia was plunged once more into war when armed factions operating from Guinea launched an assault on the power Charles Taylor had established by force three years before. They were joined in 2003 by rebels based in Ivory Coast.

Once again, the populations of Liberia find themselves trapped between rebels who reduce them to slavery and government troops for whom racketeering, pillage, rape and the harassment of civilians constitute the principal form of retribution. Hundreds of thousands of Liberians have attempted to escape the brutality of the combatants and have tried to find refuge in Sierra Leone as well as in Guinea and Ivory Coast, where the war caught up with them in 2000 and 2002. Those who cannot flee because of border closures or the pressure exerted by the various factions are forced to drift around a country in ruins, obeying the dictates and whims of the combatants. Most displaced people are eventually crammed into camps that afford little security or manage to settle in the sordid suburbs of the capital, Monrovia, which is home to 1.5 million Liberians, almost half the country's population.

At the time of writing (July 2003), Monrovia is the arena in which rebels and government troops continue to fight battles of ferocious intensity. The city, wracked by a cholera epidemic, lacks running water, food and health care. Hundreds of thousands of inhabitants, terrified of being targeted by combatants who are often drugged and prone to unpredictable behaviour, have gone into hiding to avoid the hail of bullets and shells.

Whereas Great Britain became involved in a decisive fashion in Sierra Leone and France sent its troops to contain the civil war that broke out in Ivory Coast in 2002, Liberia has been carefully placed in quarantine: the international community strives to confine the conflict within the country's borders and is content to withhold its intervention and observe this new bloodbath from the sidelines without so much as offering Liberians the possibility of securing a decent refuge in neighbouring countries. The humanitarian organisations operating in this ravaged land in July 2003 once provided rudimentary social services but are now reduced to counting the dead, tending to the wounded who manage to slip through the violence and assisting in a few camps for displaced persons thanks to the courage of their local personnel.

However, this crisis is not the result of a surge of 'African barbarity' that 'civilised' states can only deplore or try to confine to Liberian territory with a feeble show of humanitarian compassion. This crisis is closely linked to Liberia's increasing integration into the global economy and to the disintegration of a 'shadow state' that has been pampered by Washington since the Cold War. Above all, it reveals the hidden face of the international community's stabilisation policies in Sierra Leone and Ivory Coast, which drove the most intractable combatants into Liberia and encouraged them to overthrow Liberia's president.

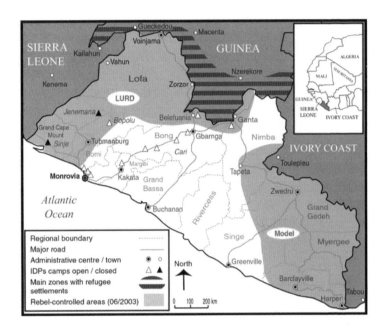

The Liberian maelstrom

In 1996, after seven years of conflict in which at least
80,000 people died, Liberia seemed to be setting foot on
the road to peace. The four main faction leaders,
including Charles Taylor, the most powerful of them,
signed a final peace agreement under the auspices of
Nigeria and the Economic Community of West African
States. It provided for an end to hostilities, disarmament
of combatants, and the organisation of elections. The
first round of the presidential elections, held without
serious incident on 19 July 1997, saw a high turnout.
Charles Taylor was elected with 75.3 percent of the vote,
following a campaign of intimidation conducted under
the slogan 'No Taylor, no peace'. Liberians felt that they
had to elect him if they were to have peace, no matter

how much blood he had on his hands ('He killed my pa, he killed my ma, I'll vote for him').

Charles Taylor's inauguration as head of state did not radically alter the system of domination he had developed as a rebel leader. Like his predecessor Samuel Doe, Taylor used state institutions as a symbolic façade behind which he consolidated a personal and highly centralised network of economic exploitation. Businesses operating in forestry, the diamond trade, or telecommunications were obliged to work in partnership with Taylor, and he used his position to protect his commercial and financial activities, maintain 'official' contacts with his foreign associates, and strengthen his coercive apparatus. This apparatus was based on the army, police, and various governmental security agencies, as well as several militias that provided services in exchange for a few emoluments. All of these claimed their reward at the population's expense: systematic taxation of civilians, pillage, rape and murder seemed to have become the standard remuneration system for the armed groups that were operating on the regime's behalf (see Box).

Legitimised by the 1997 electoral process, Taylor extended his influence to neighbouring countries. Since 1991 he had already been providing active support to the RUF (Revolutionary United Front) rebels of Sierra Leone, hosting their rear bases and their channels for diamond exports. In September 2000 he was accused of supporting a motley coalition comprising RUF fighters, Liberian forces and Guinean rebels attempting to overthrow Lansana Conté's government in Guinea. That same year, he supplied a personal bodyguard to Robert Gueï, the Ivorian general who mounted a coup d'état and remained in power for a year before being ousted from Abidjan. Furthermore, in 2003, Ivorian president Laurent Gbagbo accused Taylor of supporting rebels in the west who were threatening his regime.

Taylor's regional ambitions and his close contacts with Libya irritated Liberia's neighbours and powerful western states. The latter set about isolating his regime in the hope of destroying his capacity to do further harm. Liberia's links with the RUF were denounced on several occasions, and despite Charles Taylor's outraged denials, the Security Council imposed sanctions against Monrovia in March 2001, including an embargo on arms sales and diamonds purchases, and an international travel ban for Liberian officials and their families. In Guinea, the Conté regime received financial and military aid from the United States to drive back the rebels attempting to overthrow it. In 2001, Conakry carried the battle to northern Liberia and increased its support for LURD (Liberians United for Reconciliation and Democracy), a group of Liberian insurgents that appeared in February 2000.

An ordinary day in Liberia

An ordinary day in Monrovia. A police car dumps three swollen bodies in front of the hospital. Two of them die within the hour, the third one drags himself inside. The medical teams discover that he has been tortured. Some think they recognise him as journalist Hassan Bility, kidnapped a few weeks previously for having criticised President Charles Taylor. It proves impossible to verify this: twenty-four hours later, the patient has disappeared.

An ordinary day in Monrovia. The ATU (Anti-Terrorist Unit) descends on the capital's main market and systematically arrests all adolescents on the pretext that dissidents have infiltrated among them. Those whose families have some money will be able to buy their freedom; the others will be sent to the front-line in the north. The terrorised population keeps quiet, the security forces line their pockets, and marginalised urban youth, a potential opposition force, is usefully recycled as cannon fodder.

An ordinary day in Liberia. A pick-up truck crammed with soldiers halts at the roadside and a dozen soldiers get out. They catch a young girl and throw her into the vehicle, kicking her with their boots. They set off again, waving to a humanitarian worker.

Constituted from former Liberian factions that had sporadically attacked Liberia since 1999, LURD espouses no real aim beyond the overthrow of Charles Taylor. Its ranks include fighters from Sierra Leone and Guinea. It has rear bases and arms supply channels in Guinea, and enjoyed discreet support from British military advisers attached to the expeditionary force deployed in Sierra Leone in May 2000 to support the UN peacekeeping force. In addition to this state support, LURD obtains resources from the Liberian diaspora in the United States; by extorting money and forced labour from civilians; and by exploiting diamond deposits.

With Guinean and British support LURD succeeded in entrenching itself around the northern Liberian city of Voinjama in Lofa County in 2000-1. The fighting spread to the adjoining areas in mid 2001, displacing large numbers of people, including Sierra Leonean refugees who had fled to Liberia. The north-western third of the country was transformed into a vast no-man's-land, criss-crossed by distraught civilian populations fleeing harassment by poorly identified and poorly controlled armed groups. The movement of humanitarian organisations were restricted to routes authorised by Taylor's forces, and in November 2001, access to Lofa became impossible.

At the beginning of 2002 the government accused LURD of being behind a series of attacks on displaced persons' camps (such as Sinje, Cari and Jene Mana), as well as on the towns of Kakata, Tubmanburg and Bopulu. Some observers suggested, however, that instability and pillage were the work of armed groups operating on the government's behalf. While there was no doubting LURD's offensive, its capacities were probably exaggerated by the Liberian government in order to cover up exactions by pro-government forces. Dramatising the threat also allowed Taylor to declare himself the victim of aggression and to demand that the arms embargo be lifted and international humanitarian aid increased.

Although it is difficult to know with any certainty who was behind the attacks, they conveniently allowed the Liberian president to decree a state of emergency in February 2002. Taylor also destroyed the leadership of the civilian opposition a year before the date set for the next presidential elections. He intensified his policy of terror towards the civilian population, subjecting them to the arbitrariness of his 'Anti-Terrorist Units'. But in June 2003 LURD's military successes, together with the appearance of a new armed movement (MODEL – Movement for Democracy in Liberia) in the south-east of the country, forced the Liberian president to hole up in his besieged capital and then to open negotiations with the rebels in Ghana. Whatever the outcome of the talks and whatever Taylor's personal fate, it is hard to regard the LURD rebels, who have perpetrated so many violent abuses in the north of the country, as an alternative capable of restoring peace to the country.

Populations in search of refuge

The armed violence in Lofa and surrounding areas provoked hundreds of thousands of people to flee, both within the country and to neighbouring states. The International Committee of the Red Cross (ICRC) estimated that 60,000 Liberians were internally displaced over the first six months of 2002, and 100,000 sought refuge over Liberia's borders, half of them in Côte d'Ivoire and the rest in Sierra Leone (25,000) and Guinea (25,000). They joined the 220,000 Liberians already present in these countries since the war of 1989-1996. Recent events in 2003 (disturbances in Côte d'Ivoire, the siege of Monrovia, the conflict's expansion to south-east Liberia) have sent yet more Liberians fleeing along the roads to exile.

Targeted by the combatants' extreme violence, these populations have again endured the fear and suffering experienced several times since 1989. And crossing the border does not guarantee escape from the conflict. In the Kouankan refugee camp near Macenta in Guinea, for example, armed movements such as LURD engage in extortion and forced recruitment, even though its entrances are controlled by the Guinean authorities. The United Nations High Commission for Refugees (UNHCR), responsible for protecting and assisting the Liberians, prefers to turn a blind eye rather than confront the *laissez-faire* attitude of the Guinean gendarmes (whom it considers have already been sensitised to refugee protection via a training course it financed). The militarisation of the camps has turned them into military targets. Dislodging the LURD fighters installed among the refugees along the Liberia-Guinea border was one of the main objectives of the offensive by 'Guinean rebels' supported by Taylor.

The refugees live in such precarious circumstances in the camps that the 'law of the jungle' prevails. The most vulnerable (women, children, the old, ethnic minorities, 'recent arrivals') are victim to numerous abuses such as violence, extortion, and forced labour. These are rarely identified and combated by the aid agencies, whose laxity or turpitude often contributes to perpetuating the social violence. Under the current system for running the camps, individuals are categorised according to administrative abstractions defined on the basis of a few 'vital needs'. One representative of an international agency asked in surprise, 'What are these refugees complaining about, who emerge wild-eyed from the forest and are given free assistance?' They are complaining about the equation that all too often reduces them to a volume of water expressed in cubic metres, to a ration expressed in kilograms of crushed wheat, to health care expressed in terms of epidemiological indicators. They are complaining of assistance that reduces them to biological bodies, waiting, surviving and without rights – in short, of being the objects of a system of domination within which every kind of violence is possible (see Chapter 14).

The progressive destabilisation of the border areas has also hindered the flight of Liberians to Guinea to escape the fighting. The Liberian LURD rebels demand payment to cross the border, and try to keep back men of working or fighting age. Guinea also turns back many Liberian civilians, citing its right to ensure the security of its own territory (see Box below).

Routes of flight

One morning in November 2001, government forces attacked Awa Degbé's village in Lofa, a northern region of Liberia. The inhabitants had made the mistake of sheltering LURD dissidents. At the first sound of gunfire, they scattered into the forest. Awa Degbé fled with one of her daughters, her father and other villagers. She has had no news of the other members of her family. Some say that her husband was executed by drunken soldiers, others that her two boys were forcibly recruited by the Liberian army. She doesn't know.

Awa Degbé, her daughter and father spent several months in the forest, surviving as best they could on wild fruit and tubers. But hunger, fatigue and, above all, the sound of the battles raging throughout Lofa drove them ever further northwards, towards Guinea.

On the way, they were recaptured by the rebels and taken to Kolahun, the rebel base, to serve as domestic slaves. On Christmas Eve, government forces attacked the town. They again took flight. On the road to Guinea, the rebels had put up roadblocks to prevent people from escaping. But Awa had succeeded in obtaining the one hundred Liberian dollars – less than two euros – needed to buy two passes to the border. Don't ask her how.

She took her daughter with her but had to leave her father behind for lack of money. She reached the Guinean border, where hundreds of gaunt, distraught refugees had massed after many months spent in the forest. All were trying to flee the horror, but only a few small groups were being allowed to cross the border when the numbers swelled too high. In these borderlands of Liberia and Guinea, the right to flight proclaimed by international law was a dead letter.

Who would have been prepared to apply it? The LURD rebels needed civilians to supply them with provisions and to prove that they held the north of Lofa. The Guinean authorities had closed the border, fearing infiltration by Liberian fighters who, two years previously, had provoked violent battles in the prefecture of Gueckedou. UNHCR

> would not have been able to face an influx of refugees at a
> time when its camps were already full and the Guinean
> government was balking at opening any new ones. And
> Western states had chosen to confine the Liberian crisis
> within the country's own borders.

Civilians uprooted by fighting but unable to find refuge abroad move around the interior of the country according to the dictates of shifting battles and the injunctions of the armed groups they encounter. Some end up crammed into camps for internally displaced persons (IDPs), the locations of which are decided by the Liberian authorities according to military priorities that negate the civilians' need for protection and assistance. Others manage to settle in the insalubrious outskirts of the capital, having circumvented or paid their way through the filtering roadblocks set up by pro-government forces to stem the flood of displaced persons heading for Monrovia, who are suspected of harbouring 'infiltrators'. Many others are unable to escape the armed factions, for whom they constitute a major source of young recruits and servile labour.

The situation in areas spared by the conflict is hardly better. In addition to the arbitrariness of the security forces, Liberians have to cope with the collapse of the national economy and a complete absence of social services. Public utilities stand neglected and the capital constantly lacks running water and electricity. The government health system has only twenty-five doctors, and Monrovia has only one overcrowded hospital to serve nearly one and a half million inhabitants (half of Liberia's population).

The government budget (70 million dollars in 2002) is woefully inadequate. Its revenue is mainly derived from registration fees for ships flying the Liberian flag of convenience (such as the oil tanker, The Prestige, which sank off the coast of Spain), and royalties collected on forestry operations. But proceeds from both these sources are paid into private accounts outside the control of the central bank, on which the president has the right to draw at will. No country except Taiwan has risked granting bilateral economic aid to the Liberian 'shadow state'. As a result, almost all international aid has been channelled through NGOs and UN humanitarian agencies who struggle to keep the country's rudimentary social services going.

More generally, Liberian society seems to be the victim of a process of structural breakdown that is poorly reflected in the United Nations' 'human development' indices. Such indices do not reflect the probability of a girl born in Lofa reaching the age of fourteen without having been raped, or the proportion of Liberian children and adolescents that have never witnessed the killing of a close relative. In addition to high morbidity, these populations are victims of social disintegration: the break-up of families, collapse of community solidarity, enslavement of civilians, acceptance of rape as a feature of everyday life, and the recruitment of child soldiers. Liberia should be recognised as a crisis equally notable for the considerable daily mortality rate as for the banality and generalisation of violence linked to the breakdown of the social fabric.

In the 'heart of darkness'?

Contrary to prevailing media images of this part of the world, the violence in Liberia is not set in the 'heart of darkness', at the centre of a fantasy Africa where 'civilisation' has yet to supplant 'barbarism'. The violence, in fact, is closely linked to the country's increasing integration into the world economy. With the end of the Cold War, the Liberian ruling class faced the progressive loss of considerable quantities of foreign aid. This had notably come from the United States, which after 1945 wanted to establish a military bridgehead in the region. At the end of the 1980s Washington officially halted all financial support to Samuel Doe's regime, whose numerous acts of violence foreshadowed those later perpetrated by the Taylor regime. Deprived of this manna, the Liberian state was no longer in a position to disburse the patronage that had ensured the support of local elites and reproduction of the system.

Hastened by the end of the Cold War, state power declined, rendered the ruling class vulnerable to the ambitions of enterprising local politicians. The latter profited by the state's weakness to tap the country's resources to their own benefit, turning themselves into the dispensers of patronage. International economic actors rapidly adapted to these changes and turned them to their own advantage. Informal economic networks sprang up for the extraction of diamonds, rubber, gold and precious woods. These networks survived the outbreak of the civil war, which led to a marked increase in wood exports. The apparent chaos of the Liberian politico-military scene has never led to economic chaos. On the contrary, the links rapidly established between business circles and the military leaders have afforded the latter the economic resources they need and hastened the collapse of what little remained of the state.

The Liberian conflict also stemmed from a societal crisis that went beyond the collapse of the state. Liberian society was incapable of absorbing an under-employed and disappointed younger generation that no longer accepted the legitimacy of social regulations that were out of step with its aspirations. Faced with unemployment, the failure of the education system, and the inability of rural society to compete with life-styles seen in towns and Western countries, some young people came to see the path of arms as the surest and quickest means of acquiring the status they desired. If it was not the pen or *daba* (West African hoe), then it would be the Kalashnikov. In a context of social disintegration, increased violence, and cultural globalisation, the old images of success (such as the educated intellectual or the government official) gave way to others glorifying the 'armed man' who was cunning and resourceful and who legitimatised the principle that might was right. These young people, exploited by enterprising politicians who recruited them at increasingly early ages, then went on to stoke the cycle of collective violence in Liberia.

The matrix of the Liberian conflict is infinitely complex and its actors are more numerous than those mentioned here (mercenaries recruited abroad, the influence of regional powers such as Libya, Burkina Faso, Ivory Coast and Nigeria). This rapid sketch has simply emphasised the connections between the workings of the world economy, the frustrations of the marginalised youth, and the appetites of enterprising politicians emboldened by the break-up of the Liberian state. In this respect, it should be stressed that the Liberian crisis is not a product of the African continent's 'atavistic barbarism' any more than of a 'tribalism' deeply rooted in the culture of forest societies: Kongo versus foresters, Krahn versus Mano, Mandingos versus Loma,

Gbandi versus Kissi. While tribal and ethnic resentments today are real, these animosities in no way constitute a natural starting point for the conflict. Far from having their roots in immemorial enmities, they are the product of recent political exploitation: the acts of violence perpetrated against the Mano by president Doe in the 1980s and against the Mandingo and the Krahn by Taylor in the 1990s provoked an intensification of identity-based assertiveness and ethnic animosities. The latter are not the engine driving the war, but one technique of mobilisation among others – and by no means the most decisive one – used by the main parties to the conflict.

In the political and military equation, civilians find themselves reduced to the role of a servile labour force, a reservoir of potential fighters, and a source of material and sexual rewards for the brutal, undisciplined soldiers entrusted with improving security in the zones where economic exploitation of natural resources is underway. A veritable proletariat of violence, the rank and file combatants – some of whom are child soldiers recruited by force and subjected to particularly brutal methods of socialisation as fighters – are their own paymasters. Within the armed factions, discipline is as lax as it is cruel, and often the troops surpass their commanders. The extreme violence perpetrated against civilians must be understood in the light of this context, and as a technique of terror and domination.

Containment strategy

While the international community has launched vast projects and disbursed large sums in the 'laboratory' of Sierra Leone, Taylor's Liberia has been scrupulously ostracised with aid cutbacks, an embargo, and support for Guinea, which shelters LURD dissidents. International policy towards Liberia takes the form of a containment strategy designed to limit, as much as possible, Taylor's ability to cause trouble in neighbouring countries, while allowing his tyrannical regime to sow disorder within the country. In one sense, Liberia is paying the price for the pacification policy in Sierra Leone. The most intransigent fighters in the whole region have been driven to the north of Liberia. This has forced Taylor to revise his expansionist ambitions in order to concentrate on defending his regime, and has restricted the activity of the region's armed bands to a limited area. But how long will it be possible to confine these groups within the Liberian cauldron before they once more venture into neighbouring countries (northern Sierra Leone, the forested regions of Guinea or, more likely, western Ivory Coast)?

In June 2003 President Taylor was indicted for war crimes by the special court for Sierra Leone (see Box pp. 52-3). The decision, taken at the instigation of an American prosecutor, was announced just as negotiations among the parties to the Liberian conflict were opening in Ghana. The judicial agenda clashed with the diplomatic program, damaging chances for a peaceful settlement to the conflict. Was this a coincidence, or evidence that some powers prefer the continuation of war to engagement in an expensive and difficult intervention to halt it? In any case, few can seriously believe that containing or replacing Charles Taylor with another faction leader will enable the country to resolve the tragic impasse in which it finds itself.

This containment strategy has had obvious repercussions on the volume of aid provided to the Liberian population. While flows of humanitarian aid have poured into Sierra Leone – a showcase for the UN's activities and British diplomacy – Liberia has suffered from chronic under-funding of aid programs. By July 2002, the UN agencies in Liberia had received only 3.9 million dollars of the 15 million required for their programs at the start of the year. Yet in the same period, their counterparts in Sierra Leone and Guinea had received 58.8 and 37.7 million dollars respectively. Worse still, the principal donors were extremely slow in financing assistance to the IDPs fleeing the violence attributed to LURD. Considering that these acts were probably manipulated by Taylor to pass himself off as a victim of external aggression, they balked at providing aid, though this was vital to the victims, who were real enough.

On a more structural level the UN's deficiencies are also connected to the way it manages displaced populations. While UNHCR is responsible for protecting refugees (who have crossed an international border), responsibility for IDPs has yet to be clearly assigned. OCHA is supposed to take it on, but is a coordinating body, not an operational agency. Above all, displaced persons officially remain under the protection of their own government, even when the latter has caused its citizens to flee.

The Liberian Refugee, Repatriation and Resettlement Commission (L3RC) is the government agency responsible for IDPs. In practice, it has a monopoly on operations to identify and count the displaced. Its control over the numbers allows it to magnify the crisis and manipulate the volume of aid sent to the camps. At the end of July 2002, for example, the L3RC claimed there were 133,000 displaced persons in Liberia, while the ICRC estimated them at 60,000. The misuse of distribution cards, which are likewise administered by the L3RC, facilitates the appropriation of aid by business circles and fuels exploitation of every kind by the 'big men' in the camps. Furthermore, the L3RC is unable to ensure the safety of those living in the displaced persons camps. Not only do the Liberian security forces frequently commit violent acts in the camps, but L3RC's local staff, who include numerous veterans of the 1989-1996 war appointed as a reward for their loyalty to the regime, also profit from their position vis-à-vis the camps' inhabitants.

None of the international agencies in Liberia assumes responsibility for protecting displaced persons. In fact, many of them engage in a bureaucratic activism that dodges the issue of violence. The program to construct 'Child Friendly Spaces' in camps, financed by UNICEF, is an example. These solidly constructed buildings set in the middle of the camps are meant to provide a haven of peace for children, and were opened with much fanfare on United Nations' Internet sites. Yet at the same time, the recruitment of child soldiers continues in the camps but is ignored. To denounce it would amount to questioning the Liberian authorities' responsibility in managing the camps. A building and a few toys will hardly enable children to escape the recruiting sergeants of Taylor or his opponents.

The NGOs have not escaped the dilemmas posed by insecurity. The example of the Jene Mana camp is most revealing in this respect. In June 2001, rumours of an attack swept the camp, which was sheltering inhabitants of Lofa who had fled fighting and violence. Some

NGOs wondered whether it was best to continue providing aid, thus giving the displaced persons a false sense of security, or to withdraw, which might impel the displaced persons to flee... but where to, and under what conditions? In December, the camp was attacked. The displaced persons escaped en masse, while the equipment left behind by the NGOs was stolen by the aggressors, whose identity was unclear. While fleeing, the population of the Jene Mala camp were stopped once again by the Liberian security forces in areas south of the former camp. The same dilemma arose once more: should these people be assisted at the risk of keeping them where they were and making them the target of fresh violence? Or should they be left alone despite their poor state of health? Some medical NGOs, aware of the additional dangers to which they might expose this population already in distress, opted for a minimal deployment using scant logistical resources to avoid attracting combatants.

In June 2003 the spread of fighting to the gates of Monrovia and in south-east Liberia prevented the humanitarian organisations from reaching 80 percent of the country. Tens of thousands of Liberians fled the displaced persons camps located on the outskirts of the capital to seek refuge in the city centre. Others tried to flee towards Guinea or Sierra Leone. While food and health conditions in Monrovia deteriorated rapidly, most of the aid agencies were forced to reduce their presence and activities due to security problems. Many remembered that in April 1996, fighting in the capital ended in the theft of over 20 million dollars worth of food and equipment from aid organisations, including 489 vehicles that were used by the fighters to continue their war.

The suffering of the Liberian people is not the result of some barbarous war that has developed on the fringes of the civilised world. On the contrary, this suffering is directly linked to the current international political and economic system. First, connections established between the warlords and international commercial networks have helped to strengthen the war economy and hastened the break-up of the Liberian state. Second, the international community has limited its intervention to a calculated policy of containment that has sacrificed the Liberian population to the project of stabilising the West African region. In fact, the British intervention in, and pacification of, Sierra Leone has paradoxically entailed the immersion of the Liberian population in continued violence.

This policy has helped to ensnare humanitarian action in a series of inextricable contradictions: helping victims of the conflict at the risk of strengthening the tormentors through the unavoidable diversion of aid; aid meeting the social functions of a 'shadow state' dedicated to the enrichment of a tyrannical war leader; restricting humanitarian assistance because of insecurity and the donors' aim of preventing a revival of 'Taylorland'; assisting populations lacking food and health care, but being unable to address the daily violence to which they are subjected.

In the same vein the legitimate protests of humanitarian organisations at the absence of protection for Liberians seem futile. Are these protests inviting the UN to strengthen protective measures whose ineffectiveness has hitherto been deplored? Are they calling for a tightening of sanctions against the Liberian 'shadow state' and the diamond trade? Or do they implicitly invite the deployment of an international security force on the Sierra Leonean model, which might constitute the sole means of curbing the violence? The international response to the extreme violence suffered by Liberians is a matter of political choices that should be debated publicly by all the parties concerned. It would be inappropriate for the humanitarian organisations, as such, to voice an opinion. At most, they can play a part in ensuring that the debate takes place.

Bibliographical references

R. Banégas and J.P. Warnier, 'Nouvelles figures de la réussite et du pouvoir', *Politique Africaine*, no. 82, June 2001, pp. 5-21.

S. Ellis, *The Mask of Anarchy: The Destruction of Liberia and the Religious Dimension of an African Civil War*, London, Hurst, 1999.

C. Ero and M. Ferme (eds), 'Dossier: Liberia, Sierra Leone, Guinée: la régionalisation de la guerre', *Politique Africaine,* no. 88, January 2003, pp. 5-102.

W. Reno, *Warlord Politics and African States*, Boulder, CO, Lynne Rienner, 1998.

F. Weissman, 'Liberia. Derrière le chaos, crises et interventions internationales', *Relations Internationales et Stratégiques*, no. 23 (1996): 82-99.

8

CHECHNYA
Eradication of the Enemy Within

Thorniké Gordadzé

During the Soviet era, an imposing stone statue representing three men – a Chechen, an Ingush and a Russian - stood in a great square in the eastern part of Grozny. The statue and the square shared the same name: 'Friendship'. Today, the inhabitants and the Russian troops stationed in Chechnya call it 'Three Idiot Square'. Indeed, after eight years of extraordinarily savage war, only idiots or cynics could talk of friendship between Russians and Chechens. The despair of a population subjected to the arbitrary justice of Russian soldiers and the radicalisation of Chechen resistance – increasingly evident in suicide attacks – are now established facts, as is the profound mistrust and hatred of Russian Federation forces and a growing section of the Russian population towards Caucasians.

Victims of the conflict can only hope for a meagre humanitarian assistance which can do little in response to a policy of terror. The international climate since the events of 11 September 2001, which provided the perfect opportunity for those who, like Vladimir

Putin, claimed to be combating 'international terrorism', has evaporated hopes of bringing effective international pressure to bear on the Russian government.

The last war in Chechnya (1994-6) had ended in the military victory of Chechen combatants over federal troops dispatched to 'restore constitutional order' in this majority Muslim republic which declared its independence in 1999, after two centuries of resistance to Russian colonisation. The outbreak of the second Chechen war in October 1999 came just at the right moment: it sidelined political debate over who would succeed Boris Yeltsin and consolidated the electoral rise of his prime minister, Vladimir Putin. Four years later the small Caucasian republic is entirely occupied by federal troops and officially run by a pro-Russian administration. But Chechnya has become the stage for a vicious war – a war which is now a matter of survival and vengeance for some, of scorched earth and extermination for others, and for many a war for control of resources, looting and human trafficking.

The myth of pacification

The image of a 'pacified' Chechnya promoted by the Kremlin for over a year deceives nobody except those who want to be deceived. The rest can appreciate the reports on wheat harvests or resumption of classes in Grozny for what they are – surprisingly similar versions of the old official reports on the war in Afghanistan, with their depictions of brave Pashtun peasants working in the fields, smiling children greeting Soviet soldiers, and the daily phenomenon of dozens of 'enemy' combatants giving up their arms and swearing loyalty to the communist regime.

For the Russian government the federal population census held in Chechnya at the end of 2002 and the referendum on 23 March 2003 signalled the

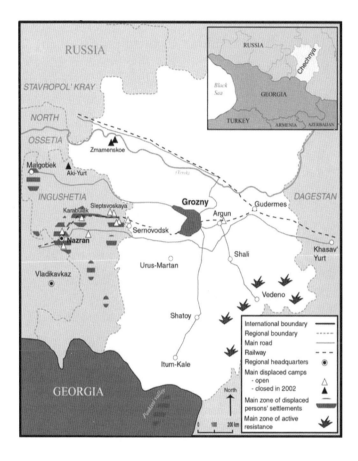

'pacification' of this small Caucasian republic. According to the census, the population miraculously increased during the war, reaching 1.04 million inhabitants compared with the one million counted in 1994. This result is all the more startling considering that between 75,000 and 150,000 people have died from war-related causes since 1994, and 400,000 more have fled Chechen territory. Independent sources estimate that the resident population is barely 500,000. Similarly, the referendum results 'surpassed the most optimistic expectations' according to Sergei Yastrzhembsky, the Kremlin spokesman on Chechnya. Figures published by the electoral commission recorded a 90 percent turnout with 96 percent of the votes cast in favour of continued adherence to the Russian Federation. These 'Soviet-style' scores, as the Russian press described them, reflect the many irregularities that marred the consultation: electoral rolls included several hundreds of thousands of dead people; the people displaced to Ingushetia were denied the opportunity to vote; and nearly 40,000 Russian soldiers (7 percent of the electorate) participated in the ballot. In reality, the referendum was designed to close the debate on Chechen independence, reaffirm the territorial integrity of Russia, and further discredit Chechen president Aslan Maskhadov, elected in 1994 in a vote recognised by the Organisation for Security and Cooperation in Europe (OSCE).

The forced return of Chechen refugees

Since the start of the second Chechen war in 1999, more than 200,000 Chechens have sought refuge in the neighbouring republic of Ingushetia. These exiles have no status and most are forced to live in appalling conditions in tented camps or vacant agricultural and industrial buildings. Since 2000 humanitarian organisations and United Nations agencies have been drawing attention to the wretched state of the tents – ragged, full of holes and without ground sheets, they are permeable to rain, snow and the cold – as well as the lack of latrines and showers.

In the spring of 2002 the Russian and Ingush governments announced that the eight tented camps – unwanted showcases of the war's consequences on civilians – were to be closed. The announcements were accompanied by pressure and intimidation. Military units established bases close to the sites and patrol in and around the camps, undermining the refugees' relative feeling of security. In December 2002, the Aki Yurt camp was brutally closed and the tents provided by NGOs torn down and removed.

Yet Vladimir Putin himself had promised that the refugees would not be forced back to Chechnya against their will. Humanitarian organisations had therefore begun building temporary accommodation for the Chechens who did not want to return in the immediate future – more than 98 percent of the 16,000 people living under canvas (90 percent of whom feared for their lives in Chechnya) according to a Médecins Sans Frontières report (February 2003).

Since the announcement of the referendum result, people are gradually leaving the camps. Families yield to brutal pressure and take the road of return, counting on government promises of financial aid (although nobody knows how or when it will be distributed) to escape the intimidation inflicted on those stubborn enough to remain.

Of the 3,000 temporary lodgings planned for over 14,000 people only 180 have actually been built and these were immediately declared illegal and threatened with destruction – the Ingush authorities claimed they did not conform to the planning code but generously offered to convert them into market stalls. Despite the protests of NGOs and the more timid complaints of UN agencies, the exiles of the tented camps have no choice but to return to Chechnya.

The Russian image of pacification is at odds with reality in Chechnya. Despite announcing the imminent withdrawal of Russian troops and their replacement by conventional police forces, the federal government maintains close to 100,000 military personnel on the territory of a now 'loyal' region. Scores of people disappear or are murdered every day in Chechnya, victims of search operations, physical abuse, and acts of violence by federal forces. Twenty or so government soldiers are killed every week. Helicopters are regularly shot down and armoured vehicles blown up by mines. To further enhance the 'pacified' image of Chechnya, the federal government is forcing refugees who live in appalling conditions in the neighbouring republics of Ingushetia and Georgia to return to their homes (see Box above). Yet the refugees, fearing the constant threat that awaits them in Chechnya, refuse to return despite constant harassment by federal forces who conduct 'cleansing' operations in the Ingush camps and aerial bombardments of the Pankissi Valley in Georgia. Their despair is so great that several hundred have written a collective letter to the president of Kazakhstan, asking him to authorise their return to live on the steppes where Stalin had deported them in 1944: Putin's Russia has given an aura of nostalgia to memories of Stalinist deportation.

The inefficiency of the Russian forces – a motor for resistance

The inefficiency of Putin's cherished police and secret services was clearly revealed when several dozen armed Chechens burst into Moscow's Nord-Ost theatre on 23 October 2002. The security apparatus maintains an impressive presence in Moscow and pursues the government policy of hunting down Caucasians, but proved incapable of intercepting – in the centre of the country's capital – a group of over forty heavily armed commandos or of thwarting an attack that had been meticulously prepared months in advance. The police, FSB (federal security service – former KGB), GIBDD (traffic police), and half a dozen specialist and anti-terrorist forces active in Moscow seem to pass most of their time extorting money from people of Caucasian origin by means of intimidation, arbitrary arrests and torture. Corruption is so rampant that anyone with money can obtain a pass signed by the security authorities or vehicle licence plates reserved for officials.

The unhindered arrival of the Chechen commandos in Moscow (most of its members were recruited in Chechnya around Vedeno, Khatuni and Alkhan-Kala) also demonstrated the impotence of the federal troops based in the republic. There are 40,000 Ministry of Defence troops in the country, supported by 32,000 Interior Ministry troops, 6-7,000 border guards, soldiers belonging to the railway army (with their World War One-style armoured train), and several thousand FSB agents spread between various special units. The GRU (military intelligence) fields elite units in the region that consist of some 10,000 operatives – the hooded men principally responsible for the imprisonment and disappearance of thousands of civilians. This vast network of around 100,000 men – which has lost more than 4,000 members according to official figures and twice that many according to independent sources – does not control the situation, as the destruction of the Russian administration building in Grozny on 31 December 2002 and the loss of several helicopters over Khankala (the federal forces' headquarters in Chechnya) last summer shows. Nevertheless, Putin and the military swore not to repeat the mistakes of the first war and from the start pursued a strategy of massive daily aerial attacks followed by the advance of ground troops, disregarding the number of civilian casualties this would provoke. Despite better preparation than in 1994, the federal troops took six months to conquer Grozny and lost over 1,500 soldiers during the operation.

The failure to overcome Chechen resistance is largely due to difficulties this enormous military machine experiences adapting to the situation on the ground, and the multitude of internal problems. Although the Russian armies in Chechnya are under a unified command based at Khankala, the units belonging to various ministries and departments act independently. This extreme compartmentalisation is partly motivated by rivalry between security services seeking to monopolise 'administrative resources' but it is also founded on the Kremlin's traditional suspicion of political power in the hands of security organisations. Moscow limits the acquisition of power by continually rebalancing their respective forces. The Russian government has not forgotten the threat of Bonapartism exemplified by General Alexander Lebed (a signatory to the agreement terminating the first Chechen war who then pursued a promising political career until his death in a helicopter accident), and is afraid of entrusting command of all the armies in Chechnya to a single general.

Corporatist rivalries among security agencies are often stirred up by conflicts linked to the illegal financial activities of the Russian forces. Confrontations frequently break out between, for example, the FSB and the army, or interior ministry troops and paratroopers. These confrontations sometimes end in pitched battles: serious fighting between Russian units broke out in Grozny in March 2001 following the arrest of a Chechen leader. One unit tried to free the rebel because it had received money from him to ignore his presence in the city. These field rivalries are even more pronounced at the top, where different clans of *silovoki* (the Russian term for all security agencies) confront each other. In Moscow there is an obvious rift between the chief of staff, who is close to the business world and the energy barons, and the minister of defence. And both are opposed to the FSB, whose control has become increasingly oppressive since Putin relied on it to consolidate his power.

Furthermore, much of the Russian military equipment is defective despite efforts to avoid the military disaster of 1994-6. Soldiers die of asphyxiation in tanks and armoured vehicles because there is no air conditioning or gas ventilation. The state of the troops is disturbing: conflicts between officers and men, discrimination against young conscripts, physical and even sexual violence practised by the older soldiers, and a high rate of alcoholism and drug abuse all take their toll. Several hundred young conscripts die every year in senselessly violent initiation ceremonies, fights, or the settling of personal grudges. Deaths also occur through drinking bouts, suicide, tuberculosis or inexperience in handling weapons, some of which are defective. Most young men try to avoid military service by resorting to corruption or desertion. Humiliated, beaten and starved, Russian soldiers avenge their miserable existence on Chechen civilians by subjecting them to even worse treatment in order to regain a sense of superiority.

Evidence suggests that the federal forces are behind the supply of arms to Chechen independence fighters. Contrary to Moscow's victorious declarations, the *boeviki* (Chechen resistance fighters) still organise bombings and launch surprise attacks on a daily basis and do not appear to suffer an arms deficit despite three years of intense military operations. Russia's official explanation is that the arms come from abroad via Georgia, accompanied by 'Islamist' volunteers. General Mironov, an FSB officer, admitted in an interview with *Moskovski Komsomolets* in December 2001, however, that the rebels import relatively few weapons from other countries and mainly use equipment produced in Russia. In fact, the Chechens are equipped with the same types of weapons as the federal forces. Since the rebels do not have any aircraft, the army has no need of anti-aircraft weapons in Chechnya, so the rebels cannot obtain them. Russian soldiers of all ranks are involved in this traffic. While ordinary soldiers may trade a grenade or a box of bullets for vodka or hashish, the officers deal in shells, mortars, rockets, information on their colleagues, and even the liberation of imprisoned rebels.

The conflict offers many opportunities for enrichment apart from the trade in war materials. Despite the almost total destruction of the country, over 1,500 mini refineries and several hundred oil wells are still functioning, each one under the protection of a colonel or a general. Dozens of road tankers and trains loaded with oil leave the republic under armed escort every day. Other lucrative practices include the 'protection' of humanitarian workers and journalists; arbitrary arrests with release upon a ransom payment; theft and pillage committed during 'cleansing' operations; large payments for leaving in peace certain villages or districts (sometimes the notorious refuges of rebel leaders); and smuggling between Chechnya and the neighbouring Russian regions. The Chechen war has become a bone to chew on for the military. Although the army has sustained heavy losses, the conflict strengthens it and the definitive cessation of hostilities could provoke serious unrest among officers.

Beyond the privatisation of the Russian army, the fundamental reason for the ineffectiveness of federal troops is the absence of the local population's support. The inhumanity of federal troops maintains the rebellion's strength.

The new face of Chechen resistance

Although the first war (1994-6) cost almost 100,000 Chechen lives (10 percent of the population) it was not then that the Russians became objects of hatred. The independence movement that appeared around 1990 had developed in the climate of opportunity created by the break-up of the USSR. It was unique in the sense that it expressed the claims of a people that had suffered constant oppression under the Tsars and later the communists; a population deported in its totality under Stalin and whose language and history had long been suppressed while other Caucasian peoples had been offered concessions like their own alphabet and the opportunity to have party cadres drawn from local people. The strength of the Chechen movement lay in the euphoria produced by the chance to finally and openly advance claims for its own culture and state.

Despite their ferocious opposition to Moscow, Chechens aged over 35 still have something in common with other populations of the Russian federation, even if it is only their communist past. The 'radical' war leader Shamil Bassaev, as 'Wahhabite' and anti-Russian as he is, astonished journalists by reciting '*Chiroka Strana Moya Rodnaya*' ('How Vast is my Homeland'), a poem that every Soviet child was forced to learn by heart, while President Maskhadov, leader of the 'moderate' wing of the resistance, can look back to his past as a colonel in the Soviet army. Despite their deep attachment to Islam and Chechnya, these leaders have personal and cultural ties that are closer to Russia than to Saudi Arabia or Afghanistan. Until the start of the second war, they seemed to envisage a future in which their republic maintained close links with Russia.

But it is precisely this generation of leaders that the federal forces are striving to eradicate. According to Kremlin propaganda, the elimination of the rebel leaders would automatically provoke the collapse of the resistance movement. Today, most of the historic leaders are dead. Yet even if Bassaev and Maskhadov were executed in their turn, there is an entire generation determined to fight on without the authorisation or direction of their elders. The Nord-Ost theatre incident illustrates this as most of the commandos were in their early twenties and were not led by a famous resistance figure. This new generation has known nothing but war. Its only image of Russia is of troops raping, killing, kidnapping and torturing. The brutality of the federal soldiers has convinced it beyond the shadow of a doubt that Russia is the eternal enemy and that its troops are 'savages' who respect nothing, not women, not children, not the elderly, not the dead.

Extreme as it may sound, young Chechens have only three choices available to them: they can flee, remain in Chechnya and wait to be killed, or take up arms and join the nearest guerrilla group. Most rebels belong to the new generation and have a completely hostile attitude towards Russia. The young *boeviki* are motivated less by religious ideals or dreams of political independence than by the urgent need to survive, the desire for vengeance, or the need to preserve their dignity as free individuals. It would be more accurate to describe them as antifederalists than as Islamists or independence fighters. Unlike their elders, who had some experience of peace and a normal life, they are ruthless and extremely radical. It will be much more difficult for the central power to negotiate with them if such was its intention. As one of Maskhadov's representatives stressed to one of the few Russian members of parliament favourable to opening negotiations: 'with these young people it will be too late, they will kill you and us at the same time.'[1]

The Kadyrov report

According to a report commissioned by President Kadyrov, head of the pro-Russian Chechen administration, 1,314 civilians were murdered outside of any armed confrontation in 2002 alone – over 100 summary executions a month since the official 'pacification' of the republic. Three thousand corpses were buried in 'mass graves', a term that the pro-Russian administration had refused to use until then.

This report, which revealed a higher number of victims than even cited by Russian human rights organisations like Memorial, confirms – if there was a need – the intensity and cruelty of counter-insurrectionist violence. The stories told by refugees and the few journalists to visit Chechnya had already shed light on the *zatchiski* or mopping-up operations conducted by masked men who travel in armoured vehicles with unidentifiable plates. Their job entails the rape of men, women and children, torture inflicted directly on site in specially adapted troop carriers (less visible than the 'filtering camps'), and the slaughter of

---

[1] As recounted by Yuri Shekotoshikhin, a Russian deputy of the Yabloko party, to whom Akhmed Zakaev, a representative of Mashkhadov, once said : 'Yura, don't miss this chance [to negotiate]. Maskhadov and I grew up in the Soviet Union and studied at Soviet university. With these young ones it will be too late; they will kill you and us too at the same time" (Y. Shekotoshikhin, 'Marodyory' in *Novaya Gazeta*, November 11, 2002).

civilians of all ages using the latest refinements like the 'human fuse' which explodes leaving the corpse almost impossible to identify.

Recognised now by the pro-Russian authorities, this unprecedented violence is even leading victims to participate in their own torture in order to relieve the torment of suspense: in the little village of Tsotsin-Yurt in the Argun region, the inhabitants themselves proposed dates for the next *zatchiski*.

The most obvious sign of Chechen radicalisation is the increase in suicide attacks, and the growing participation of women in them. Such attacks were extremely rare in the first war and many Chechens regarded them as contrary to their interpretation of Islam. Today, women are ready to blow themselves up to kill a general renowned for his atrocities, or drive lorries stuffed with explosives into Russian command posts.

Unlike the 1994-6 war or even the 2000 campaign, the rebels are now active in every part of the territory. There is no front line any more, nor any clear distinction between rebel and civilian. Contrary to Kremlin statements, most rebels are not hiding in the high mountains or dense forests but live in Grozny, Gudermes, Alkhan-Kala and Star Atagy. Federal control in the mountainous regions of Vedeno and Nojay-Yurt is limited to a few hundred metres around troop positions. As the resistance has become more diffuse, it has also become more effective. Some rebels even become incorporated in the police or pro-Russian command posts to earn money. Even so, they do not stop hating their employers. Russian troops are equally consumed by hatred: they harbour a profound mistrust of the Chechen police and refuse to mount joint operations for fear of being betrayed.

The growing reference to Islam as an ideological spearhead of the resistance is an equivocal phenomenon. It is primarily a psychological weapon in the war against an occupier who is ignorant of this religion and who has an embittered fear of it. The spread of Islam, which has affected those who, like Maskhadov, have never been ardent followers, is also connected to the Chechens' desire to emerge from their isolation. As there is no support from the West, Islamists from the Gulf, Europe and the Middle East are *de facto* the only people who are prepared to help the resistance. The new order thus invalidates the rebellion's division into 'moderates' – pro-Western nationalists personified by President Maskhadov – and 'radicals' – Islamists turned towards the *Umma* (community of believers), represented by commanders like Bassaev. The Americans, who still officially support a negotiated end to the conflict, declared after 11 September that they were 'disappointed' by Maskhadov. Considerably weakened by the loss of his most loyal allies, Maskhadov was left with no choice but to make his peace with Shamil Bassaev in August 2002. Even Islamists from Arab countries, who were relatively poorly regarded by the Chechens, began to attract respect, as they did not hesitate to sacrifice their own lives in the 'defence of oppressed Muslims'.

Finally, the recourse to Islam is not only instrumental. Permanently confronted with an extreme situation in which the prospect of death is omnipresent, the population and combatants are becoming increasingly attached to religion. Commanders are now adopting the role of spiritual guide in order to give the troops metaphysical support and to make them accept hunger, danger and cold. It is rare for a preacher to become a commander: the 'puritans' of the pre-war era, accused of having served as a pretext for the Russian intervention, do not enjoy much popularity.

Chechen society is certainly more detached from Russia today than is any other country in the Russian Federation. Chechens cannot reconcile themselves to life under occupation, and those who live in Russian cities are regarded as potential enemies by the rest of the population.

The Russian population, the state and the war in Chechnya

An overwhelming majority of Russians now believe that Chechens are 'savages', an instinctively violent race that only understands the language of arms. Racist attacks have doubled in intensity in Russian towns where foreign nationals from Asia, Africa, the Caucasus, central Asia, and even the former Soviet republics of Ukraine and Moldova are daily assaulted, beaten up or murdered. These are not isolated acts or perpetrated solely by marginalised skinheads. The Moscow police and many 'ordinary' citizens do not hesitate to express their disgust at seeing Russian towns 'invaded' by 'blacks' (from the Caucasus and countries further south). A popular journalist working for a public national television station can refer on air to the UN Secretary-General as a 'monkey' without arousing public indignation.

The racism of the 'educated classes' has different sociological roots to the form practiced by idle, shaven-headed youths. Indeed, the Soviet education system had instilled in citizens the idea that racism was a typical product of Western, capitalist society. The educated middle classes, plagued by an inferiority complex in relation to Western Europe, now openly display their racism in the belief that the denigration of 'blacks' or 'orientals' will finally establish that Russia is a European nation and worthy of taking its place among the 'whites' and the 'civilised'.

The stranglehold exercised by the government over the media (especially television) has thus proved to be effective. The unpopularity of the first war amongst the Russian population was principally due to the much greater freedom enjoyed by the media during the Yeltsin era. Today the Russian public is unaware of the situation in Chechnya. It is only exposed to information approved by the authorities who resort to doctored films or documents of dubious provenance in which 'Chechen fanatics' decapitate hostages, usually Russian. Major television shows like beauty contests are punctuated by plays featuring elite commandos adept at martial arts thrashing purported terrorists in front of a euphoric audience. The hatred of 'the Chechen' as the incarnation of the enemy of the Russian state and nation is so strong that the lies disseminated by the authorities provoke no reaction from the Russian public. This is a major difference with the war conducted in the Yeltsin period.

This voluntary blindness goes hand in hand with the rehabilitation of a patriotism that glorifies the Soviet past and martial values. Thus, despite its flagrant inefficiency in Chechnya, the army is once again extremely popular. Russians are prepared to forgive it anything, including the corruption, lack of professionalism, and extreme human rights violations in Chechnya. The Western media show mothers refusing to let their sons fight in the Chechnya, but omit to mention the thousands of Russians who feel pride in seeing their sons leave for the Caucasus. It is significant that the Russian public was so uncritical of its government after it condemned 150 hostages to death by sanctioning the assault on the Nord-Ost theatre. The images of young Russians singing and photographing each other in front of the theatre, bottles in hand, a few hours after the assault by the 'Alpha' units show that the radicalisation of youth is not confined to Chechnya.

The Nord-Ost hostage crisis put the finishing touches on the transformation of Russia into an 'anti-terrorist state', a state whose *raison d'être* and principal function is to hunt down terrorists. Human rights, education and the general well-being of the population are now secondary issues. Public freedoms are steadily being eroded. A recent law decrees that the bodies of dead 'terrorists' (including those who die in prison) will no longer be returned to their families. Hence any 'terrorist' can now be murdered while in detention without any medico-legal investigation into the cause of death. The Duma has just voted in a law (not yet ratified by the executive) which reinforces control over the media. The authorities will be able to close down press agencies accused of 'favouring terrorism' no matter what kind of material they release.

Colonel Budanov, 'hero' in Moscow,
'barbarian' in Chechnya

On 26 March 2000, the day Putin was elected as the Kremlin's new master, Colonel Yuri Budanov was celebrating his daughter's second birthday. A bout of heavy drinking at the Tangi-Chu headquarters in the Urus-

Martan region was followed by a jaunt to the small village nearby. When Visa Kungaev heard the armoured vehicles arriving, he woke his eldest daughter, 18-year-old Elsa, before seeking refuge himself. Budanov and his men burst into the house, pounced on Elsa, beat her and took her back to the base. She was left alone with the colonel and when he called his men an hour later, Elsa Kungaeva was dead.

The same night, her father went to Urus-Martan to see General Gerasimov, the zone commander, who personally went to arrest the Colonel. An investigation was opened – it was to be the first and only investigation into the conduct of a Russian army officer for such crimes in Chechnya. The evidence against Budanov was overwhelming. He admitted strangling the girl but denied raping her although the autopsy revealed that she had been vaginally and anally raped an hour before her death.

The rapes were omitted from the charge sheet. According to the new official version, Budanov strangled the girl in a fit of rage because he suspected her of rebel activity. The Colonel benefited from an impressive mobilisation of support. General Shamanov, governor of the Oulianovsk region, called his act 'heroic', fellow officers demanded his release, and he enjoyed an astonishing degree of sympathy from the Russian public.

At the start of the investigation in February 2001, two psychiatrists had found Budanov to be 'mentally competent' at the time of the crime. Although some had hoped for a guilty verdict that would expose the Russian army's impunity in the Caucasus, a new examination was ordered. Experts from the Serbsky Institute of Psychiatry – responsible in its time for the internment of dissidents – concluded that the colonel had not been in control of his actions due to 'temporary derangement'. This was enough for the Rostov tribunal to acquit him in December 2002, a verdict that aroused no public indignation. Since then further expert opinion has been requested by the plaintiff and the court case has resumed.

Before the tragedy at the Nord-Ost theatre, the Kremlin's tone had perceptibly shifted. Whereas in June 2001 Putin had fiercely defended the 'combing operations', he acknowledged for the first time in June 2002 that the federal power bore some responsibility for the tragedy in Chechnya and that it would be more appropriate to 'put a stop' to the *zatchiski* instead of perfecting them. Putin had even begun to rein in the military and had sent the head of the government accounting office to investigate the army's misappropriation of public funds.

But the theatre crisis ended the many peace plans and semi-official meetings with Maskhadov's emissaries. Putin seems to have already selected the future Chechen president, Ahmed Kadyrov, currently Interior minister in the pro-Russian Chechen administration. The referendum organised in Chechnya in March 2003 had the notable aim of smoothing and legitimising Kadyrov's accession to the presidency by way of the ballot box. It is possible, however, that Putin is making the same mistakes as his predecessors. Inspired by colonial ethnography and the memoirs of Ermolov (conqueror of the north Caucasus in the 19th century), he seeks at times to co-opt the 'old guard' while at others he courts the leaders or the muftis, but there is no guarantee that Kadyrov has the means to earn respect.

The consent of the international community

The genocidal dynamic unleashed in Chechnya is supported by the silence, indeed the consent, of the 'international community'. Relations between the European Union, the United States and Russia are too important to be impeded by the Chechen question.

Certainly, these states and international authorities are obliged for the sake of appearances to admit that 'violations of human rights' are being committed in the Caucasian republic – Putin himself acknowledges them. 'Abuse' features in every report compiled by the US State Department, the OSCE, the European Parliament, the Council of Europe and other organisations. But references to 'abuse' and the 'disproportionate means' used by Moscow do not convey the extent of the violence and discreetly reduce the deliberate policy of terror to a series of regrettable errors.

The war in Chechnya does not exist for the UN Security Council since it has never met to debate it. The UN General Assembly which, given the Charter and the Acheson Resolution of 1951, could have called an extraordinary session to discuss the situation, has not ventured that far. The Secretary-General has had ample opportunity to draw the Security Council's attention to the conflict but has yet to do so. Certainly, some diplomatic pressure has been brought to bear on Moscow, but only during the course of the year 2000. Russia was condemned before the UN Human Rights Commission, and the Council of Europe's Parliamentary Assembly caused a stir by suspending the Russian delegation's right to vote and asked the executive to begin suspension proceedings against Russia and submit the case to the European Court for Human Rights. In November 2000, France and the US called for the immediate return of the OSCE to Chechnya, from which it had withdrawn in 1998.

Nonetheless, the pressure has not been backed up by any concrete action or sanctions. Russia was not excluded from the Council of Europe and no state referred the matter to the European Court of Human

Rights. The OSCE briefly returned to Chechnya in the summer of 2001 but was pressured into leaving on 31 December 2002, when the Kremlin refused to renew its mandate, a move that aroused little more than vague protests from the European Parliament. According to Western diplomacy, any significant action against Russia would be both hysterical and counter-productive: it is absolutely essential not to weaken the Kremlin's strong man, or to make the former great power lose face, for fear of compromising the country's 'democratic evolution'. It was thought better to encourage the Russian authorities to conduct their own investigations into the 'human rights violations'.

Since 11 September 2001, the silence of the 'international community' concerning the war crimes and crimes against humanity committed in Chechnya has turned into consent. As Sergei Kovalev, the former dissident and honorary president of the Russian human rights organisation Memorial, emphasised in January 2002, 'bin Laden has presented Vladimir Putin with a personal gift'. In other words, he has enabled Putin to position the Chechen conflict within the framework of an international fight against terrorism and pass off the war as a simple policing operation. During his electoral campaign (in an interview with Larry King) George W. Bush declared the action of the Russian army in Chechnya 'not acceptable', and advocated cutting off aid to Russia in order to 'condemn the – you know, the killing of innocent women and children'.[2] But now Bush considers Vladimir Putin a 'good friend in the fight against terrorism'. According to the new American

---

[2] Cf. F. Zakaria, 'This is Moral Clarity', *Washington Post*, 5 November 2002.

strategic doctrine,[3] 'Russia is engaged in a promising period of transition; it seeks a democratic future and an ally in its war against terrorism.'

As for the Council of Europe, it effectively discarded its values at the end of 2002 by awarding the medal of merit to Vladimir Kalamanov, Kremlin representative for human rights in Chechnya. At the time of the EU-Russia summit in November 2002, a European diplomat claimed in private that 'relations between Europe and Russia are too important to be dominated by the human rights question'. As a consequence, the Chechen question disappeared from the agenda at international political conferences. France, whose firm stance had nearly cost it the diplomatic wrath of Putin, (who refused to visit Paris for several months in 1999-2000 after the French criticised the Russian 'anti-terrorist operation' in the Northern Caucasus), rejoined the ranks in July of 2002, citing its need to develop bilateral relations with Russia.

Impossible humanitarian action

If the reports by UN agencies and NGOs are anything to go by, it is easy to believe that a powerful international presence is being deployed in Chechnya: food, shelter, water, health, education – all the fundamentals of a humanitarian response – are being provided by 20 organisations including the main UN agencies (OCHA, WFP, WHO, UNICEF, UNHCR, UNDP). Money is generously spent: ECHO, the humanitarian office of the European Commission, principal donor in the region, has allotted 90 million

---

[3] *The National Strategy of the USA*, Washington, DC, 20 September 2002.

euros to the Chechen crisis since 1999, 25 million of which was for 2002 alone. The 'needs' of Chechen civilians therefore seem to be 'covered'. Poul Nielsen, the European Commissioner for Humanitarian Affairs, recently claimed that aid organisations were in a position to deliver humanitarian aid to the interior of Chechnya and the surrounding areas, only conceding that 'it was difficult'. But he assured his audience that it could and would continue to be done.

But this show of publicity can no longer deceive. Apart from the fact that deliveries of medicines or reconstruction materials can do little in response to a policy of terror, humanitarian assistance contributes in a very marginal way to the improvement of the population's material conditions. Because of the insecurity, most agencies are reluctant to send representatives to supervise aid programs. 'Ground visits' seldom last more than a couple of hours and are restricted to meeting the local authorities in Grozny. The few NGOs who do send international personnel live – or rather furtively operate – in constant fear of attacks, of being kidnapped, of exposing their local staff or the people they assist. The list of security incidents and accidents attests to an omnipresent climate of dread: the arrest and brutal interrogation of ICRC staff at a military roadblock in November 2002; the attack on a Danish Relief Council convoy; the kidnapping in July 2002 of Nina Davidovitch, representative of Druzbha, a Russian NGO; and the kidnapping of Arjan Erkel, MSF head of mission in Dagestan in August 2002. As this book goes to press, we still do not know who is holding Arjan and for what reason. All that we do know is that the Russian authorities, who hold primary responsibility for the safety of aid workers on their territory, have done little to assist in securing his release. Most MSF aid activities remain suspended until Arjan is freed, raising the question of whether those opposed to aiding Chechen civilians are behind the abduction. In reality the amount of aid that reaches the Chechen population is derisory; insecurity and misappropriation ensure that it does not correspond to the needs generated by the violence and war. It is impossible, for example, to deal efficiently with medical emergencies because the risks involved in moving around prevent patients and medical staff from reaching the hospitals, and the health centres are too dangerous for the war wounded and are consequently avoided. Assistance to Chechen refugees in the neighbouring republics is equally problematic: in Ingushetia, the Russian authorities deliberately keep displaced people in deplorable conditions, hoping to incite them to return to Chechnya, and increasingly restrict the working space of humanitarian organisations (see p. 188).

By refusing any confrontation with Russia, UN agencies are complicit in the Kremlin's game by maintaining the illusion of a return to 'normality'. The 2003 UN consolidated appeal states that the forced closure of a displaced persons camp in Chechnya in July 2002 'has led to a mutual understanding of humanitarian principles concerning the return of displaced persons.' [4] This 'understanding' was expressed in December 2002 by the expulsion of residents of the Aki Yurt camp in Ingushetia. The UN also 'expects the overall situation to improve by the end of 2002 and would not be surprised if marked advances were noted in 2003.' Meanwhile, the devastation of Chechnya continues.

---

[4] OCHA, *Mid-Year Review of Consolidated Inter-Agency Appeal*, 2002, North Caucasus.

Bibliographical references

Comité Tchétchénie, *Tchétchénie, dix clés pour comprendre*, Paris, La Découverte, 2003.

FIDH, *Tchétchénie : la normalisation, un discours de dupe*, Paris, March 2003.

F. Jean, 'Tchétchénie : guerre totale et complaisance occidentale', *Relations Internationales et Stratégiques*, no. 23, Fall 1996, pp. 24-33.

F. Jean, 'Tchétchénie : la revanche de Moscou', *Esprit*, February 2000, pp. 37-54.

T. Gordadzé, 'Les nouvelles guerres du Caucase (1989-2000) et la formation de l'Etat post-communiste', in P. Hassner and R. Marchal (eds.), *La guerre entre le global et le local*, Paris, Karthala, 2001.

Médecins Sans Frontières, *Les exilés cachés d'une guerre sans témoins*, Paris, December 2001.

Médecins Sans Frontières, *Sans l'ombre d'un choix. Le retour forcé des Tchétchènes en Tchétchénie*, Paris, May 2003.

9

DEMOCRATIC REPUBLIC OF CONGO
Victims of No Importance

Marc Le Pape

Since July 1998 the Democratic Republic of Congo has been the theatre of the 'first African world war'. In May 2003, despite the signing of ceasefire agreements, the intervention of foreign armies continued in the east of DRC and militia confrontations and massacres occurred in Ituri region. The suffering of the Congolese has accumulated from the ravages of armed confrontation, foreign occupation, epidemics, forced population transfers, and economic distress. UN intervention has been predominantly in the diplomatic arena and the monitoring of peace agreements. Acts of violence against civilians have been observed, recorded, and publicly exposed, but the United Nations Mission in the Democratic Republic of Congo (MONUC) has not been 'configured' to curb them. Furthermore, Western states have failed to act decisively to put an end to acts of war committed by Uganda and Rwanda.

The regional conflagration

Within a matter of a few months, an armed offensive
emanating from Rwanda and eastern Zaire in October
1996 led to the fall of President Mobutu, and Laurent-
Désiré Kabila seized power on 17 May 1997. This
offensive was carried out by Congolese opponents and
the Rwandan army. Uganda supported the rebels to a
lesser degree, as did Angola – more belatedly but in
decisive fashion – and Burundi. Rwanda's commitment
was primarily due to the desire of the new authorities in
Kigali to intervene militarily in Kivu (an eastern region
of Zaire) in order to dismantle the Rwandan refugee

camps that had been established along its border since July 1994. Many of those who organised and carried out the genocide of the Rwandan Tutsi had found refuge in the camps and reorganised themselves. With rear bases located near or inside the UNHCR camps, they had been launching murderous guerrilla operations against the Rwandan army and civilians. In October-November 1996, the camps were methodically attacked by Kigali's troops and their occupants put to flight or repatriated under duress. Those who escaped were mercilessly pursued across the DRC Zaire by Rwandan troops: some 200,000 of them are estimated to have perished during the chase. The UN Security Council condemned the massacres, but asked the very governments responsible for the killings (the DRC and Rwanda) to investigate the atrocities.

The union between the new Congolese government and its allies collapsed on 27 July 1998: L.-D. Kabila ordered the Rwandan and Ugandan troops to leave the country and unleashed a series of pogroms against Tutsi of both Congolese and Rwandan origin. On 2 August and the days that followed, mutinies broke out in the eastern DRC and Kinshasa among contingents of Rwandan and Banyamulenge soldiers (the Banyamulenge being Rwandophone Congolese long settled in South Kivu). The Rwandan and Ugandan armies quickly intervened. They invaded Kivu and took Kisangani, located over 500 km from the border, on 23 August. But the front that posed the greatest immediate threat to Kinshasa was that opened in the Lower Congo by an airborne commando of Rwandan soldiers intent on seizing the capital. Only a massive intervention by Angola made it possible to thwart the attempt. From August onwards, Zimbabwe and Namibia also entered the war on the DRC's side,

Zimbabwe sending troops and Namibia delivering arms. In September, Sudan committed itself militarily to Kinshasa's side, thereby providing Uganda's president – whose government was being challenged by several insurrectionary movements backed by Khartoum – with an argument to justify his country's armed intervention.

By mid-October 1998 a third of the DRC was in rebel hands. Following the fall of Kindu, the administrative centre of Maniema Province in the east, the diamond-yielding region of Kasai and the town of Mbuji-Mayi, in the centre, were under threat. In time, the whole south-eastern part of the country (the province of Katanga) risked falling into rebel hands. In February 1999, an offensive was launched against Mbuji-Mayi, where Kinshasa's allies had reinforced their numbers and equipment, especially their aerial component (battle helicopters and fighter-bombers sent by Angola and Zimbabwe). The rebel and Rwandan forces occupied part of Kasai and North Katanga, but Mbuji-Mayi did not fall. The war continued simultaneously in the province of Equator, where Uganda was supporting the Congo Liberation Movement (MLC – le Mouvement de Libération du Congo), distinct from the Congolese Rally for Democracy (RCD – Rassemblement Congolais pour la Démocratie) with which Rwanda was allied. In January 2001, the Congolese government controlled half the country, while the rebels, Uganda and Rwanda controlled the other half.

By this stage, it was clear that an international war was underway, the 'first African world war'. Laurent-Désiré Kabila's decision to expel Ugandan and Rwandan troops from the DRC had immediately provoked their counter-attack, and then, via the play of alliances and interests, a regional conflict. Since then, it has been the military options and political choices of the region's heads of state – in other words, international factors – that predominantly determined events imposed on the Congolese. Even so, the parties engaged in the international conflict often exacerbated local animosities or played on old or current rivalries between actors in Congolese political life. They thus ignited centres of violence whose expansion they could not always control, to which the recent upsurge in massacres by militias in Ituri attests. These were typical war strategies linked to territorial occupation.

International mediation

The Congo war gave rise to many attempts at mediation. The most significant was the ceasefire agreement signed at Lusaka on 10 July 1999 by most of the international parties to the conflict, and then by the two main rebel movements (RCD and MLC), who joined the process in August. Although constantly violated between 2000 and 2002, this agreement formed the basis of attempts to resolve the conflict. It proposed 'inter-Congolese dialogue' on how to govern the country and provided for the departure of foreign troops from DRC territory and the disarmament and demobilisation of foreign armed factions active within the country. This latter clause responded to demands of the Rwandan government, which was exposed to attacks by armed groups organised and trained on Congolese territory (former Rwandan army forces, known as ex-FAR, and *Interahamwe* militias, both implicated in organising and perpetrating the 1994 genocide). The agreement also defined the tasks of MONUC (created in 1999): it was to supervise the disengagement and withdrawal of foreign armies; investigate ceasefire violations and undertake measures to enhance its respect; disarm, demobilise, repatriate, resettle and reintegrate ex-combatants; and identify perpetrators of war crimes and crimes against humanity and bring them before the International Criminal Court. In February 2000 the Security Council strengthened MONUC (Resolution 1291), which henceforth could number up to 5,537 soldiers, including 500 observers. But it stipulated that this deployment would only become effective if the parties respected the Lusaka ceasefire agreement and on condition that a plan for the disengagement of forces be established. In the same resolution, the Security Council authorised MONUC to take the necessary action 'as it deems it within its capacities', to 'protect civilians under imminent threat of physical violence'.

Joseph Kabila's accession to power following the assassination of his father on 16 January 2001 permitted some concrete progress in the Lusaka process to begin. In February, the new Congolese head of state accepted a plan for the disengagement of armed forces and gave his support to the deployment of MONUC's team. Judging that 'the conditions relating to respect for the ceasefire have been met', the United Nations began actually deploying their civilian and military personnel in February. Nonetheless, it would be a year and a half before Rwanda and the DRC signed a draft agreement in Pretoria (July 2002) over the simultaneous withdrawal of Rwandan troops and dismantling of groups of *Interahamwe* militiamen and ex-FAR. By 9 October 2002 around 90 percent of the 23,760 Rwandan soldiers officially present in the DRC had been withdrawn, according to MONUC. On 6 September 2002 the

Congolese and Ugandan Presidents ratified an agreement on the departure of Ugandan troops. These agreements have been violated regularly since being signed. The Rwandan and Ugandan military interventions have not ended in eastern Congo, where Rwandan Hutu armed groups continue to pursue a war against the Kigali regime. The *Maï-Maï* – a term used in the 1960s to designate militias that allied themselves with the Mulelist revolt against Mobutu's army in South Kivu, and henceforth applied to any group of young armed people more or less at odds with their societies of origin – continued to harass the rebel and loyalist troops who, on both sides, perpetrated numerous acts of violence.

The Congolese

Numerous dispatches, first-hand accounts and investigations published during the war describe the fate of populations caught up in battles and subjected to the prolonged presence of rebel, foreign or governmental armed forces. The following extracts of news dispatches illustrate the sort of information published about attacks and counterattacks on towns:

> *Agence France Presse, 6 October 1998. Offensive against Kindu (Maniema), in eastern DRC*
>
> The rebels claim that on Tuesday morning they launched an offensive against Kindu, which is being bombarded by mortars and is the scene of street fighting. The rebel commander, Arthur Mulunda, stated that the offensive was launched from the right bank of the Congo River, to the east of Kindu. According to him, the rebels first bombarded the town with mortars, starting at 3

am, then attacked with land forces at dawn. 'The government forces are resisting,' he added, and the civilian population 'is in flight, using the road and the railway line.'

[According to other dispatches, the rebels claim to have committed 9,000 men to this battle. Agence France Presse reminds readers that 'journalists are forbidden access to the front, which makes it impossible to verify information on the conflict.']

Agence France Presse, 8 June 1999. Capture of Manono (Katanga), in the southeast of the DRC

Since 7 June, Manono has been in the hands of rebel Congolese troops, backed by Rwandan soldiers. In Manono, the streets are empty, and the shutters and doors of houses stand wide open. The only signs of life are the few lamps lit at night in houses where newly installed soldiers are quartered. There is no life at all on the wide avenues bordered by mango trees. Today, following a month of battles and bombardments, the population has completely deserted the town.

'The population has fled to the bush. We are very afraid of the bombardments. We will only return if the bombing stops.'

'The Zimbabwean planes, MiGs and Antonovs, came almost daily. They sometimes dropped ten bombs and then left, but could return again the same day.'

Agence France Presse, 11 April 2001. Bombardment of Nyunzu (Katanga), in the southeast of DRC

Since December, Nyunzu, under siege by the Congolese Armed Forces (FAC – Forces Armées Congolaises, loyal to the Kinshasa government) and the tribal Maï-Maï militias, has received almost no supplies. On 20 December, at 6.00 in the morning, four FAC battalions attacked

Nyunzu. The battle raged for almost two weeks. Mortar shells rained on the small town's former colonial villas and avenues shaded by mango trees: '176 bombs in twelve days.' 'Everyone hid in the houses, we had nothing to eat or drink.' The attackers repelled and the blockade began. Food shortages set in. 'No sugar, no salt, no beer, almost no cassava, because nobody could go out to farm, we were really hungry.' It was not until nearly four months after the attack that the assailants' grip began to loosen.

During this war, the capture of towns was constantly highlighted in the public arena as evidence of the opposing armies' victories and advances. The descriptions of attacks shed light on the nature and scale of the battles: encirclement, aerial bombardments, heavy shelling, street fighting. In some cases, the blockades and bombardments lasted for months. In others, towns were taken and retaken by belligerents. Often, troop movements, confrontations, or the threat thereof caused villagers to flee to nearby towns for refuge where, in the end, they found themselves trapped by encircling troop movements. These displaced persons, mostly farmers who sold their produce in urban markets, abandoned their crops and stopped trading, causing the rupture of food supplies to the towns. The disorganisation of trade between urban and rural areas, together with the disruption of commercial circuits on a local and regional scale, contributed to the emergence of food shortages.

In numerous cases, such as Manono, it was urban residents who departed en masse from towns threatened by or under attack. Their survival depended on help from villagers, themselves overwhelmed by the number of people needing assistance, and often exposed to violence by rebels or deserters. Armed men pillaged and burnt villages and mistreated the population who, whenever the soldiers approached, left their houses to hide in the forest. In North Katanga, for example, where there was a strong concentration of government soldiers and Maï-Maï militiamen due to the proximity of the front line, the Congolese lived in constant fear of violence. At the slightest warning of Congolese soldiers or Maï-Maï approaching, villagers fled to refuges hidden in the bush, from whence they continued to cultivate their fields. Many villages remain deserted along the main roads frequented by troops. The Congolese sleep in the bush and might emerge in the morning to inspect the state of their crops and their belongings.

Total war and international passivity

External intervention in the eastern provinces of North and South Kivu was continuous since 1996. Kigali claimed the right to intervene to protect its border and to pursue the *génocidaires* who had taken refuge in the DRC, but in practice the Rwandan forces, like the Ugandan troops also present in the region, constituted an army of occupation. They reached Kisangani, Kasai and Katanga, all situated great distances from the border that needed protecting. In reality troop concentrations and targets indicate that the economic exploitation of occupied areas was a principal goal of intervention. As a number of United Nations investigations have documented, the illegal exploitation of Kivu's natural resources and the plundering of its installations to benefit Rwandan and Ugandan military oligarchies constitute one of the major stakes of the conflict.

From 1996 onwards Kivu's inhabitants developed numerous forms of civil and armed resistance to the foreign occupation. The Rwandan troops and their rebel allies responded by waging total war against the populations: arrests, torture, summary executions, mass repression against villages, pillage, burning houses to provoke flight into the forest, rape, and harassment of civil society organisations (interrogation, intimidation of activists, murders). These practices were not confined to Kivu and were widely known. Information spread rapidly about massacres perpetrated by rebels allied to Rwanda in eastern DRC in reprisal for Maï-Maï attacks against them. According to Catholic missionaries, 633 people were murdered en masse in Kasika in August 1998 irrespective of age or gender (thirty or so, according to the attackers), 500 at Makobola in December 1998, and 300 at Katogota in May 2000 (31 according to an anonymous UN official). Numerous facts and investigations make it possible to draw up a horrifying tale of the various forms of cruelty perpetrated against the Congolese by all armed forces involved in this war.

Although UN Security Council Resolution 1291 (February 2000) authorised the UN Mission, under Chapter VII of the UN charter, to take all measures necessary 'to protect civilians under imminent threat of physical violence', Kofi Annan announced in April 2001 that 'MONUC has neither the mandate nor the means to ensure the safety of the civilian populations'.[1] The means were certainly lacking – in June 2002 MONUC's numbers were still below the target set by resolution

---

[1] United Nations Security Council, *Seventh Report of the Secretary-General on MONUC*, 17 April 2001 (S/2001/373).

1291 – but had not the protection mandate, albeit restricted, been passed by vote? Annan also stated that 'the equipment, training and configuration' of the Mission's contingents had not been designed to provide rapid protection to civilians, but admitted that where sizeable UN contingents were deployed (as at Kisangani), the population 'would expect' them to protect civilians. As the precedents of Rwanda and Bosnia have shown, such expectations are dangerous and in vain. Despite the promises contained in the United Nations' resolutions, clearly protecting Congolese civilians was not the Security Council's priority.

The scale of atrocities committed against non-combatants was rapidly made public by local and international NGOs, churches and, later, UN observers, but no sanctions were imposed against the states occupying eastern Congo. The behaviour of the Rwandan and Ugandan armies in the DRC provoked no reduction in aid granted to these countries by the European Union – nor by Britain and the US; the latter saw in the Presidents of Rwanda and Uganda a 'new generation of African leaders' pursuing a veritable 'African renaissance'. As if to be pardoned for its inertia during the genocide in Rwanda in 1994, part of the 'international community' accepted, until recently, Kigali's justifications: Rwanda, by intervening militarily in the DRC, was merely protecting its border and pursuing the *génocidaires* on the ground. The international community used this rationale to permit the Ugandan and Rwandan troops to do as they pleased.

Nevertheless, confronted with the massacres committed in Ituri in May 2003 and following the withdrawal of Ugandan troops, the UN Security Council adopted on 30 May a resolution authorising a Chapter VII deployment of an 'interim' multinational force in Bunia. The mission is limited to the protection of the airport and displaced persons in town. Acting under French command and the auspices of the European Union, this force was due to withdraw on 1 September 2003 and hand over to MONUC contingents which are currently being assembled.

The battles of Kisangbani, 1998-2002

The Congo war began on 2 August 1998 and by 23 August Kisangani had fallen into the hands of the Congolese Rally for Democracy and its Ugandan and Rwandan allies. The capture of this town of 700,000 inhabitants, which had two airports and was the regional centre for control of diamond marketing channels, constituted an important strategic military and political phase in the war. Uganda and Rwanda quickly exploited the rivalries among Congolese rebel leaders, each supporting the emergence of a movement favourable to it and over which it would hold sway. They thus provoked a split in the RCD between a faction close to Uganda led by Wamba dia Wamba (RCD-Kisangani) and another (RCD-Goma) allied to Rwanda and run by Émile Ilunga.

On 22 May 1999, four days after the split in the RCD, there were fierce exchanges of fire in Kisangani between the Congolese factions and their respective allies. In July, Wamba dia Wamba announced that he might sign the ceasefire agreements under negotiation in Lusaka, a signing opposed by the leaders of the RCD-Goma. Between 14 and 16 August, the troops of Uganda and Rwanda confronted one another at Kisangani. Each side tried to impose the hegemony of the rebel faction it supported. The urban battle, with both armies using heavy weapons, left at least 300 civilians dead, mainly victims of bombardments. The confrontations between the Rwandan and Ugandan armies resumed in May and June 2000. From

5 to 10 June, the town was under fire, with combatants using tanks, rocket launchers, heavy machine guns and grenades. Hundreds were left dead and thousands seriously wounded or traumatised, while thousands of houses were destroyed or damaged and thousands of people displaced. In August 2000, the UN Secretary-General sent a team of observers to the DRC 'in order to assess the loss of human life and the material damage inflicted on the civilian population of Kisangani' as a result of the battles. The confrontations had left 760 civilians dead.

In his report of 21 September 2000 to the Security Council, Kofi Annan declared that Rwanda and Uganda had indeed withdrawn their forces to a distance of some 100 kilometres from Kisangani. Nonetheless, he explained, the military elements of the rebels allied to Rwanda were in control of the town, which was therefore not truly demilitarised, contrary to the commitments made.

One year later, in June 2002, the Secretary-General once more asked the RCD-Goma to 'immediately demilitarise' Kisangani which had been the scene of military acts of extreme brutality in May. On 14 May, dissident soldiers had seized the local radio station and issued a call to rise up against the 'Rwandan invaders'. When the soldiers loyal to the RCD-Goma regained the upper hand, they summarily executed civilians, soldiers and policemen suspected of not being sympathetic to them; victims had their throats cut and were mutilated. At the time, MONUC had not completed its 'deployment' in Kisangani and was unable to protect civilians, but it nonetheless gave refuge to seven people who said they would be in danger if they fell into the hands of the RCD.

The Security Council's Resolution 1291, recommending the protection of civilians, dated back to 24 February 2000. Yet it was only in mid-June 2002 that the UN brought its team in Kisangani up to the planned level of 1,150 soldiers. Slowness and caution were the option on which the Security Council had agreed.

Investigations into the consequences of a total war

The war's consequences have been observed, measured and described in a number of investigations. Carried out at the initiative of various international actors (international NGOs present in the DRC, European Union, World Health Organisation, United Nations), they all shared the same diagnosis: the primary health care system was in terrible shape; endemic illnesses (AIDS, sleeping sickness, malaria) were spreading rapidly; epidemics (measles, cholera) were multiplying; and the nutritional situation was serious for both town residents and the hundreds of thousands of internally displaced persons. In 2000, the number of Congolese exiled within their own country, mainly in the eastern DRC, was estimated at over two million. They sought refuge with friends, relatives or strangers, exacerbating their hosts' precariousness and dragging them into poverty. Among the displaced were a large number of children, often separated from their families. Health services were in a total state of collapse, unable to respond to the suffering endured by an increasing number of Congolese. The economic chaos caused by the war aggravated poverty and hence the vulnerability of the population. Such were the terms of the diagnosis.

One document played an essential role in the public debate on the scale of the Congolese disaster – a report on retrospective mortality undertaken in the eastern DRC in 2000 and 2001 by the International Rescue Committee (Mortality in Eastern DRC: Results from Eleven *Mortality Surveys*, May 2001 and April 2003). According to this study, 2.5 million Congolese lost their lives between August 1998 and March 2001 as a result of the war from a population of 19.9 million living in the eastern provinces directly affected by conflict and occupation (North and South Kivu, Maniema, Katanga, Eastern Province). The deaths were mainly due to sickness and malnutrition, with some 350,000 caused by direct acts of war by all parties. Far from passing unnoticed, these data were taken up, and hence legitimised, by the international media, and became for many Congolese a tool in the political fight against the foreign occupiers, whose cruelty they served to demonstrate.

More recently a new epidemiological study conducted between August and October 2001 by the Belgian section of MSF confirmed the serious harm caused to life and living conditions (*Accès aux soins et violences en RDC – Access to health care and acts of violence in the DRC*, December 2001). It showed that in Basankusu in Equateur Province, military operations, pillage, burning and bombardment of houses, devastation of crops, and population displacements killed 10 percent of the population within the space of one year (2000), including a quarter of all children under the age of five. Mortality was mainly linked to malnutrition and the increase in infectious diseases, with only 4 percent directly linked to acts of violence. Nonetheless, the investigation states that in more than four of every five homes, at least one person had been subjected to violent practices characteristic of total war: property destruction, beatings, torture, rape, wounding by weapons, imprisonment, and forced recruitment. Pillage and property destruction were the two most widespread types of violence. In 15 percent of homes, one or more person had been a victim of torture (before 2001), and in 13 percent, at least one person had been sexually abused. Violence this serious was particular to confrontation zones and areas located near the front lines.

The humanitarian response to the tragic situations described by Congolese and international aid organisations was greatly limited by the risks and difficulties of access to conflict areas where civilians faced the greatest danger. In April 2001 six members of the International Committee of the Red Cross (ICRC) were killed by bullets and mutilated with knives while travelling for work purposes in the region of Bunia, in the north-eastern DRC, and in May 2003 two MONUC observers were murdered in the Ituri region where confrontations and massacres have recommenced. Some belligerents, states and armed groups refused to open areas under their control to international NGOs, deliberately maintaining a deterrent atmosphere of insecurity. In addition to security constraints, there are formidable logistical constraints, due in particular to the dilapidation or destruction of transport infrastructure, a factor which necessitates frequent recourse to air transport. As a result, assistance operations, even when confined to a single hospital or health area, involve considerable financial cost.

Most of the reports published by international NGOs present in the DRC end with the following findings: there is an 'immense gap' between what they are doing and the scale of the catastrophe, 'the needs are enormous and resources insufficient'. These findings, while completely correct, are at the same time couched in traditional NGO rhetoric. In their quest for funds and support, NGOs tend to stress the enormity of the tasks to be accomplished and hence the resources that must be raised: the image of an immense gap is aimed primarily at mobilising the most powerful institutional donors. But don't such claims overstate the role of humanitarian organisations? In addition to publicising the Congolese tragedy in the international arena, aid organisations have conducted numerous operations since 1998: support for hospitals and health areas; assistance to displaced persons and Congolese refugees in Zambia and the Central African Republic; food aid; emergency medical relief in battle zones; and responses to epidemics. Yet these operations were unable to accomplish something that only the Congolese and Western states, or inter-state organisations (European Union, United Nations) have the capacity to implement: the restoration of a public administration paying those in its employ, the re-establishment of communication routes, and the rehabilitation of public buildings, facilities and housing which were looted and ravaged by the war. Considering these necessities alone (there are others), it is already clear that the task is a matter for national and foreign political power. Without commitment from such quarters, the humanitarian organisations will always be 'faced with an immense gap'. For all that, their actions have not been merely symbolic, for they supplied much needed assistance – and for a long time were the only ones providing it – often in the areas most exposed to conflict, violence, epidemics and economic distress.

Bibliographical references

Centre d'étude de la Région des Grands Lacs d'Afrique, *L'Afrique des Grands Lacs, annuaire 1999-2000*, Paris, L'Harmattan, 2000.

Centre d'étude de la Région des Grands Lacs d'Afrique, *L'Afrique des Grands Lacs, annuaire 2000-2001*, Paris, L'Harmattan, 2001.

Médecins Sans Frontières, *RD Congo. Silence on meurt*, Paris, L'Harmattan, 2002.

R. Banegas and B. Jewsiewicki (eds.), 'RDC, la guerre vue d'en bas', *Politique Africaine*, no. 84, December 2001.

Jean-Claude Willame, *L'Odyssée Kabila. Trajectoire pour un nouveau Congo?*, Paris, Karthala, 1999.

10

COLOMBIA
Violence versus Politics

Michel Agier

Violence has long been embedded in the Colombian national conscience as a distinctive cultural feature periodically dominating the country's history and collective memory since the mid-nineteenth century. Yet the current war is different from previous cycles of violence. Colombian guerrilla movements – which appeared during the 1960 in a regional context marked by Castro's victory in Cuba and the prevalence of ideologies recognising armed force as a legitimate means to transform political systems – have undergone a profound transformation since the mid-1970s. The explosion in drug trafficking and racketeering has dramatically increased their resources while at the same time dissociating them from social struggles from whence they originated.

Faced with an upsurge of armed violence, the Colombian government enlisted the support of paramilitary groups, who, themselves implicated in narcotics business, proved to be dubious allies. The exacerbation of the conflict was marked by the increasing targeting of civil populations and hence the decomposition

228

of social relations as witnessed by the increase in criminality, the erosion of traditional hierarchies, and the spread of mafia-like norms and practices.

Since the mid-1990s the conflict has annually generated hundreds of targeted attacks and collective massacres, and approximately 25,000 murders and 3,000 kidnappings. Tens or even hundreds of thousands of civilians are also forcibly displaced each year (approximately one million between 1995 and 2000).

These figures are characteristic of a dirty war which today has no other motivation than the control of resources, land and local populations. The conflict unites or opposes – depending on the case – guerrillas, paramilitaries, drug traffickers, death squads, and at least part of the government's forces, to the detriment of civilian populations caught in the crossfire. Under such circumstances, any attempt to 'humanise the war' is an action against the war itself.

The deep-rooted nature, extent and duration of different forms of violence in Colombian social life make it particularly difficult to define the priorities and most appropriate sites for humanitarian action. Viewed from an international perspective, the role of the United States seems paradoxical. On the one hand, as the principal market for Colombia's drug yield, the US facilitates the arming of the warring factions. Yet on the other hand, it supplies the Colombian army with considerable financial, logistical and training support within the contexts of 'Plan Colombia' and the post-September 2001 'anti-terrorist struggle'.

The roots of the violence and the present extent of the war

A brief historical overview is required to understand the complexity of the current context. The creation of the Conservative and Liberal parties in the mid-19th century furnished the framework for the emerging Colombian political system. Their permanent and often violent confrontation dominated national life until the 1970s. From their inception, the two parties incorporated regional factions controlled by *caudillos* and *caciques* – regional overlords who, through their family connections and economic and political influence, were in a position to weaken the emerging central administration and engage in ferocious power struggles. The parties were all the more efficient locally because the state had difficulty establishing its infrastructure and institutions throughout the territory. Having formed societies and militias early on to direct or contest decisive election, the parties were able to block all democratic political expression – particularly electoral – despite the existence of a constitution and institutions of parliamentary democracy in the country for many years.

The dysfunctional nature of this two-party system, the frustrations and hatreds it engendered, and attempts to challenge it sparked periods of violence of varying intensity. The most lethal of these – the 'thousand day war' (1899-1902) – resulted in 100,000 deaths. Half a century later, in 1948, extreme violence flared up again after the murder of the Liberal leader Gaitán, then on the point of introducing social and political reforms that potentially threatened the patronage-based and conservative edifice of bipartisanship. The assassination triggered a long series of score settlings and acts of vengeance throughout the country that involved the Conservative government's political police, the Liberal party's self-defence militias, and gangs of hired killers (*pájaros*) working for both parties. This was the period of *La Violencia* (1948-64), during which 200,000 people (300,000 according to some sources) died and hundreds of thousands more were forcibly displaced.

In the early 1960s the Liberal and Conservative parties arrived at an arrangement that guaranteed the alternation of power. *La Violencia* came to an end and the political system began to function in an apparently normal and democratic manner. This quickly provoked frustration, however, as popular demands, particularly peasants' concerns, were not represented in the political process. As in many other Latin-American countries at that time, popular movements opted for revolutionary armed struggle as the best way to advance their claims, and several extreme-left guerrilla groups began a clandestine war in the 1960s. In 1964 the FARC (Fuerzas Armadas Revolucionarias de Colombia – Armed Revolutionary Forces of Colombia) regrouped peasant self-defence guerrilla bands formed by the Communist and Liberal parties during La Violencia. The ELN (Ejército de Liberación Nacional – National Liberation Army, Guevarist) emerged in 1962, followed by the EPL (Ejército Popular de Liberación – Popular Liberation Army, Maoist) in the late 1960s. Finally, the M19 (Movement of 19 April, a more critical, intellectual and urban group) was created in the early 1970s. The guerrillas benefited from a certain public sympathy throughout the 1960s and 1970s but did not succeed in obtaining broad popular support.

The 1980s marked the start of a new period of extreme violence. The guerrillas gradually consolidated into a vast warlike enterprise based on the exploitation of various resources. They forged economic and military links with the drug networks (the FARC, for example, ensured the protection and transportation of illicit crops and, at least in part, the processing of the coca and poppy harvest). They also engaged in racketeering of rural town administrations, large plantations (the EPL controlled the Urabá banana plantations), and the national oil industry (an important resource for the ELN). Kidnapping developed as an economic activity during this period. By the middle of the decade, paramilitary formations had begun to contribute to the conflict. They were an offshoot of the anti-guerrilla 'peasant self-defence' committees (often supported by the army) and of the clandestine squads, composed partly of serving or retired soldiers and police, who were recruited to carry out killings that the forces of order could not be seen to commit overtly. While the FARC guerrillas were closely linked to the drug economy, a large number of paramilitary groups were the direct issue of the old Medellin and Cali 'cartels'. In 2001, the leader of the Colombian paramilitaries admitted that 70 percent of their income came from narcotics traffic.

The internal war that rages today sees the two main forces, guerrillas and paramilitaries, engaged in interminable confrontations to hold or contest positions in almost every part of the country. The major guerrilla groups (FARC and ELN) had over 20,000 combatants in 2000 and possess sophisticated weapons and equipment. The various paramilitary groups are becoming increasingly autonomous in relation to their original sponsors and went as far as federating in 1997, forming a powerful national organisation, the AUC (Autodefensas Unidas de Colombia – United Self-Defence Forces of Colombia), which claims over 10,000 members. Of the 30,000 combatants belonging to illegal armies at least 12,000 are minors, many of them disaffected teenagers from urban peripheries or rural areas, attracted by the income and status these war-oriented groups provide. Throughout the 1990s the armed organisations became more professional in their military strategies and concentrated on territorial and economic goals. Drug trafficking increased and the state and legitimate army lost much of their credibility in the spheres of law and order and territorial control. By 2000, guerrillas and paramilitaries were active in 822 (75 percent) of the country's 1,050 municipalities. At that time, 40 percent of national territory was thought to be under the control of illegal armed groups (see map p.238).

The internal war had become much more a 'war
against society' (the term employed by sociologist Daniel
Pécaut) than a conflict between adversaries and
defenders of the established system. Indeed, the tempo
of this 'dirty war' has increased dramatically since the
second half of the 1980s: 25,000 murders (30,000
according to some sources, excluding those reported
missing) and hundreds of massacres occur every year.
The massacres are largely the work of paramilitary forces
who use mass killings as a systematic method for
capturing a village and installing a reign of terror, but the
guerrillas themselves are no longer concerned with
sparing the lives of the civilian population, particularly
when they retake an area occupied by paramilitaries.
When the FARC bombarded the village of Bojayá in the
Chaco in 2002, 109 inhabitants who had sought shelter
in a church lost their lives. For several years, the FARC
has been using land mines to mark out its territory, a
practice that results in several hundred amputations
annually. All armed groups carry out targeted
assassinations of political figures (from town councillor
and mayor to minister and presidential candidate) as well
as clergy, union leaders, journalists, judges and academics.

Each year since 1999 3,000 kidnappings accompanied
by ransom demands have occurred (over 25,000
between 1990 and 2001). The guerrillas are primarily
responsible but some are the work of paramilitaries and
criminal gangs. Besides targeted political kidnappings
(the ELN specialises in the abduction of groups), other
forms of kidnapping include the 'lucky dip' in which
vehicles are randomly stopped and anyone who seems
likely to fetch a ransom is abducted. The abduction of
children or supposedly wealthy people by gangs who
then sell their hostages to guerrillas or paramilitaries is

motivated as much by financial as by political considerations. For several years, Pax Christi, a Dutch NGO, has been conducting a major international campaign against the kidnappings. The organisation also attempts to address the issue of complicity, notably on the part of multinational corporations and their insurers, who are prepared to accept this form of blackmail.

Violence versus politics

The national mythologising of violence is largely a product of *La Violencia* and has engendered a fatalistic attitude that is particularly widespread among lower-income groups. Violence is regarded as a plague that may strike at any time, an historical phenomenon beyond individual control. The sixteen consecutive years of *La Violencia* witnessed constant cycles of revenge that entailed countless mass killings. A community spirit reigned among the armed bands: vocabulary, nicknames and ritual declamations pronounced before the massacres helped to maintain solidarity and bestowed a sense of individual as well as political identity on the participants. The ritual character of the massacres was emphasised in various ways: choice of location (the patios of targeted houses), organised torture sessions, death as a form of sacrifice, symbolic and repetitive mutilation with its own specialised lexicon, the search for a style in the arrangement of the corpses, and the 'signature' of notes or objects left at the killing site.

The ritualistic horror of these mass murders still resonates in Colombian collective memory. If a culture of violence exists in Colombia today, it cannot be traced back – as many Colombians believe – to ancestral practices that would explain the existence of a land of violent people. It is rather the result of the gradual formation over the last 150 years of a memory of macabre acts and ritualised massacres that have created the figure of a general enemy by altering the humanity of the body of the current enemy. If there is a culture of violence, it stems from the gradual constitution of a specific vocabulary designating the practices of execution – in effect, from the assembly of a specialised memory of violence which overshadows the causes of major and minor conflicts. This collective memory is now activated in the most bloodthirsty manner by a loose conglomeration of gangs of hired killers in the pay of powerful landowners, drug barons and sometimes political parties, by 'self-defence' groups (i.e. paramilitaries), and by the urban gangs responsible for *limpieza* – 'social cleansing' meaning the elimination to order of beggars, street children, male and female prostitutes and other 'marginals'. The old political alliances and oppositions have lost their relevance: every gesture involved in the relationship between friend and enemy is now mediated through this specialised collective memory.

The widespread belief in the myth of 'atavistic' violence, the specialised memory of violence, and the impunity of participants in this 'dirty war' (government forces, paramilitaries, guerrillas and drug traffickers), authorises ordinary criminal behaviour. Violence, even murder, has thus become the predictable outcome of any type of conflict from petty delinquency to neighbourhood or family disputes. Intra-family violence, such as the physical abuse of women and children, rape, infanticide, incest, traffic in children, and sexual exploitation, has worsened. Every social problem, whether conflict over land or work or student strikes, is rapidly transformed into a new front for violence. The mere possibility of expressing social protest is itself called into question by threats of violence, which are felt by everyone. In recent years the phenomenon has become generalised and elusive in terms of its origins: it has lost the regional and thematic character that formerly distinguished it (political violence in eastern and Andean rural areas) and is now more prominent in the cities (Medellin, Cali, Bogotá), or in certain regions such as the Pacific coast that were previously unaffected (see map p.241).

In the poor quarters of cities, where the police rarely venture unless there is a major outbreak of violence, large numbers of 'popular militias' have been established to protect residents from neighbouring gangs. These militias are often converted into criminal organisations and enforce their own law through intimidation and extortion. The official police, known as *La Ley* (the law), sometimes behave in the same fashion: when a colleague is murdered they don masks to become *encapuchados* (hooded ones), and raid the neighbourhood to exact lethal vengeance on the killers and their families. There are also armed persons, often no older than twelve or thirteen, who circulate between criminal *pandillas* (gangs), local militias, guerrillas and paramilitaries. Permanent channels exist to facilitate the move from one organisation to another and this ensures that the network of violence spreads to almost every part of the country. This diversification and distribution of violence makes it difficult to distinguish between 'political' and other crimes.

As the political dimension of the conflict has been largely obscured, conventional political language is of little use when analysing the clash between guerrillas and paramilitaries. Although guerrilla leaders still officially claim to be guided by an extreme-left social and political ideology that opposes the extreme-right security-centred and authoritarian ideology espoused by the paramilitaries, this is far from the case. The guerrillas have become increasingly distanced from their origins as representatives of a social movement, first of peasants (the FARC of the early 1960s), then of its urban offshoots (the other guerrilla groups that emerged between 1960 and 1970). This detachment has reached breaking point: nobody today believes they are fighting a

Confrontations between paramilitaries and guerillas (1998-2002)

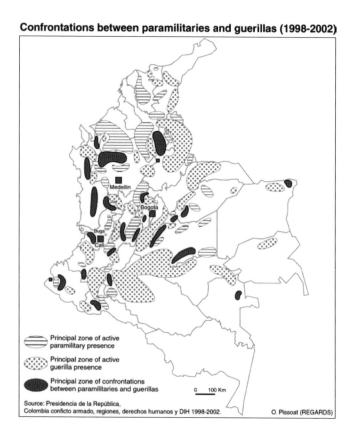

Principal zone of active paramilitary presence

Principal zone of active guerilla presence

Principal zone of confrontations between paramilitaries and guerilas   0   100 Km

Source: Presidencia de la República,
Colombia conficto armado, regiones, derechos humanos y DIH 1998-2002.   O. Pissoat (REGARDS)

'just war' although some still feel that it was so, notably in rural areas where the guerrillas publicly supported social claims and presented an obstacle to paramilitary excesses. The political result of today's war is that politics has been confiscated by the war.

Forced displacements – a fact of war

Current estimates put the number of people displaced by violence since the mid-1980s at more than two million. Quantitative estimates are controversial,

Homicidal violence in Colombia (1982-1998)

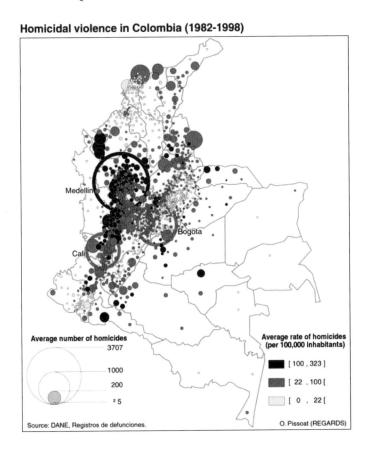

Average number of homicides
- 3707
- 1000
- 200
- ² 5

Average rate of homicides
(per 100,000 inhabitants)
- [100 , 323]
- [22 , 100 [
- [0 , 22 [

Source: DANE, Registros de defunciones.   O. Pissoat (REGARDS)

particularly so as no rigorous or objective study has ever been undertaken. According to government sources, 400,000 people were forcibly displaced between 1995 and 1999. CODHES (Consultoria para los Derechos Humanos y el Desplazamiento – Consultancy on Human Rights and Displacement), an NGO founded in 1992, has been providing regular updates of forced displacements since 1995 and puts the figure at 1,123,000. Government figures indicate that 320,000 were displaced in 2000-1 although CODHES estimates the number to be double.

The spread and diversity of the violence in Colombia is reflected in the mixed profiles of the people forced to flee from it. Among the two million Colombians displaced between 1985 and 2000 (approximately 5 percent of the total population) are peasants who abandoned their homes and land at the approach of guerrillas or paramilitaries; other peasants fearing army reprisals because they had yielded to the threats of drug traffickers and planted coca; and farmers forced to abandon their land after it was contaminated by chemicals sprayed to eradicate illicit crops. Inhabitants of small towns or the margins of cities flee to escape the crossfire of hired killers, and one finds just as many ex-guerrillas as former paramilitaries among the displaced. Youths flee their associates in the *pandillas* (gangs) as do members of 'social cleansing' and other militias. The established populations of reception areas are, rightly or wrongly, often suspicious of the newcomers: in their eyes, displaced people are morally soiled by the events they have fled and are seen as representatives of the dirty war as much as survivors of it.

Almost all areas of the country have now been affected by forced displacements, whether as places of departure or arrival. Tens, even hundreds of thousands of *dezplazados* have flocked to the peripheries of urban centres. The outskirts of Bogotá alone absorbed 350,000 homeless people between the mid-1980s and the late 1990s. Smaller towns close to departure points are just as affected as the capital. Most *dezplazados* end up in a town, occupy slums known as *invasiones*, and try to find support and ways of surviving locally, often by turning to the parallel economy. Women play a major role in the survival of families since it is easier for them to find temporary employment, for example as domestic servants and street sellers. Organised attempts at resettlement are rare. Some examples of community initiatives do exist in rural areas and include the establishment of *haciendas* (agricultural centres for displaced people) and the creation of 'peace communities' on land made available by the government. Many find it difficult to survive over the longer term, however, due to economic hardship and the proximity of conflict. There are no formal camps for displaced people, but certain emergency zones have become permanent, such as public buildings that house the *dezplazados*.

The issue of forced displacements has recently received unprecedented exposure and visibility in Colombia. About forty NGOs currently work in this field. A magazine, *Exodo*, is published by the Grupo de Apoyo a Organizaciones de Dezplazados (Support Group for Displaced Persons Organisations) and in 1997, a law recognised the 'socio-demographic and humanitarian significance' of the problem (Law 387, June 1997). This law states that every displaced person must obtain a *certificación* card entitling them to a minimum of assistance – a sum of money covering the cost of three months' food and rent (renewable once), and the enrolment of any children in a state school. But the meagre resources the government allots to the program drastically limit the number of beneficiaries. Moreover, the government's clampdown on the informal sector primarily penalises displaced people who then face further victimisation (humiliation, persecution, imprisonment and extortion).

The return of the *mano dura* and international confusion

Outraged by the mindless violence of combatants, the tragic social consequences of the dirty war, and years of fruitless peace negotiations, Colombians partly united around Alvaro Uribe, a young candidate from the right, in the 2002 presidential elections. Elected from the first round (marked by a high abstention rate) and having had little to do with traditional party politics, Uribe is an advocate of the *mano dura* (hard hand). Once linked to the so-called self-defence groups, he claims that violence can be curbed by reinforcing the role of the army, and encourages public informing. In September 2002 a month after Uribe's investiture, masked people appeared on television and received money for naming the perpetrators of acts of violence they had witnessed (the accused were always 'insurgents', never criminals or paramilitaries). The new administration plans to organise a network of one million civilians equipped with communications equipment and possibly weapons. Although President Uribe has committed himself to combating paramilitaries, these methods may indirectly recreate what the government claims to be eliminating and further erode the idea of a non-combatant, thereby indirectly sanctioning attacks on civilians.

'Plan Colombia', launched by the preceding Pastrana government, is essentially supported and financed by the United States. It has been just as ineffective in the battle against drug cultivation as it is cruel to peasant populations: aerial fumigation contaminates their land, forcing them to migrate, and they are not entitled to compensation. Between 1999 and 2000 the United States helped to destroy 90,000 hectares of coca, yet the CIA estimates that in 2001, 120,000 hectares were still entirely devoted to coca cultivation compared with 25,000 hectares of cannabis and coca plantations in 1981. Concurrently, the US remains the main market for a clandestine drug economy whose existence and profits depend on prohibition. There are 14 million drug users in the United States and cocaine use has risen considerably since the late 1990s. Plan Colombia has become redundant. As a result of Uribe's decision to join America's 'anti-terrorist' struggle after 11 September, US military aid is now directly targeting organisations declared to be terrorist (guerrillas and paramilitaries). But the old links between Uribe and the paramilitaries are likely to lead to an unequally applied anti-terrorist strategy, and the 'war on evil' rhetoric might make violence against non-combatants more acceptable if the recipients are located on the 'wrong side' of the front line.

The vigilance of international human rights organisations is an important tool in the search for a real exit from a war in which civilians are the victims 90 percent of the time. Given the turn the dirty war has taken − confrontations involving civilian massacres, the abduction and murder of non-combatants − the war constitutes a permanent violation of international humanitarian law, and any initiative to 'humanise' the conflict is a direct action against the war itself. Humanitarian organisations can only play a marginal role. The intense polarisation of the struggle around the friend/foe duality that is ceaselessly recreated through extreme violence renders particularly delicate the recognition of humanitarian neutrality. In practice, insecurity confines most aid organisations to the towns: the rural zones are left to the rare aid operators who, through regular contact with the various forces on the ground, are able (at least in appearance) to convince the warring sides of their neutrality and the necessity for delivering aid to civilians. But even then, it is doubtful whether the actions of aid organisations have any significant impact given the destabilisation of social relations by the dynamics of violence. Humanitarian actors can nonetheless play a part in revealing the human cost of the confrontation, and contribute to forcing it into the arena of public debate.

As for the problem of drug cultivation, it will not be resolved by the repressive and socially destructive fumigation system. The policy of manual crop substitution could be more effective if accompanied by agricultural reform. The multinational drug trafficking networks must be tackled, which requires international acknowledgement the *co-responsibility* of producer and consumer countries (the US, Europe). Within such a framework, the legalisation of drugs – a weapon against clandestine networks – would considerably reduce the financial resources available to armed groups. Social reconstruction is just as important as support for peace negotiations and the fight against drug trafficking, and is the aim of localised projects that promote the growing of alternative crops. The 'Peace Laboratory' in the Middle Magdalena region (an ELN controlled zone where the AUC is active) is the largest peace project to participate in a scheme that combines agricultural and social goals. In 2002 the European Union agreed to support this initiative with 35 million euros spread over three years.

There is some optimism on the Colombian political scene concerning initiatives to form a 'civil society' movement that occurred during the upsurge in violence. This movement seeks to rekindle the flame of radical protest and social and political struggle but rejects all forms of violence, and opposes all illegal armed groups in the name of human rights. Even so, whatever turn the war may take in political and military terms, Colombian society has been profoundly and irrevocably altered by this latest cycle of violence which, by its atrocities, has added another chapter to earlier, unresolved episodes. The memory of the unsung dead of *La Violencia* has been overlaid by the social cost of the current dirty war – violence has permeated every aspect of society and huge numbers of people have been forced to flee the conflict zones and struggle for survival in small and large towns.

Bibliographical references

M. Agier, 'Perte de lieu, dénuement et urbanisation, les desplazados de Colombie', *Autrepart,* no. 14 (2000), pp. 91-105.

A. M. Losonczy, 'Violence sociale et ritualisation de la mort at du deuil en Colombie', *Autrepart,* no. 25 (2003).

D. Meertens, 'Populations deplacées en Colombie et Insertion urbaine', *Annales de la Recherche Urbaine*, no.91 (2001), pp.118-27.

J.P. Minaudier, *Histoire de la Colombie de la conquête à nos jours*, Paris, L'Harmattan, 1997.

D. Pécaut, *L'Ordre et la violence. Evolution socio-politique de la Colombie entre 1930 et 1953,* Paris, Editions de L'EHESS, 1987.

D. Pécaut, 'Guerre, processus de paix, polarisation, politique', *Problèmes d'Amerique Latine,* no. 44 (2002) pp. 7-30.

G. Sanchez, 'La Guerre contre les Droits de l'Homme', *Problèmes d'Amerique Latine,* no. 44 (2002) pp. 63-79.

11

ALGERIA
The Utility of Terrorism

Chawki Amari

Since the start of hostilities between radical Islamic groups and government forces, the Algerian civil war has cost the lives of more than 100,000 people and devastated whole sections of society. Although the current regime is no longer threatened by terrorist violence, the conflict is far from over: more than 1,500 civilians were murdered in 2002. For many observers Algeria's slide into war was the consequence of an ineptly managed transition to democracy. According to this view, the Algerian government, confronted with an Islamist victory in the 1991 legislative elections, had no choice but to take exceptional measures to guarantee the survival of the Republican state. This reading of the conflict allowed the international community to justify its unfailing support for the total war the Algerian generals unleashed on their opponents. The first 'war on terrorism' could then unfold behind closed doors without arousing any international reaction apart from some sanctimonious indignation at the brutality of the massacres imputed to Islamists. Few questioned the Algerian government's responsibility for the origins of the terrorism and the crimes inflicted

on the civilian population. Yet this was far from negligible. By
refusing to acknowledge this aspect of the conflict, Western states
and international organisations effectively sanctioned the sacrifice of
thousands of Algerians, hostages to the confrontation between the
regime and the terrorist violence it nurtured.

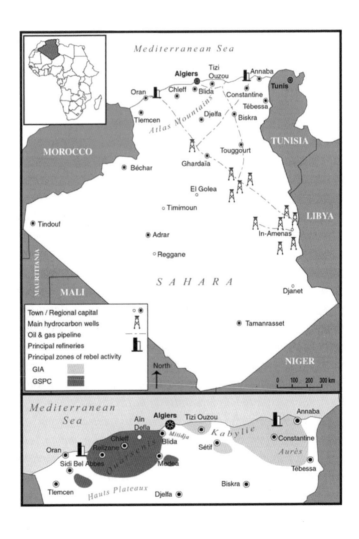

The genealogy of Islamic violence

As soon as Algeria gained independence in 1962, the leaders of the National Liberation Front (FLN – Front de Libération Nationale), embarked on an authoritarian project of social transformation. For the army and its state, the imperative was to construct a modern 'socialist, Arab, and Muslim' Algeria. The revolution was driven by a policing conception of political action, and ignored the country's cultural, linguistic and religious plurality as well as its diverse historical legacy (notably Berber and colonial). From 1965, security services began to infiltrate every level of Algerian society and impede any possibility of autonomous political expression. Nevertheless, social harmony was preserved for a time through the significant expansion of the country's social services and the launch of a public-sector job creation program that was financed by oil and gas revenues.

The fleeting emergence of the first Islamist guerrillas in the early 1980s signalled the system's decline into crisis. Falling oil prices, over-investment in vast industrial schemes, and heavy dependence on imports pushed the country to the brink of defaulting on its debt repayments. The authorities introduced timid liberalisation measures but these did little to curb the crisis or limit the job loss caused by the progressive dismantling of public projects. However, the reforms did trigger the rapid enrichment of an oligarchy that had arisen through military patronage. With the death of President Houari Boumedienne, army corruption and its division into rival clans became obvious. People close to the regime flaunted their wealth, provoking deep resentment in the population towards the *nouveaux riches*.

As resources dwindled, the FLN-State attempted to stem the growing tide of protest by courting advocates of Islamic fundamentalism. Restrictions on political dialogue in the 1980s made religion the privileged sphere in which to express and give shape to social conflicts. Political Islam disseminated by Arab volunteers – brought in to further the policy of Arabising national education – and by 'jihadists' who had fought in Afghanistan began to target the ills of Algerian society. They denounced the idea of 'progress', described as the monopolising of power and the economy by government elites, and offered an alternative project for an 'ideal society' whose reference to the Qur'an was much more effective than the FLN's modernist slogans. Concerned by the growing influence of political Islam, the authorities clumsily sought to pre-empt it by adopting some of its demands: they banned alcohol and revised the status of women, reducing them to 'minors' under male tutelage.

Popular protest turned to tragedy in 1988, when riots in Algiers left hundreds dead. The government pretended to yield to pressure from the street and initiated a transition to a multi-party system that was adopted by referendum in 1989. But the security services strengthened their presence within the many parties, organisations and newspapers that emerged, and waged intense campaigns of manipulation and propaganda. In 1989, the government took the crucial step of legalising the Islamic Salvation Front (FIS – Front Islamique du Salut), the major religious party, in the hope of countering the heavily divided secular movements who favoured the democratisation of political life.

The FIS took advantage of its new legitimacy and consolidated its strategy for the conquest of power. It infiltrated the main administrative bodies and engaged in charitable works. Exploiting the deficiencies created by the withdrawal of the welfare state, it delivered material aid to populations suffering the effects of the economic crisis and the collapse of social services (it delivered significant aid to the victims of the Tipaza earthquake in October 1989). The party gained in confidence and moved between 1989 and 1991 towards a rigorous and menacing Puritanism without arousing any particular reaction from the authorities.

The consequences are well known – the FIS triumphed in the 1990 municipal elections and the first round of the 1991 legislative elections. Five days before the second round, a military coup terminated the electoral process and forced President Chadli Bendjedid to resign. Thus the generals dragged the country into civil war: veterans of Afghanistan and radical Islamic sects seized their opportunity and exhorted the FIS and similar groups to take up arms. As Islamists adopted the path of armed resistance, the security services raided mosques and herded thousands of suspects into internment camps in the middle of the Sahara. Thousands of young men possessed by a profound and long-held sense of injustice joined the underground movement, where they forged strong bonds and created nation-wide networks. A ruthless war was underway and the civilian population was destined to bear the brunt of it.

The first 'war on terrorism'

Supported from the outset by segments of the population, the armed Islamist militants established themselves in Algiers and its environs. The regime excluded all political means to deal with the crisis and opted for total war. In 1993, it set up an anti-terrorist corps and undertook the re-conquest of the 'liberated areas'. The notion of 'terrorist' was extended to any youth suspected of sympathising with the guerrillas. Suspects were put on file and arrested. Roundups at the doors of mosques became the rule; brutal interrogations and disappearances multiplied.

The years 1993 and 1994 constituted a turning point as the radicalisation of Islamist violence led to the collapse of public support. The methods of brutal but selective intimidation employed at the beginning of the conflict (executions of secular intellectuals and relatives of the security forces, for example) had given way to wholesale violence – marketplaces, cafés, trains and other public places were bombed; vehicles were stopped at false roadblocks and their passengers murdered; men, women and children were killed en masse – shot, decapitated, mutilated, burned or torn apart by bombs. Terrorists exhorted helpless civilians to choose sides or face 'punishment' for their lack of commitment to the struggle against the state.

These forms of terrorism were particularly prevalent in areas to the south of Algiers (Mitidja, Médéa) and to the west of the city (Chleff, Aïn Delfa, Relizane) and led to large population displacements. They reached unprecedented levels in 1997, just as the army and the AIS (Armée Islamique du Salut, the armed wing of the FIS) were negotiating a truce. Six to eight hundred people, most of them women and children, were massacred in the villages of the Mitidja and the Ouarsenis within the space of a few weeks. The ease with which the terrorists were able to commit their crimes right outside army barracks – and as peace negotiations were underway – aroused suspicions. Who really ordered these massacres? Were they independent operations by the Armed Islamic Group (GIA – Groupes Islamistes Armés), an Islamist splinter movement opposed to the FIS and known for its extreme brutality or, as certain defectors from the security services later claimed, had they been fomented by government agents? Uncertainty became a fixture of Algerian life, clouding analysis and understanding of the conflict.

Regardless of who was responsible, the fact remained that the state could not protect civilian populations. Villagers in the interior lived in the double fear of unintelligible terrorist atrocities and army counter-offensives involving aerial bombardments of hills where terrorists might be hiding and vast, violent sweeps of the countryside. But with the exception of these strong-arm measures, the army devoted most of its efforts to protecting towns and major roads and defending oil industry infrastructure.

Terrorist pressure diminished in the late 1990s chiefly because a huge number of civilians had been armed. Bolstered by the rescheduling of its debt in 1994, the regime constructed a veritable civil war apparatus and armed more than 200,000 volunteers recruited from the villages. Organised into 'communal guards' or 'legitimate defence groups' under army control, these 'militiamen' (or 'patriots', according to the point of view) assured the security of isolated hamlets and played a prominent role in stifling the war economy of the Islamists, suffering heavy losses in the process.

The arming of civilians, however, had serious consequences. From settling scores to constructing false roadblocks, the 'patriots' added to the ravages of war. Several militiamen were relieved of their duties or arrested for racketeering, theft, rape, murder or mass killings. In effect, the militarisation of Algerian society contributed to its further destabilisation by introducing violence into ordinary social relations and creating new divisions in social hierarchies. Moreover, it rendered impossible the maintenance of neutrality as civilians were forced to choose sides and therefore expose themselves to reprisals from their adversary. This was the price paid for pushing the Islamists back into the uninhabited zones. By 2001-2 regions where no one, not even the army, had dared to venture were secured. Peasants gradually returned to the fields they had abandoned because of violent battles or terrorist aggression and the price of fruit and vegetables, which had peaked in 1994-96, began to fall.

The Islamist network, fragmented by combined pressure from the security forces, civilian militias and the army, gradually disintegrated. The 1997 truce between the AIS and the army prepared the ground for a wider reconciliation, confirmed by Abdelaziz Bouteflika when he became president in 1999. Since then, 10,000 Islamists have laid down their arms and benefited from a presidential amnesty provided for by the 'law on civil agreement' approved by referendum in September 1999. But up to 3,000 combatants belonging to autonomous units of the GIA (active to the south of Algiers) and the Salafist Group for Preaching and Combat, a rival organisation active to the east of the capital, are still at large.

Relatively disorganised and isolated, these small units do not threaten the survival of the regime. But they continue to sow terror. Although the number of victims has fallen (1,500 deaths in 2002), not a day goes by without the murder of a civilian, a policeman, a soldier or a 'terrorist', usually in the countryside or a suburban area.

The cost of the confrontation

According to international human rights organisations, the conflict has cost the lives of more than 100,000 people since 1992. Five percent of the population (1.2 million people) have been displaced by the violence and 7,000 are officially listed as 'missing' – a figure disputed by some sources who claim it may be as high as ten or twenty thousand. To this provisional assessment must be added the lasting consequences of the militarisation of society and the imposition of a liberalised economy on the ruins of Algerian socialism.

By devoting vast human and financial resources to the 'war on terrorism', the state deliberately chose to ignore the challenges posed by economic and social degradation. Reforms initiated in partnership with international monetary institutions in order to 'modernise' a crisis-ridden centralised economy have methodically eluded the question of their social consequences. According to official statistics, 1,500 businesses have collapsed and 510,000 workers have lost their jobs since 1994. The unemployment rate was approaching 30 percent in 2000. Household income fell by 36 percent between 1987 and 1995 while the proportion of families living in absolute poverty (less than one dollar per person per day) has doubled and now stands at a quarter of the population. Those at the bottom of the social ladder have no alternative but to turn to the black market and corruption in order to assure their daily survival and this affects society as a whole. As a local commentator puts it, 'If you are not corrupt, you must be rich.'

The upturn in macro-economic indicators at the close
of the 1990s was achieved at the price of heavy cuts in
social service budgets. Combined with the spread of
corruption, the budgetary reductions had a profound
effect on the health system and have eroded one of
socialist Algeria's main assets – access to free and
relatively modern health care (see Box).

The collapse of the Algerian public health system

Access to free and relatively modern health care, once one
of the principal assets of socialist Algeria, is suffering from
cuts in social service budgets, administrative
incompetence, and the spread of corruption.

The closure of many community screening centres
opened in the 1970s has led to the reappearance of
endemic illnesses – tuberculosis, for example – that had
once been eradicated. The rural exodus and consequent
changes in eating habits led to fresh outbreaks of diabetes,
a disease that is now assuming epidemic proportions.
Hospitals and health centres are being abandoned,
equipment is breaking down, and 90 percent of the budget
is spent on staff wages.

Medicines have become a luxury. Their prices shot up
with the liberalisation of the pharmaceutical market and
social security offices can no longer afford to refund
prescription charges. A two-week course of antibiotics
now costs a third of the minimum monthly salary.
Pharmaceutical imports (a market worth 500 million
dollars a year) are monopolised by the state and private
businesses close the centre of power. Many generals have
invested in this sector, using front men (often their own
children). They benefit from large credit facilities,
transport and customs clearance and can rely on the
complicity of the health minister to approve the import of
new drugs even if it entails excluding equivalent treatments
from the list of refundable medicines. As a result, many
Algerians are turning to traditional medicine, which is

more accessible than the rundown, overworked, and relatively expensive health care system. The new law on health care, postponed after strong opposition in 2002, should come into force soon and confirm the dismantling of the public health service.

Algeria – condemned to violence?

In this context of socio-economic breakdown and residual armed violence, riots erupted in the Kabylie region in 2001 and unrest soon spread to most of the country, including areas thought to be stable. These protests were usually led by groups of young men pursuing social, economic and political grievances (such as police brutality, the incompetence of local administrators, contempt for regional identities and customs), and signalled that Algerian society was retaking some initiative. Until then, the fear of terrorist and anti-terrorist violence had forced entire sections of society to adopt a 'wait-and-see' attitude. The relative calming of the armed conflict allowed the social fractures previously overshadowed by the regime's authoritarianism and the 'war on terrorism' to come to light. Public protest, however, also gave the government fresh room for manoeuvre and it mounted campaigns of manipulation and propaganda that allowed it to play off one segment of society against another and consolidate its position as referee. The riots have so far caused more than 100 deaths and provoked thousands of arrests.

Is Algeria condemned to a violent political and social life? The brutality of the civil war and the social conflict, unique in the Maghreb region, may give that impression. Algeria has 30 million inhabitants, 20 million of whom are under 30 and constitute 80 percent of the

unemployed. The annual arrival of 100,000 young
people on the job market is certainly a destabilising
factor and may account for the considerable increase in
petty and serious crime. The despair and rancour of a
particular age group cannot, however, explain the
brutality of Algerian social and political life.

One explanation can be found in the authoritarianism
of a discredited political system. Algeria has a relatively
free press but the major news media, television and
radio, are state monopolies. It is difficult to point to a
political party or organisation that is not connected to
the networks of government patronage. Just one
officially recognised trade union exists to represent
workers' claims. In such circumstances, violent protest
may seem the only way of expressing a demand for
change or for participation in the political process. The
country's violent past tends to reinforce this view.

Wholesale violence, from the devastation wreaked by
colonial conquest and occupation to the ordeal of the
war for independence, is embedded in Algerian political
history. The war of independence, which cost the lives
of 300,000-400,000 people (proportionally equal to the
losses sustained by France in the First World War) and
displaced millions more between 1954 and 1958, is still
fresh in the collective memory. Moreover, 12,000 people
lost their lives during the internecine strife that followed
liberation, and at least 50,000 French army auxiliaries
(the *Harkis*) were slaughtered between the summer and
autumn of 1962. Islamist militants were quick to base
their strategies on the model provided by the National
Liberation Army and used the same arms caches and
guerrilla tactics. Similar kinds of attack were mounted in
an attempt to enlist public support for a struggle defined
as an effort to restore popular sovereignty that had been

confiscated by a pro-Western and atheistic junta. The terrorist groups even included some children of *Harkis*, bent on avenging their marginalisation or the elimination of their parents after liberation. In fact, a final explanation for the violence in political and social relations may be found in the suppression of any debate on the substance of the Algerian political community. In its determination to construct an 'Arab, Muslim and Socialist' Algeria, the FLN-state ensured that the contradictions inherent in the nation building process were stifled by a forced consensus that took no account of the Berber and colonial legacies. Perhaps the violence expresses the frustrations engendered by a political project that failed to build a community reflecting the country's true social plurality.

The fears of Western countries

The Algerian state, through its authoritarianism, its system of patronage and its corruption, is an active participant in the diffusion of violence. It bears responsibility not only for the genesis of armed Islamism but also for the violence committed by the various security services acting clandestinely or in the government's name. By electing to combat militant Islamism on a strictly military level, it failed to address the potential for violence present in the country and plunged it into a fratricidal war the repercussions of which are still felt.

Nevertheless, the Algerian regime has never lacked international support and has rarely attracted open criticism. United Nations Human Rights Commission reports regularly highlight the management styles of Algerian decision makers and their repeated failure to observe human rights but criticism is never followed by sanctions. In fact, the opposite is true: in 1994, the country obtained the support of the IMF, World Bank, European Community, and the G7 states to reschedule its debt. The financial package, valued at $ 6,000 million, enabled the regime to reconstitute a sizeable cash reserve and then invest most of it in the 'war against terror'. Intense media coverage of the Mitidja massacres in the summer of 1997 did result in a semblance of pressure from the UN and the EU but that was soon abandoned after a flying visit by a UN fact-finding commission and a delegation from the European Parliament. Their conclusions were very reserved in comparison with the damning reports published every year by human rights organisations.

The surprising degree of tolerance the international community extends to the Algerian authorities is largely the product of the conflict's distorted representation in the West. Panic-stricken by the prospect of 'Islamic terrorism' and the possibility of its exportation (particularly to France), European countries also fear the 'migratory peril' associated with the risk of regime collapse. The generals are thus allowed to manage the crisis as they see fit – as long as they guarantee to keep it within their borders. France, the former colonial power, has played a key role in this alignment, assisted by certain intellectuals who regard the Algerian generals as 'defenders of the Republic' against 'Islamic barbarity'.

Commercial interests are also a factor in the tolerant attitude of western countries. France is Algeria's main export market and its biggest source of imports. Some southern European countries (Spain, Italy, Portugal), having rejected the option of nuclear energy, are heavily dependent on oil and gas supplies. In fact, the conflict has never threatened hydrocarbon exports and European countries congratulate themselves on doing business with a partner so 'reliable' that it succeeded in doubling exports in the middle of a civil war. It is obvious that the regime can only benefit from greater international support as the 'war on terrorism' extends to every part of the globe. The United States, previously at loggerheads with Algeria over Western Sahara, the Palestinian question and other issues, seems to have revised its attitude. The fight against the 'Islamist International' and attention to Algerian oil reserves, certainly of secondary importance but nevertheless of interest to Texan companies linked to George W. Bush, have brought the two governments closer together.

Humanitarian inaction

International attention did not afford the suffering Algerian people the slightest humanitarian consolation. The regime instinctively tried to block the entry of humanitarian NGOs to the country from 1992 onwards, suspecting them of seeking to destabilise central power by questioning its conduct in the struggle against terrorism. Algeria has always been suspicious of attempts by NGOs to gain access to countries at war, believing that, in most cases, they constitute a bridgehead for a less disinterested form of intervention. Western advocacy of a 'right to humanitarian intervention' has encouraged Algerian leaders to fall back on a rigid conception of national sovereignty. Furthermore, Algiers has always preferred to help others and regularly sends aid to countries struck by disaster.

The Bab-el-Oued floods of November 2001

On 8 November 2001 torrential rains fell on Algiers and surrounding areas. Two days later, the water that had accumulated in the Bouzaréah hills overlooking Algiers Bay poured into the town. Bab-el-Oued, a community at the foot of the old Casbah, was inundated. Torrents of mud bristling with cars, buses, rubble and tree trunks swept away everything in their path. The damage was considerable: 1,000 dead, as many injured, and many more left homeless. Relatives of the missing stood on the seafront, waiting for the tide to return the bodies that had been washed out to sea.

Given the disrespect for building regulations, the dilapidation of public infrastructure, and the deforestation of the hills, the tragedy had been entirely predictable. The government received warnings from the meteorological services but took no preventive measures. It preferred to blame the disaster on the former colonial administration that built the road leading to Bab-el-Oued – literally 'the door to the river'. The state was incapable of coordinating aid efforts. A large part of the donations generated by a surge of national and international solidarity was misappropriated. The government compounded its incompetence by placing many obstacles in the way of foreign-led aid operations.

On 14 November a Médecins Sans Frontières cargo plane flew to Algiers. It carried 13 tonnes of emergency aid including plastic sheeting, blankets and medical kits. Volunteers and cargo remained blocked for several days as customs insisted on procedural formalities. The team finally retrieved part of the cargo and entered the damaged areas of Algiers and the Wilaya of Chlef, 100 km. west of the capital, which had also suffered flood damage. Amongst other things, MSF installed emergency potable water systems to limit the risk of epidemics.

More than a year after the tragedy, inhabitants of Bab-el-Oued still sleep in tents amidst rubble and unstable buildings, still exposed to the risk of flooding at any time.

At the national level, all emergency aid operations are confided to the Algerian Red Crescent (ARC). This imposing state-controlled body is not only responsible for raising and distributing funds but also for medical, sanitary and food operations. Having long refused support other than that furnished by the Red Cross movement (ICRC and IFRC), it is now cautiously establishing relations with other partners. The ARC is also the unavoidable interlocutor for any humanitarian organisation that wants to operate in the country. There is no doubt that the Algerian Red Crescent provides valuable support for populations ravaged by war but, given the scale of the crisis, its cumbersome bureaucracy, patronage and political priority – to act as a showcase for the redistributive capacities of the state – reduce its work to a series of stopgap measures.

The national voluntary sector, a network of over 4,500 organisations that work with war victims, families of the missing, the handicapped, local area movements, and women's groups also plays an important part in assisting those who have suffered from the conflict and economic crisis. It is hampered, however, by a serious shortage of funds and remains vulnerable to infiltration by the authorities and political parties.

Algeria seems to be adopting a more cooperative attitude to international humanitarian aid now that Islamist violence has decreased. Some NGOs like Terre des Hommes, Handicap International and Caritas have begun operating under close surveillance. The regime is now prepared to accept limited foreign assistance when disaster strikes (the Bab-el-Oued floods in Algiers, the Aïn Témouchent and Tipaza earthquakes in the west). Given their limited capacities to assist disaster victims, the authorities would have found it difficult to refuse outside assistance without risking popular protest.

Although the Algerian government has relaxed its grip in recent years, it remains extremely circumspect in its relations with international organisations. Partly responsible for the Algerian tragedy, it knows that more openness to foreign observers could act against its interests. Hence the space now offered to humanitarian NGOs is in practice non-existent. Unable to move freely, aid organisations are restricted to supplying unaccountable distribution networks and have no control over the final destination of their aid. Corruption and misappropriation have become so systematic and widespread over the last ten years that the impact of any action designed to assist populations is extremely limited.

So what role might humanitarian organisations play in the Algerian tragedy? They have no place at massacre sites, unless it is to bring assistance to survivors or to those who escaped. Optimists point out the dissuasive effects of an international presence in the conflict, hoping that the proximity of witnesses might stay the executioner's hand. Treating the poorest, who have been sacrificed to the privatisation of public health services, also constitutes a form of intervention. Sensitive humanitarian action in Algeria is possible as long as it is accepted by those for whom it is intended. The Algerian population broadly shares its government's suspicion of humanitarian action. Although fascinated by Western models of development, most Algerians are convinced that the crisis can only be overcome by 'internal' means. Having fought a war of independence, Algeria exhibits a strong desire to free itself of all international supervision, and campaigns for a rebalancing of relations with Europe. Furthermore, the social consequences of IMF and World Bank pressure coupled with international socialism's condemnation of the Algerian government have simply convinced more sceptical Algerians that the world is aligned against them. Nationalism is therefore an attractive option for a significant part of the population. The Algerian siege mentality is also exacerbated by Western policies toward 'brother countries' like Iraq and Iran, and the West's approach to the Palestinian question which is judged as biased and unacceptable. Algerian society is thus impregnated with a culture of emancipation. Its defiant attitude towards the 'international community' is illustrated by the reluctance of Algerian citizens to take up EU offers of business development aid (unlike their Moroccans and Tunisian counterparts who willingly accept this institutional manna). The belief that international pressure in the form of an enquiry or sanctions might persuade Algerian leaders to behave more humanely – or that foreign humanitarian aid could significantly reduce the suffering of the population – is politically sensitive because it clashes with the independent tradition to which Algeria adheres. If humanitarian action is ill conceived or prevented from forming partnerships with Algerian organisations, it risks provoking a backlash that can only reinforce the nationalist sentiments that help to keep the oligarchy in power.

Bibliographical references

O. Lamloun, 'L'enjeu de l'islamisme au cœur du processus de Barcelone', *Critique Internationale*, no. 18 (2003), pp. 129-42.

J. Leca, 'Paradoxes de la démocratisation. L'Algérie au chevet de la science politique', *Pouvoirs*, no. 86 (1998), pp. 7-28.

L. Martinez, 'Algérie: les massacres de civils dans la guerre', *Revue Internationale de Politique Comparée*, vol. 8, no. 1 (2001), pp. 43-58.

L. Martinez, *La guerre civile en Algérie: 1990-1998*, Paris, Karthala, 1998.

POINTS OF VIEW

12

Iraq: in Search of a 'Humanitarian Crisis'

Rony Brauman & Pierre Salignon

The military intervention in Iraq was still in the planning phase when the first humanitarian shots were fired. Aid organisations were offered US government funds to join the 'coalition' and play their humanitarian role under the protection and coordination of 'Operation Iraqi Freedom'. In bringing humanitarian organisations on board, the White House wanted to demonstrate its attachment to moral values and its concern for the civilian population, just as Colin Powell had done when he addressed American NGOs in October 2001 during 'Operation Enduring Freedom' in Afghanistan: 'As I speak, just as surely as our diplomats and military, American NGOs are out there serving and sacrificing on the front lines of freedom… I am serious about making sure we have the best relationship with the NGOs who are such a force multiplier for us, such an important part of our combat team… [We are] all committed to the same, singular purpose to help humankind, to help every man and woman in the world who is in need, who is hungry, who is without hope, to help every one of them fill a belly, get a roof over their heads, educate their children, have hope, give them the ability to dream about a future that will be brighter, just as we have tried to make the future brighter for all Americans.'[1] The message was perfectly clear: we share the same values and objectives so let us combine our forces. This appeal to join the 'civilised' side was naturally followed by the creation of an 'Office of Reconstruction and Humanitarian Assistance' (ORHA), controlled directly by the Pentagon, to which NGOs only had to present themselves in order to serve the liberated Iraqi people.

Rather than cautioning against the appropriation of humanitarian action by a belligerent party to the conflict, several European humanitarian organisations responded by expressing their opposition to the war. In France, the Red Cross called for 'the unrelenting pursuit of efforts aimed at reaching a peaceful solution that would avoid subjecting populations to new and cruel hardships,' while a consortium of NGOs[2] questioned the necessity of going to war 'given the possibilities for the peaceful disarmament of Iraq.' In Great Britain, Oxfam stated its 'opposition to a military strike on Iraq because of the massive *humanitarian crisis* that it might create,'[3] and, while nonetheless preparing for post-war reconstruction,

---

[1] Colin L. Powell, *Remarks to the National Foreign Policy Conference for Leaders of Non-Governmental Organisations*, State Department, Washington DC, 26 October 2001.
[2] Action Contre la Faim, Médecins du Monde, Handicap International, Première Urgence, Solidarité and Enfants du Monde.
[3] Authors' emphasis.

announced that it would refuse all funds offered by belligerent countries. Nobody thought to ask these NGOs on what information or strategic analysis they based their assertions, nor what instrument Oxfam and others used to measure the intensity of a 'humanitarian crisis' caused by bombing in comparison to the crisis produced by Saddam Hussein's dictatorship. In the United States, by contrast, most NGOs accepted government funding, refrained from judgement on the forthcoming war, and held themselves ready to intervene in Iraq when the time came.

In both Europe and the US, these positions had the double distinction of being in phase with public opinion in their respective countries and in contradiction with certain principles generally accepted by the humanitarian movement. NGOs (particularly American) that chose to be financed by their governments for the Iraq intervention accepted to reduce their role to that of sub-contractor to a belligerent party, a debatable choice to say the least. There is a long-standing tendency of NGOs to act as mere service providers of governments and international institutions: a tradition so solidly established in some NGOs through their jargon, discussion forums, and exchanges of personnel, that it is difficult to see differences between public and private institutions other than administrative ones. This tendency has been exacerbated in Iraq by the US government's increased use of private profit-making companies to undertake functions that were formerly the exclusive preserve of NGOs. Many NGOs fear that they will lose out to private companies, which are already claiming larger amounts of the 'NGO market', and hence prefer to play the role requested of them to preserve their 'market share'.

Neither pro-war nor anti-war

To give NGOs their due, it is true that in Europe they were under great pressure to pronounce an opinion on the war at a time when feelings were running high. Some NGOs faced internal pressure from members who expected their organisation to express their own opinions, defend international law, and clearly distance themselves from the US-British position. External pressure came from the media: not a day went by without invitations for aid officials to offer their 'expert' opinions on the probable 'humanitarian consequences' of the war, to describe preparations and operational scenarios, and often to speak on the conflict's background. It is equally true that the singularity of the situation led it to be treated in a different manner than previous crises. Hour by hour media coverage of the diplomatic 'thriller', set against a background of massive street demonstrations all over the world, turned it into a spectacle in which everyone became an actor well before the first bombs exploded. In this climate of extreme polarisation, there was all the more temptation for humanitarians to align themselves with their respective societies since morality, international law, and human rights were at the heart of both the pro-war and anti-war camps. Médecins Sans Frontières did not escape this debate: supporters of a public anti-war position had been reinforced in their conviction by the organisation's receipt of the Nobel Peace Prize in 1999. Nevertheless, those who considered this position to be illegitimate and incoherent were ultimately in the majority.

For humanitarian actors, such considerations are, or should be, immaterial. Unless humanitarians oppose all wars, or, on the contrary, defend the principle of war in defence of human rights, they had no valid reason as humanitarian organisations to take a stand for or against this particular war. No more so, in any case, than for or against other armed conflicts. The first Gulf War, triggered by Iraq's invasion of Iran in 1980, aroused no declarations of this kind, nor did the numerous wars that bloodied the world in the 20 years that followed. The denunciation of war crimes in Chechnya or the 'humanitarian alibi' in Bosnia did not imply judgement on the justness or lack thereof of these wars, but on the responsibilities of combatants and states. We should remember that modern humanitarian action developed out of armed conflicts in the nineteenth century by asking, 'who needs help because of this war?' instead of 'who is right in this war?' These origins are not recalled as a dogma to condemn some heresy, but to stress the continued importance of this position if aid is to be effective.

Warning! Impending disaster

The UN agencies were deeply affected by the climate of disapproval of the war. Expressing concern in February at the lack of mobilisation of donor countries that hindered contingency planning (for 600,000 refugees), Ruud Lubbers, the High Commissioner for Refugees, was one of the few UN officials to speak out before the war. With the UN pushed aside, others were reticent to comment for fear of appearing to condone the war or of being perceived as Washington's 'colonial office'. Stephen Johnson, deputy director of the UN Office for the Coordination of Humanitarian Affairs (OCHA), raised justifiable concerns at the UN's participation in a 'clean-up operation' following acts committed by the world's 'most powerful states': 'under certain circumstances, we would have to ask how happy we were with that role. Do we want to play that role, and is that what we were set up for?' Anxiety of a different kind was expressed by Yussuf Hassan, UNHCR spokesman in New York, who was disturbed to see funds for 'vital operations' in Angola, Afghanistan and Ivory Coast diverted for preparations in and around Iraq.

But these legitimate concerns that preceded the war were interspersed with catastrophic scenarios that both reflected the difficulty experienced by UN agencies in openly expressing disapproval of the war and fundraising imperatives. The predictions of their spokespersons transformed a political problem into a simple question of funding for a relief operation. Once the war began, the UN led the field in an unprecedented bidding contest to see who could come up with the most catastrophic predictions of its impact. The interruption of food aid distributions under the 'oil for food' program, combined with destruction from the bombing, prompted UNICEF to claim that nearly 100,000 children under five were in danger of losing their lives. The World Health Organisation forecast increases in cases of cholera and other diarrhoeal diseases and estimated that 400,000 civilians were at risk. World Food Programme spokesman Trevor Rowe broke all records by saying: 'What we're looking at is having to feed, eventually, 27 million people. That is the whole population of Iraq. So, what we are envisioning is an enormous programme, probably the biggest humanitarian operation in history.'

Few NGOs avoided the temptation of being alarmist. Although the president of the French Red Cross spoke out against 'certain dramatic depictions of the plight of civilians', he simultaneously launched, 'in view of the predicted humanitarian disaster', a public appeal for funds. Many organisations in the US and Europe did the same: fundraising campaigns were launched notably by CARE International, Oxfam, CAFOD, Save the Children, Christian Aid and Action Aid. Many believed the consequences of 12 years of sanctions magnified the risks and that a tragedy was unavoidable. CARE declared that damage to electricity and water treatment plants during the 1991 conflict had caused more deaths than the war itself. Charles MacCormack, president of Save the Children (US), announced that 30 percent of children were suffering from malnutrition before the war and that clearly their situation would not improve. His French counterpart at Action Contre Faim, Jean-Christophe Rufin, denounced coalition troops using 'hunger as a weapon' in their conquest of Iraqi towns.

Iraq had already accustomed us all to the vastness and mystery of figures. We still do not know how many died in the war of 1991 for none of the protagonists provided a figure. The 'Desert Storm' allies do not intend to tarnish the sheen of victory by acknowledging an inevitably sombre death toll, while for the Iraqi government to do so would be an admission of weakness, unthinkable in a dictatorship. The same applies to the number of Shi'a and Kurdish victims of the violent repression that crushed their rebellions in 1991, whose bodies are only now being found. Sanctions, by contrast, gave rise to exceptional numbers: the figure of 500,000 children dead as a consequence of these measures is advanced without any evidence to support such a horrendous accusation. Journalists and NGOs continue to quote it as a proven fact, yet no study or serious inquiry has evaluated the high mortality the sanctions allegedly provoked. The collective punishment of a population, even led by a tyrant, is, of course, profoundly unjust. The sanctions' main effects seem to have been both to reinforce the regime's control over the population through food distributions organised by the Ba'ath party, and to provoke the economic decline of the country's middle class. Sanctions enfeebled Iraqi society and consolidated its regime, which is quite enough to condemn them unreservedly – there is no need to resort to figures that are straight out of Ba'ath party propaganda.

It seemed as if disapproval of America's Middle East policy found expression through the operational lexicon employed by various organisations, each one drawing the appropriate accusation from its specific vocabulary. This was also reflected in NGO appeals to the UN, which was suddenly transformed into the shrine of all humanitarian virtues. Most European NGOs beseeched the UN to adopt the leading role in managing the 'humanitarian crisis', and some, like Rufin of ACF, wanted the UN to secure access roads to create 'humanitarian corridors' along which NGOs could safely transport aid. Although it is understandable that everyone, except America's leaders, hoped to see the UN return to the operation's forefront, it is perplexing, to say the least, to see such disdain for reality. Can we really imagine Blue Helmets ensuring the armed protection of relief convoys in Iraq during a war? Can we see the UN ensuring coordination in a conflict from which it was actively excluded? Can we ignore the UN's limits and deadlocks in providing humanitarian aid during the wars in Afghanistan, Angola or Liberia? Is it so easy to forget that in the latter two countries, the UN took part in blocking aid destined for civilian populations?[4] Under no circumstances could such requests have responded to the problems raised. A UN text dated 21 March warned against any confusion of roles: 'anything that could give the impression that the UN is a sub-contractor [of the armed forces] must be avoided.' The document notably excluded any military escort for UN convoys. This seemed an astonishing reversal to those who remember that the same UN defended the military protection of humanitarian convoys in all preceding crises.

Confusion was at its height during the five weeks of military operations with 'massive' or 'targeted' bombing raids, contradictory announcements, political tensions, propaganda, and collateral damage. ICRC, which had been working in the country since the war with Iran, continued as best it could to maintain water supply systems, particularly in Baghdad and Basra. With this prominent exception, little humanitarian activity was undertaken as military operations raged. The MSF team in Baghdad was paralysed when Iraqi police arrested two of its members at the very moment when the al Kindi hospital was swamped by an influx of wounded. Hence it was unable to carry out its work even though a consignment of materials and medicines had been delivered by truck from Jordan while Baghdad was under attack. Members of the British organisation Islamic Relief and several journalists were also arrested. Although no precise count of civilian and military losses is possible, civilian casualties caused by the bombing of 'Operation Shock and Awe' seem to have been relatively limited.

---

[4] See corresponding chapters in 'Situations'.

When spin doctors embrace humanitarianism

As in previous conflicts involving Western forces, humanitarian rhetoric provided the most visible component of the coalition's 'psychological operations'. Like the food airdropped in Afghanistan in October 2001, food aid and bottled water supplied by allied troops during the siege of Basra became the object of intense media attention. The magic of words transformed the landing of troops, munitions and provisions at Umm Qasr into a 'humanitarian operation': due to fears of a 'humanitarian crisis' resulting from the encirclement of the neighbouring city of Basra, the offensive was accelerated to resolve the crisis and to distribute 'humanitarian aid'. It is high time we realised that the term 'humanitarian', when employed in such conditions, is purely propaganda. Under the laws of armed conflict, it is the responsibility of the occupying power to meet the vital needs of the population and treat prisoners properly. These are legal obligations, not humanitarian gestures: calling the provision of water and food to Iraqi civilians a 'humanitarian act' is equivalent to claiming that sparing the life of prisoners of war is a 'humanitarian act'. For an act to be humanitarian, it should be freely given and be neither obliged by law nor owed as compensation for harm done. Giving people goods of which we have ourselves deprived them is not a donation, but restitution. To refuse to do so constitutes theft. Humanitarian law simply records this fact.

For those governments like Spain, Italy and Lithuania that were eager to demonstrate their commitment to the US but were not in the position to offer military support, 'humanitarian' action served as the link. Turkey, reproducing what it did during Operation Desert Storm, invoked a humanitarian pretext in an attempt – unsuccessful on this occasion – to justify a military presence in Iraqi Kurdistan. It is true that the eight war objectives established by the Pentagon included 'putting an end to sanctions and immediately providing 'humanitarian' aid, food and medicines to displaced persons and the many Iraqis in need'. But after twelve years of sanctions imposed by the US itself, this objective reeked of cynicism.

In such a context, where the use of the word 'humanitarian' by the coalition forces did not seem to pose a problem for anyone (except the NGOs) it is noteworthy that nobody thought to qualify as 'humanitarian' the distribution of provisions that Saddam Hussein began before the war broke out. This food was just as useful to recipients as that provided by the coalition, but in this case, its usefulness could not be the only criterion by which this transfer of goods qualified as 'humanitarian'. Saddam Hussein's intention was obviously not to ease the lot of his compatriots and that was enough to prompt all commentators to refer to this food as 'provisions' and not as 'humanitarian aid'. What secret hierarchy of values come into play when the delivery of provisions by US-British troops is dressed up in this convenient adjective while it is refused, for the same operation, to the Iraqi administration?

Whatever the case, the confusion caused by the misplaced use of this all-purpose word did not disappear with the end of military operations, far from it. The chaotic situation created by the war – looting, score settling, general insecurity – was also described as a 'humanitarian crisis'. It is a curious term, applied exclusively to a context of misfortune (always exotic) to denote a disorder that rescuers (always Western) are supposed to remedy. Given the advantages such a convenient expression affords, it is hardly surprising that the spin doctors employed by heads of state and high commands are so fond of it: in one context it permits the response to be confined purely to relief like during the genocide in Rwanda; in another it justifies military intervention, as in Kosovo. Wherever it is applied, it is an elegant version of 'thing' or 'whatsit', in other words what Roland Barthes described as 'an indeterminate value of signification in itself empty of meaning and therefore susceptible to receiving any meaning.'[5] It is more surprising to see the term figuring so prominently in the vocabulary of NGOs for its use reflects the basic communicative strategy – propaganda, in other words – of political power. Some humanitarian NGOs have doubtless adopted it for the sake of convenience, seeing it as an immediately intelligible way of designating their natural place and of legitimising their actions even before they are carried out. In this sense, the use of it serves their interests. But they reap short-term benefit because the first to profit from the confusion to which they thus contribute are those who use humanitarianism for other ends.

Desperately seeking a humanitarian crisis

In the absence of deliberate and repeated attacks on civilians which might have generated massive population displacement and an acute collective emergency, the problem of immediate relief amounted to re-establishing

---

[5] Barthes refers to the concept of *Mana* discussed by Lévi-Strauss. Roland Barthes, *Mythologies* (Paris, Seuil, 1957).

the water supply and treating the injured. Although ICRC was able to act quickly on water supply as its specialists had worked in this field since sanctions started, the injured faced a different situation in spite of the 33 public hospitals in Baghdad which are capable of providing Western standards of care. Basic care is assured by a large number of doctors' surgeries and private clinics, a sector that has flourished for several years due to the traffic in medicines and materials created by the sanctions. When Baghdad was attacked, most directors and qualified doctors disappeared from the hospitals, leaving the wounded in the hands of a reduced staff of volunteers and young trainee surgeons. It was a classic situation and justified the despatch of expatriate medico-surgical teams to serve in the critical period of a war whose evolution was unpredictable.

Although no precise evaluation has been undertaken, the number of injured seems to have been relatively low. It is estimated that between 1,500 and 2,000 casualties still required treatment in the days following the cessation of air strikes, at a time when the city was prey to looters. Some hospitals, especially military, were totally devastated while others were defended tooth and nail by their staff or protected by groups of armed Shi'as. Private clinics were spared and some of them, as well as certain public hospitals, were in direct receipt of looted materials. Despite the chaos, much of the medical infrastructure still functioned although only at 10 percent of its capacity because severe disorganisation caused a dramatic fall in the quality of care. Only the private sector functioned in a more or less normal fashion, ensuring, for example, almost all caesarean births[6].

What kind of humanitarian relief should be provided in a context where medical staff are present but cannot, or are reluctant to, work and where the material means are available? Deliveries of drugs and medical equipment are always welcome and photogenic but are of little use, to which the piles of unopened cases encumbering hospital corridors and pharmacies attest. The reorganisation of a city's public life is beyond the capacities of aid organisations, and no NGO could envisage working under the armed protection of American forces unless it wanted its staff to become prime targets. More generally, humanitarian aid is unjustified in countries rich in skills and material resources, which are undergoing physical reconstruction and socio-political change. Of course, 'humanitarian needs' can be found in Iraq, as in almost all countries of the world, but they bear no relation to the enormous budgets put at the disposal of NGOs by the European Commission and the US government as an incentive to participate in the reconstruction of Iraq. Most NGOs realised this shortly after the termination of the 'military phase'.

You enjoyed Somalia…?

As May drew to a close, the main NGOs began announcing their forthcoming withdrawal from Iraq. They were motivated by three reasons: the difficulty of operating in chaotic and unsafe conditions compounded

---

[6] MSF, *Bagdad : OPA sur les hôpitaux publics*, Assessment Mission Report, Paris, 5 May 2003.

by omnipresent political pressures and hidden agendas; other, more pressing priorities in the world; and finally the uneasiness induced by having to work under the control of a military administration of occupation.[7] MSF teams observed the intensity of power struggles between former hospital managers, consultants, the new guard of volunteers, new managers, and self-proclaimed management committees, all conducted against a background of rumours about US intentions and pressure from mullahs in Shi'a areas. These severe tensions negated the practical possibility of serious involvement in health structures. Moreover, no humanitarian organisation could serenely countenance the frightening disproportion between budgets allotted to 'humanitarian aid' in Iraq, which had few urgent needs, and the paltriness of sums available for critical situations, notably in West and Central Africa. Refusal to cooperate with US authorities – even more understandable for American NGOs that feared being confused with their government – began to be expressed by those NGOs that had been openly against the war from the start, and in the name of that opposition. It was these NGOs that made the above-mentioned appeals to the UN to ensure the coordination of humanitarian aid.

In fact, humanitarian organisations would have felt at ease in their roles (supposing that they had a real task to accomplish) if the scenario predicted by US strategists had been realised. But unlike Kosovo and East Timor, where the majority of the populations welcomed the troops as liberators, most Iraqis, like the Somalis before

---

[7] David Bank, 'Humanitarian Groups Spurn Iraq', *Wall Street Journal*, 29 May 2003.

them, regarded the coalition forces as invaders. The US administration's unease at the unexpected difficulties encountered is evident from the unprecedented media restrictions that USAID unsuccessfully attempted to impose on American NGOs including the right to filter all contacts with journalists. Furthermore, in an address to US NGOs, USAID director, Andrew Natsios, said that NGOs under US contracts are 'an arm of the US government' and that they should do a better job highlighting their ties to the Bush administration if they want to continue receiving money.[8]

Humanitarian aid organisations cannot, of course, choose their interlocutors. They can only compromise with whatever form power may take, whether a guerrilla command, military authority, international administration, or a government. Their only concern should be to obtain sufficient freedom of movement so that they are able to assist the victims before serving political interests.[9] To do so, it is essential that the population concerned perceive them as acting independently of the powers that be, especially when that power is the object of widespread hostility. This fundamental problem exists in US occupied Iraq just as it did when Saddam Hussein was in control. Humanitarians should not be concerned with assessing the legitimacy or legality of a power – on what basis could they do so? – but with the population's perception of their autonomy vis-à-vis that power. This explains, above and beyond actual needs, why an NGO can work

[8] Jack Epstein, 'Charities at odds with Pentagon: Many turn down work in Iraq because of US restrictions', *San Francisco Chronicle*, 14 June 2003.
[9] R. Brauman, *Humanitaire: le dilemme*, Paris, Editions Textuel, 2002, p. 53.

in occupied Palestine but feels it cannot do so in occupied Iraq.

With more troops deployed, resistance continuing, reconstruction slowed and 'democracy' still a slogan, tensions between occupiers and Iraqis infect everything. It is probable that we are moving towards a 'Palestinisation' of the situation in Iraq but it is unlikely that NGOs will find the minimum conditions required for the delivery of effective aid. Rather than being a field of action of humanitarians, Iraq risks turning into a lasting minefield for everybody.

13

Kosovo: the End of an Era?

David Rieff

The Kosovo crisis raised at least as many questions as it decided. It was presented by the leaders of the major Western powers as having marked a turning point in the history of modern conflict. Here was a war undertaken, as the British prime minister, Tony Blair, put it at the time, in the name of 'values, not interests'. In other words, it was a war of altruism, the sort of war in defence of populations at risk and against the perpetrators of massive violations of human rights and international humanitarian law (as distinguished from wars over money, territorial aggrandisement, or national defence) that seemed to conform to the precepts of a new human rights-based internationalism. In this more than somewhat fairy-tale-like version of events, at a time when even as intelligent a figure as Vaćlav Havel could insist that the NATO air campaign against Serbia, even the bombs themselves, had 'an exclusively humanitarian character', truth was bound to be the first casualty. Of course, this is always the case in war, but never more so than in so-called *humanitarian* war, when humanist rhetoric becomes an integral part of the military campaign as it unfolds, and as the fundamental element in the moral warrant for the war effort itself.

Obviously, in retrospect, events in Kosovo seem far more complicated. To insist on the point is not to deny the stark facts that led to the NATO intervention in the spring of 1999. There is little question that from the moment Slobodan Milošević's regime in Belgrade abolished the autonomy of Kosovo that it had been granted during the latter period of Tito's rule in Yugoslavia, a political and human crime began to unfold in the province – a crime, moreover, conceived of in ethnic terms against the overwhelming majority of its inhabitants, the Kosovar Albanians. Over the ensuing years, this criminal and racist conduct affected the bulk of the population more and more pervasively, so that, by the mid-1990s, it was a simple statement of fact to insist that Milošević had created an apartheid state in Kosovo in which a small minority of Serbs (by then generally estimated to comprise fewer than 7 percent of the population) enjoyed most essential rights – education, health care, etc. – routinely denied to their Kosovar neighbours. Given the general intransigence of the Belgrade regime; the fierce attachment to the Orthodox patriarchate in Serbia to Serb dominion over the so-called holy sites of Kosovo; the fact that the same Serb paramilitaries who had served as Milošević's shock troops in the campaigns of ethnic cleansing in Croatia and Bosnia in the early 1990s were now active in the province, and the view, prevalent in Serbia, that, demography or no demography, Serbs held a sort of mystical deed to the province (the comparison with

Israelis and the West Bank is all too painfully obvious), there is little likelihood that conditions would have changed *without* a war.

Political developments within the Kosovar Albanian polity during the period support this view. The comparatively moderate, pacifist, and accomodationist approach of Ibrahim Rugova was increasingly viewed with disdain by a younger and more militant generation of Kosovar nationalists who were increasingly rallying around the hard-line independentist views of Adam Demaci and the fledgling guerrilla movement of the Kosovo Liberation Army (the UCK, to use its Albanian initials). And the UCK was itself aligned with powerful Kosovar clans and, at least to some extent, in criminal activities both in Yugoslavia and in Western Europe. By 1998, the group was conducting hit and run attacks in several parts of the province, though it remains unclear whether, in doing so, they genuinely hoped to gain battlefield success or, instead, to elicit a harsh enough campaign of retaliation from Serb forces to guarantee an ideological victory over Rugova in the internal Kosovar Albanian political competition. What is clear is that, after seeing what Milošević had done (or allowed to be done) in Bosnia and Croatia, few ethnic Albanians could have been under any illusion over what course he would take in Kosovo.

This is not justify what Milošević did do, or to occlude the fact that – again the comparison with Palestinians under Israeli rule comes to mind – given the desperation of their everyday situations, armed resistance, no matter how desperate, quixotic, or criminal, would seem like the only course that brought with it honour and self-respect, at least to people in the their teens and twenties. To the very last moment, Milošević showed no hint of softening his line. Indeed, the return of Serb paramilitary fighters from their former hunting grounds of Bosnia and Croatia actually made it imperative for the Belgrade authorities to give them something to do. For this, Kosovo was ideal. In any case, Milošević had no pressing reason to moderate his behaviour. In effect, he had been given a pardon by the West for his leading role in the wars of Yugoslav succession, above all the murder and displacement of hundreds of thousands of Bosnian Muslims. There was no real reason for him to suppose that Washington or Brussels would suddenly take exception to a policy that, by the time the Kosovo conflict began in 1999, was already a decade old.

He was wrong, not least because Western leaders, notably US President Bill Clinton, had come to regret their inaction during the Bosnian slaughter. More prosaically, a set of institutional arrangements that had been put in place by the great powers in order to stave off the need to intervene – notably the so-called Kosovo Verification Mission – and a pervasive, though perhaps inchoate sense (one that Milošević clearly never understood) that a second Bosnia must not be allowed to take place, created the preconditions for the intervention that eventually took place. And of course, this decision was buttressed by the fact that renewed violence in Kosovo coincided with NATO's fiftieth anniversary. The notion that NATO could brook Yugoslav defiance at that particular moment was unrealistic from the start, particularly given the fact that, to varying degrees, three of the principal Western leaders – Clinton, Blair and France's Jacques Chirac – now regretted their nations' passivity during the Bosnian war. Like Saddam Hussein, though perhaps with more reason, Milošević had radically misconstrued the relation of force between himself and the great powers at which he had enjoyed thumbing his nose for so long.

And the Western leadership was responding to a real upping of the ante by the Serbs. Some opponents of the war insisted that the only emergency in Kosovo was created by the NATO bombing, or that Milošević's decision to forcibly deport some 800,000 Kosovars to Albania, Macedonia and Montenegro was only undertaken because of the West's attack, and would not have taken place otherwise. This appears to be untrue. According to both German intelligence officials and Greek diplomats representing a government (and a nation) that remained to one degree or another vehemently pro-Serb, the Belgrade authorities had always intended to deport a large number of Kosovars (the usual figure was 350,000) so as to either restore what they viewed as the 'natural' demographic balance of the province (i.e. one in which Serbs were a substantial rather than a demographically trivial proportion of the population), or to permit an eventual partition of the province on terms favourable to the Serbs. In other words, while the NATO bombing did create a short-term exodus in the sense that the mass deportations followed rather than preceded it, it is unfair and inaccurate to claim that without the bombing there would have been no crisis at all. For in 1999 the Milošević regime remained committed to the same campaign of ethnic cleansing to which it had devoted so much blood and treasure in the early 1990s in Bosnia and Croatia. The real question was one of timing.

It was because they perceived this, and were, when all was said and done, determined, however reluctantly, not to stand idly by as another campaign of ethnic cleansing unfolded, that the Western powers had little choice but to intervene. Would Milošević have acted as he did had the West been tougher with him at the time of the Dayton Peace Agreement of 1995 that ended the Bosnian war, not to speak of having acted forcefully in Croatia and Bosnia anytime during the previous four years? Probably not. But it is impossible to be certain. For in retrospect, Milošević does not appear to have been a particularly canny politician. To the contrary, from the perspective of a Yugoslav patriot in particular, it seems clear that his principal accomplishment was to preside over first the diminution, then the ruin, and then the disappearance of his own country. For now that Montenegro and Serbia are separating, and Kosovo will either remain the ward – half protectorate, half self-governing dependency – of the European Union, the United Nations and the United States, Yugoslavia has for all intents and purposes disappeared. That Milošević, who now sits in a prison cell in The Hague and is unlikely ever to live again as a free man, shares the ruin of Yugoslavia does nothing to alter this.

So it is not difficult to support the motivations of, and the necessity for, the Western intervention in Kosovo in 1999. In terms of classic just war theory, or for that matter, the decent and defensible imperative for European nations of maintaining a democratic order in Europe and in stamping out ethnic fascist rebellions of the type Slobodan Milošević represented, the campaign was eminently justifiable. In contrast, what was not sustainable at all was a *humanitarian* justification for the conflict. And yet remarkably, it was in those terms, and not those of traditional just war thinking, national interest, or even the simple, commonplace belief that democratic countries in a given region had the right and, indeed, the duty to end aggressive criminal behaviour of

neighbouring states, that the NATO action was
presented. When, for example, Václav Havel proclaimed
that the bombing campaign was impelled by no 'material
interest,' it was as if he assumed that the moral case for
war could not have been made successfully had the
opposite been the case. Havel, at least, had a reasonable
claim to actually being a moralist as well as a politician,
and, as such, at something of a slant to his own times.
The fact that career politicians like Clinton, Blair and
Chirac spoke in same terms suggested, however, that
something far more pervasive and commanding within
Western political culture was compelling the use of a
humanitarian justification as the ultimate sanction for
what, by any standard yardstick, came as close to being a
just war as anything that took place in the late 1990s. It
was as if humanitarian imperatives and the need to
enforce human rights norms offered the only credible
moral warrants (besides self-defence, obviously) for war
to which a Western politician could appeal.

   That the imperatives of humanitarian action and
human rights were by no means always the same and
were sometimes even contradictory, as is instanced by
the fact that relief workers must win the co-operation of
the types of thugs it is the sworn duty of human rights
activists to denounce categorically, was clear to activists
and practitioners in the know. But politicians could
hardly be expected to respect the imperatives of an
'independent' humanitarian space or the necessary
absolutism of the human rights approach to politics. To
the contrary, what Kosovo demonstrated was the
respect these values continued to command with the
Western public, and the ease with which these ideas had
been appropriated by Western policymakers. The use of
this rhetoric as a warrant for the conflict constituted one

more demonstration of Napoleon's maxim that in war the moral was to the material as three to one. On the ground, humanitarian aid workers might wonder and grow indignant over the fact that their vocation was being presented as the pretext for the bombing, but the matter by then was out of their hands. In this larger, geopolitical sense, the use of humanitarian language to provide an ideology for the bombing represented an important step in what was already a long process in which the independent humanitarian ideal – whether in the form exemplified by the International Committee of the Red Cross or that of Médecins Sans Frontières – was giving way either to the humanitarianism of the American type in which NGOs were seen and tended to see themselves as either servile subcontractors or valued collaborators with governments, or to the millenarian conceptions of Bernard Kouchner who saw in the collaboration of aid workers and states an Archimedean lever for justice and world-wide political transformation.

Kouchner was not wrong. A war of values, not interests, to return to Tony Blair's sonorous phrase, is, almost by definition, a crusading venture. After all, wars of interest are usually limited affairs, to be judged in the cold logic of benefits and costs. In contrast, wars of values imply that what is appropriate in a place like Kosovo will also be appropriate in Sierra Leone, or Congo, or, perhaps, Iraq. They have no limits, other than the obvious prudential ones (no sensible person calls for an intervention to end abuses in Chechnya or Tibet). And each such conflict, rather like a judicial decision that establishes a legal precedent, is viewed by its proponents as a basis for future conflicts. Unsurprisingly, one of the main criticisms made by intelligent people both at the time and since of the

Kosovo war was, in effect, why Kosovo and not, say, Sudan? Equally unsurprisingly, some of the same rhetoric used to justify what the West did in Kosovo was used by the US government to justify the war in Iraq. Thus do the millenarian ambitions of the human rights and humanitarian movements find themselves appropriated by the projects of the new imperium?

Again, none of this automatically invalidates the war in Kosovo. But it should give relief workers, human rights activists, and their supporters in the West pause. For if the humanitarian ideal is that easily co-opted by power, what is its real nature? Or, to ask the question even more harshly, is there something within the humanitarian idea that makes it peculiarly susceptible to this kind of political appropriation?

Certainly, the case can be made that there is, and not only because of the perception that humanitarian action and human rights are the secular religions of the international new class (the phrase is that of the American legal scholar, Kenneth Anderson). Humanitarian action, which has attracted young people who, in earlier generations, would have been drawn to the meta-political accounts of Communism, proclaims itself to be anti-political, or, at least, extra-political. Its allegiance, it asserts, is to the victims, to those in need. It does not judge the moral worth of those it seeks to assist, only to see that they are assisted. Though doubtless not intended in that way, such an idea obviously coincides with the Western neo-liberal consensus that the great political questions have been resolved, that there is no longer a place for ideology (except, of course, the ideology of the free market, which is declared to be non-ideological), and that the mission of democratic states in the world is to defend and propagate rights. To be sure, those rights can be extended, and here the views of the activists and political establishments often diverge, but the basic idea is that we all agree on how the world should be – all of us, that is, except a few wicked characters like Slobodan Milošević, Mullah Omar, or Saddam Hussein, and their minions.

And perhaps we do. Most of us anyway. At the very least, there is an increasing consensus – at the United Nations, among NGOs, in foreign ministries in the West – that humanitarian action, democracy building, conflict resolution, human rights, are all part of the 'tool kit' for the betterment of the world. Bernard Kouchner has devoted his life to this ideal, and, fittingly, he was named the UN's proconsul in Kosovo after the war ended and the Serbs withdrew from the province. For it is Kouchner's brand of humanitarianism that has prevailed in the chancelleries and at the UN Security Council. But with the idea of the tool kit comes the idea that humanitarian principles – above all the need to act exclusively on the basis of need – must, when necessary, be subordinated to larger goals. Thus, during the Kosovo war, most relief agencies in effect became subcontractors to the NATO war effort. These groups took NATO countries' funds, and, in effect, acted as subcontractors to one of the belligerent sides in the conflict. In this, Médecins Sans Frontières was a notable exception, in that it took no funds from the European Union countries, the European Commission, or the United States. But even MSF could not suddenly stop being part of the humanitarian system, and in this sense its gesture was more symbolic than real. Willingly or unwillingly, it still participated in the larger effort, and, to beneficiaries, it was probably largely indistinguishable from other relief groups that were taking NATO countries' funds. In fact, the humanitarian system is strong enough and entrenched enough to accommodate even its dissidents.

That process has only accelerated since the Kosovo war. In Afghanistan, for example, the subordination of relief groups to the dictates and agendas of the US military was, if anything, even more pronounced. But Kosovo set the tone, and the willingness of agencies to go on operating in the province long after the war was over and virtually all important humanitarian needs had been met testifies to their increasing subordination. To be sure, institutional self-interest plays a role in the sense that relief NGOs cannot successfully resist the agendas of their donors and, in many cases, need the funds generated by large scale and amply funded relief efforts to underwrite their headquarters expenses. But these questions of perennity and self-interest are secondary. The lesson of Kosovo remains larger and more dispiriting. For Kosovo challenges even the possibility of an independent space for humanitarian action. And nothing that has occurred in the province since, even as the political situation has stabilised and, at least to a certain extent, improved, suggests any alteration in that grim circumstance. To the contrary, in Kosovo, as in Afghanistan, and now in Iraq, most humanitarian agencies have co-operated eagerly in their own subordination to state power. Perhaps no other outcome was possible. Perhaps, once the world really came to be conceived of as a place in which the forces of good confront the axis of evil, the anti-politics of humanitarian action, with its emphasis on people's needs, not their moral worth, was bound to be transformed and instrumentalised. For states, it seems, humanitarianism is too valuable to be left to humanitarians. But this does not make the loss any less severe.

14

Humanitarian Spaces: Spaces of Exception

Michel Agier & Françoise Bouchet-Saulnier

The disclosure in February 2002 of certain information from a study commissioned by the British organisation Save the Children Fund (SCF-UK) concerning the 'Exploitation of vulnerable children and young people in the camps for internally displaced people in Liberia, Guinea and Sierra Leone', immediately provoked a unanimous but short-lived moral outcry.

The subjects of SCF-UK's study were 'children' according to the 1989 UN Convention on the Rights of the Child – those aged under eighteen. The passage to adult life, in Africa and elsewhere, often takes place before this age and not only for refugees: 'street children' are forced to live and work independently from an early age, while marriage or pre-nuptial maternity for girls of all social classes may occur during adolescence. Most victims of sexual violence in the camps studied were aged between 13 and 18. Furthermore, overt paedophile activity or rape accompanied by threats and physical violence were, if not totally absent from the collected testimony, the exception rather than the rule. The accounts described a very general form of 'sexual exploitation' typified by elementary, unorganised prostitution: a direct exchange of 'sexual favours' for a little food, some plastic sheeting, a blanket, a bar of soap or perhaps a little money.

The strictly *moral* condemnation of strictly *sexual* misdeeds is therefore misplaced: it takes into consideration only a tiny part of the facts and says nothing about the social milieu that produces them. Moreover, the events cited emerged from indirect testimony and no suspects, victims, or direct witnesses were named. Some months after these revelations, quickly described by the media as 'sex scandals', 'humanitarian rape', and 'the sleazy side of humanitarian aid', the affair ended with no charges being brought for lack of evidence. The UN's internal affairs office produced a vague report in October 2002 acknowledging that, while sexual abuse had certainly occurred and some aid workers might have been implicated in it, there was no evidence of systematic abuse although a 'very real' problem existed.

Refugees and 'big men': the camps as regimes of exception

The events brought to light by the accounts on which the British agency's report are based are sadly too banal within their context to belong to that category of indiscriminate and widespread perversion, debauchery and other forms of sexual harassment the French,

European and American press are so fond of reporting. The implication of UN and NGO 'international staff' (i.e. *whites*) in the sexual abuse of refugee children merits no official mention and does not appear in SCF-UK's published report. Their alleged involvement is important from the perspective of the white, post-colonial conscience, more or less clean or dirty, which currently preoccupies Western society. Yet if it is proven that Western staff have been involved, it is, given the context, just one more humiliation to add to the many that combine to produce an overall state of social distress for the majority, and impunity for a few. It is this overall state that we need to explore further.

The 'sexual exploiters' of refugee children are mainly adult men belonging to the social groups that wield some form of power in the camps. Although much has been made of the reference in the SCF-UK study to certain NGO and UN agency staff (workers of national and local origin and refugees employed by NGOs), other groups are equally involved in the abuse of sexual power: police and soldiers of national armies, regional units of UN peacekeepers, teachers (nationals or refugees) in schools run by governments or NGOs, refugee representatives (community or religious 'leaders'), and refugees engaged in commercial activities in the camps. Any man who has a job, some income, and access to the camps (traders, diamond miners, plantation workers etc.) may feature on this list. On the whole, we are dealing with the groups that habitually occupy 'higher' positions in the social world of the refugee camps; the young people interviewed by the compilers of the SCF-UK study call them 'big men'.

On the surface, the camps appear as almost ordinary social microcosms although they are cast from a hybrid, artificial mould: severe shortages may be the norm but there are also the rough outlines of social hierarchies, some attempt at an informal economy, prostitution, and churches of various kinds. They sometimes take the form of camp-towns, vast and deceptively temporary communities. Their difference, which facilitates all the abuse, lies in the deterioration of social life in and because of the war that ceaselessly supplies them, and in the existence of a special regime to govern the life of the refugees herded into them, remote from our gaze.

In these types of camp, as in others, prostitution and child sex abuse are fuelled not only by material destitution but also by the loss or dislocation of the social context that sustained the great majority of refugees. All refugees, particularly women and children, often the isolated survivors of massacres, are physically and socially affected and weakened by the loss of relatives killed at the place of departure or during the journey, and by the dispersal of families through flight, hunger or disease. This vulnerability enhances the absolute power possessed by anyone in the camps with a little money or food. In these conditions, there is no 'rape' or harassment or explicit pressure. The very context exempts the 'big man' from the stigma of guilt.

Created as emergency solutions, the camps gradually come to constitute the framework of daily life for their 'inhabitants' over the course of long, very long years, or even decades. The refugees, pawns in the hands of time and politics, then find themselves permanent residents of these spaces of exception. They are denied the right to travel or work in the countries where UNHCR (United Nations High Commission for Refugees) sites house them, although some may be given special, temporary permission to leave the camp and others will sneak out. As they are neither citizens of the country they have fled nor of the country that shelters them, they are entitled to no 'rights' other than those dictated by the individuals who hold power over their lives. The effects of this exceptional regime are not always negative: humanitarian agencies have developed awareness programs addressing women's health, sexual abuse in and around the camps, and domestic violence. They may run peace education programs, create post-trauma therapy groups and so forth. Nonetheless, in some camps or part of a camp, certain individuals will write their own rules.

In one camp situated in an African country that could well have featured in the Save the Children study, UNHCR delegates its powers to the national branch of a large international religious NGO. This organisation employs national, local and refugee staff; they are accustomed to working in the camp and might pass from one NGO to another. One of these workers, a refugee who arrived at the camp more than twenty years ago, is specifically responsible for transit centres. Transit centres receive the exhausted, hungry and often sick refugees who have just arrived from the border. They are the outposts of the humanitarian chain and vital to its efficient operation but they are also this man's 'territory'; he is the only person from the NGO who visits them regularly. He moves around the centre, sparingly handing out bars of soap to some, cooking pots to others; he does not issue blankets very often; new refugees may have to wait two days to a week for food. The NGO agent pushes people around, swears at others, accuses one person of 'lying', calls another a 'thief', because she asks for a plastic sheet he claims he gave her the day before. The allocation of patches of ground on which to erect four poles and a tarpaulin stamped UNHCR is the responsibility of the same man who distributes, apportions, regroups or separates the refugees by pointing a finger, shouting at those who complain. The protesters have only been living in the transit camp's tents a month but he seems to know them well already: he threatens a youth he suspects of being a troublemaker and a thief, kisses a young woman, is hugged by a young man, freely enters the tents and stays as long as he likes. If the abuse of power, probably sexual, takes place at that moment, it arises from a profound social misery exacerbated by political exclusion; it is typical of a 'power over life and death' situation. UNHCR delegates to the NGO who delegates to a single person 'on the ground' who applies his law, hence one of the components of a vast regime of exception is established.

The refugee camps are not lawless zones but zones of exceptional laws and powers where everything is possible for the people in control. In the same camp, several volunteers from international NGOs including Médecins Sans Frontières and the Jesuit Relief Service, complained about misadministration to UNHCR. Five of the camp's administrative staff – one of them personally responsible for distributing food to the 25,000 refugees on the site – were informally acknowledged as guilty of misappropriation of food or money and sexual abuse. Their contracts were terminated and they were ordered to leave the camp although no legal charges were laid against them. As for the 'man on the ground' mentioned earlier, he resigned and left hurriedly after providing a written denunciation of the extensive misappropriation of money and materials that he had observed within the NGO administration of the camp where he had been employed. UNHCR does not currently give a figure for the total number of refugees living in camps throughout the world. It claims it takes into consideration about 22 million refugees of different statuses and its latest reports estimate the total number of refugees and people displaced by wars and violence at 50 million. The figure is probably higher if we take into account all the 'invisible' refugees, the clandestine travellers who may find themselves in a camp at some stage in their wanderings. But beyond this, all places of containment, whatever ostensible purpose they serve, are concerned: prison camps, refugee detention camps, waiting areas in airports, transit centres near borders. They are all parts of an expanding and consolidating network of human confinement[1].

Humanitarian spaces – even military-humanitarian spaces, as in the Australian model of detention centres – are set apart from our spaces of ordinary life. The attention we direct at them is ego-centred in a centre-periphery fashion: our attention is only concerned with the details of internal life on the humanitarian periphery insofar as they call into question the centre itself. Is the 'scandal' of the sexual exploitation of minors quite simply supposed to disappear when we proclaim the innocence of white people? If our morality is upheld, the operation, the perversions, and the corruptions of humanitarian sites can then be attributed to a *regime of exception* in which injustice and its perpetrators act freely according to their own 'order of things'. In the best of cases, a relationship of strength is established inside the

---

[1] Cf. M. Agier, *Les réfugiés : aux bords du monde*, Paris, Flammarion, 2002.

camps so that modes of authority may be defined in a more open manner.

Whereas detached moral denunciation sustains the stigma, a critical and engaged attention to these worlds of exodus, camps, and their multiple problems, would be more productive. On reflection, what seems of real value is not the denunciation of one more 'sex scandal' simply to salve one's conscience, but the resistance, by all possible means, to the establishment of a global and permanent regime of exception reserved for the millions of undesirable people we confine in camps and restrict to ports or islands and other quarantine zones because we have given no thought to their situation or to the possibility of an inclusive policy that would reintegrate them into the world.

It is also significant that the reappearance of these populations in the public debate centres on sexual violence. Such an approach is limited to the individual and intimate aspect of the violence endured and obscures both the collective dimension of sexual violence and the political abandonment of these people. It is not enough to establish the body as a sacred space if no political and legal rampart exists to enable individuals to defend their physical integrity.

The implication of humanitarian aid workers in this form of violence has also produced a particularly shocking inversion of the roles between rescuers and tormentors. Looking beyond its emotional impact, this symbolic shock should encourage efforts to think through and comprehend the functions and limits of humanitarian action and supplement it with other forms of political and legal responsibility vis-à-vis the populations concerned.

Protected people or assisted victims

The 1990s marked an evolution in refugee care; the focus turned to various aspects of material assistance, like the elaboration of technical standards for aid and the question of armed escorts for aid convoys. Behind the apparent enthusiasm, the issue of legal protection of refugees – respect for their rights – actually regressed. Border closures and forced repatriations compelled endangered populations back into conflicts where they were turned into human shields, used as bait for international aid, and reduced to a reservoir of human beings deprived of all rights and subjected to every form of violence and injustice. The disappearance of legal protection for these populations has increased their exposure to physical danger and poses problems to security management in the camps.

An unprecedented movement of refugees took place in the African Great Lakes region after the genocide of Rwandan Tutsi in 1994. Within the space of a few weeks, 2.5 million people crossed the borders into Tanzania and Zaire. This mass of people was subject to the domination of local and national leaders who had organised the genocide. For a long time, the challenge of establishing an aid system capable of assisting a refugee influx of this magnitude overshadowed the distress caused by continuing physical abuse and political control. The camps soon lost their veneer of humanitarian spaces and were exposed as pure spaces of exception where control was in the hands of criminals and physical violence was accompanied by misappropriation of aid on a massive scale. Despite the complaints of some aid workers and requests by the UN Secretary-General, no government would agree to furnish military contingents to guarantee security in the camps and arrest the leaders responsible for the genocide. This refusal contributed to the further deterioration of a situation that was already transforming the camps into places of oppression, symbols of international political irresponsibility where the refugee, deprived of the security of the refuge, became a human shield for criminal strategies.

The attack on these refugee camps by the Rwandan army and Zairean rebels in 1996 was a deadly military response to the unresolved issue of international protection for refugees. Since then, various international initiatives have sought to learn from this tragedy by attempting to clarify the obligation to safeguard and improve the quality of humanitarian action.

The SPHERE project was initiated after the Great Lakes crisis by a group of NGOs concerned about the quality of humanitarian action. The project's charter affirms that assistance and protection cannot be separated. In practical terms, however, this project concentrates solely on assistance component. SPHERE's preamble stipulates that populations have the right to a satisfactory level of assistance but contains no details on the practicalities and methods required to secure this 'right'. Thus the project's real contribution lies in the formulation of technical standards for refugee assistance: it sets the minimum standards NGOs should observe in the provision of water, sanitation, food rations and nutrition, shelter and health. Some donors have also sought to use this project as a tool for evaluating the work of NGOs. This initiative might improve the professionalism of humanitarian actors but, by focusing energies on technical debates, it risks obscuring more fundamental problems concerning the quality of relief action. It seems difficult to talk of the quality of relief action without first referring to the extreme violence suffered by refugees and the silence, even the abdication, of many actors when faced with the objectives and responsibilities that the protection of populations entails.

It is also difficult to set standards for relief without addressing the funding problems of certain operations. In many cases, the provision of sufficient relief to endangered populations is hampered by the inadequacy or reduction of international funding. This is notably the case with budgets intended for aid to refugees and displaced people in West Africa. Should NGOs then refrain from all relief for fear of infringing operational standards? Standardising relief operations would be efficient if states were bound to a funding mechanism for UNHCR.

The responsibility to protect refugees and displaced populations is problematic due to the confusion surrounding the use and meaning of the term 'protection' at the international level. This confusion affects legal and military aspects of protection. While some consider that the term implies recognition and defence of a legal status that guarantees minimum rights to marginalised populations, others regard it as implying various national or international peacekeeping activities or the recourse to force to assure the physical safety of refugees.

In reality, the term 'international protection of refugees' designates a responsibility entrusted to UNHCR to supervise the bestowal and respect of rights that are guaranteed by international conventions to people whose lives are under threat. According to international law, these people have the right to flee their countries and take refuge elsewhere and should not be compelled to return to a place of danger. This fundamental right is complemented by a series of secondary rights such as the rights to demand asylum and receive aid. The purpose of an internationally recognised legal status is to ensure that refugees who have effectively lost the benefit of national rights by leaving their country are not placed outside the law (having no rights at all) and abandoned to unfair treatment. The International Committee for the Red Cross (ICRC) is invested with a similar responsibility for international protection but this only applies to victims of armed conflicts who have not fled their country of origin.

The physical safety of refugees or victims of armed conflicts is not, however, the object of any specific international mandate. During the 1990s various UN military operations were launched and justified by, amongst other things, the fact that massive violations of human rights or humanitarian law in certain countries constituted a threat to peace and international security. These peacekeeping missions did, therefore, have a mandate to protect humanitarian aid and populations.

The confusion between protection and security, which persisted due to the ambiguity of these peacekeeping missions, was cruelly dispelled by various massacres. When the enclave of Srebrenica in eastern Bosnia was attacked in 1995, more than 7,000 people under the protection of UN contingents were massacred and another 25,000 deported. In 1994, when the genocide of Rwandan Tutsi began, UN soldiers present were not issued with the orders or the means necessary to oppose the killing. Instead, the UN decided to reduce its number of troops in the country. Subsequent UN investigations concluded that UN missions could not guarantee the protection of endangered populations given the UN's current structural and operational state, and the absence of binding obligations on its member states.[2] A major review of UN peacekeeping operations came to the same conclusion.[3] To be sure, it acknowledged that peacekeeping forces should be invested with an implicit authorisation to bring an end to violence when they witness crimes against civilians, provided that they have the necessary means to do so. But its conclusion advised against entrusting such protective missions to peacekeepers because this seems neither possible nor desirable. In practice, protection objectives are reduced to a level determined by available means and not the inverse, as the example of the DRC (Democratic Republic of Congo) demonstrates. The mandate of UN peacekeepers in the DRC established criteria for the possible use of force to protect the population, but this is limited to situations where civilians are under imminent threat of physical violence in zones covered by UN infantry battalions, and only then if the UN forces believe they have the necessary capabilities.

Finally, the report on sexual violence in West Africa reveals that the presence of international or regional armed forces should not be regarded as a guarantee of a population's safety but as a potential source of violence and abuse.

[2] *Report of the Secretary-General pursuant to General Assembly Resolution 53/35: The Fall of Srebrenica* (A/54/549, 15 November 1999) and *Report of the Independent Inquiry into the Actions of the United Nations during the 1994 Genocide in Rwanda* (15 December 1999).
[3] *Report of the Panel on United Nations Peace Operations – Brahimi Report* (A/55/305, 21 August 2001).

Confronted with the difficulty of ensuring that populations are protected from massive violence, states have chosen to weaken their obligations in this regard. Border closures during the US offensive in Afghanistan illustrated a new international consensus that no longer recognises an endangered population's right to escape. Deprived of the legal option of survival through flight, these populations are dependent on the mercy of people-smugglers and become the subjects and objects of various forms of commerce.

These victims are forced to live on the battlefield where they are held to ransom, physically abused, and used as human shields or labour pools for different military strategies. Official sources claim that this deterioration of refugee rights will be countered by the development of a law designed to protect populations subject to internal displacement. But the day-to-day existence of people displaced by conflict is governed by the arbitrary nature of aid provision, the difficulty of access to national or international institutional protection, and constant prevarication and harassment. In such conditions how do we ensure that rights are actually observed?

Towards a future other than humanitarian

Humanitarian action is often portrayed as a victory for generosity, humanity's revenge on suffering and poverty. But it is essentially the hidden face of the violence of conflict and social fragmentation. As it relieves distress, it reveals the inability of societies to manage violence, exclusion, change and conflict. Called upon to give barbarism a human face, humanitarian action has, over the last twenty years, been presented with a growth and expansion in the scale of this challenge. Between 1990 and 1995, for example, the European Union's humanitarian aid budget increased sevenfold. During this period, humanitarian organisations rapidly became aware that this material growth was insufficient to relieve the suffering of populations. Certain organisations like Médecins Sans Frontières have exposed the danger inherent in turning humanitarian action into a substitute for political action.[4] Contrary to prevailing ideas, humanitarianism is not the radiant future of humanity but the most basic form of dialogue and social construction. By successive, apparently innocent steps, humanitarian action tends to transform individuals-subjects into depersonalised victims-objects and to replace law with charity. In the name of urgency, pragmatism, proximity to the victims, and the generous character of its intentions, humanitarian action runs the risk of damaging relations of responsibility and reciprocal rights and duties that most durably structure human life, and which limit the phenomenon of individual or collective violence. Having experienced the omnipotence of their actions of substitution, aid organisations are now experiencing their impotence in the search for solutions.

In the struggle against this erosion, which can lead from generosity to injustice and then to the abandonment of populations, it is important that humanitarian space does not simply become a space of exception where references to the rights and responsibilities of the various participants are rendered superfluous by generosity and pragmatism. Refugees living in relatively stable humanitarian territory like

---

[4] Rony Brauman, *Humanitaire: le dilemme,* Paris, Textuel, 2002.

camps regard NGOs and other organisations present as their natural 'social partners'. Despite the prohibitions and restrictions placed on active communal or political life by camp authorities, boycotts of World Food Programme (WFP) food rations have been, on occasion, organised and strike action has been known among refugees working as 'community volunteers' for NGOs. This kind of disorder can be frightening in the context of confinement that the camps represent, but is a manifestation of the existence of human subjects who are exercising their right to life and appealing for a revision of their legal status.

Humanitarian law has long sought to establish a balance between the provision of aid and services and the protection of populations in situations of armed conflict.[5] The texts do not speak of victims but of protected persons. The right of the different categories of protected persons to receive aid is integrated into a specific framework of responsibilities assigned to various political, military and humanitarian actors. Humanitarian law thus provides a dynamic framework for relief actions. It balances the power and responsibilities of aid workers. It compensates for the unilateral nature of pragmatic or moralistic approaches by forcing us to consider the diverse forms that individual vulnerability can assume. Morality springs from the individual while the law is the product of negotiation between individuals. And effective as a pragmatic approach might be from an operational perspective, it reduces individuals to their existence as victims.

---

[5] Françoise Bouchet-Saulnier, *The Practical Guide to Humanitarian Law* (Lanham, MD, Rowman and Littlefield, 2002).

Some attempts to rebalance the relationship between humanitarian organisations and victims are underway. One project is examining the possibility of creating a humanitarian mediator to hear complaints lodged against aid agencies by victims, renamed 'beneficiaries' on this occasion. But it is illusory to try and regulate the relationship between rescuer and victim since it is, by definition, a relationship of exclusive dependence. Alternatives to this dependency must be created so that endangered populations are offered the prospect of a future other than humanitarian.

In West Africa, as elsewhere in the world, humanitarian organisations are eager to adopt codes of good conduct in order to protect vulnerable people from the abuse of power. This kind of voluntary restraint is understandable and justified in terms of professional ethics but it cannot replace a collective response to the extreme vulnerability and extensive violence to which some populations remain condemned. Preserving the purity of humanitarian actors will not resolve the challenge of establishing a legal and practical framework for survival that preserves the dignity of endangered populations and their rights to seek asylum and protection. Humanitarian action has progressively evolved. Created to bring aid and protection to populations in danger, it has, in some cases, contributed to their imprisonment in spaces of exception and arbitrary justice. Far from upholding international law and order, the continuing presence of these spaces of exception reintroduces inhumanity to the heart of all societies.

15

Justice and Humanitarian Action : a Conflict of Interest

Eric Dachy

On 1 July 2002 the treaty establishing the International Criminal Court (ICC) came into force. This permanent court will judge 'the most serious crimes of concern to the international community as a whole', including acts of genocide, war crimes, crimes against humanity and crimes of aggression. In contrast to the Nuremberg (1945) and Tokyo (1946) tribunals or the *ad hoc* jurisdictions created for the former Yugoslavia (1993) and Rwanda (1994), the ICC will be a permanent court with universal jurisdiction. Numerous humanitarian organisations actively lobbied for the creation of this court, arguing that the fight against impunity for authors of mass crimes constitutes a logical extension of their action. The participation of aid organisations in the development and functioning of international justice, however, carries several contradictions. Humanitarian and judicial approaches are not necessarily compatible. The ICC's statutes stipulate that the Court can only accept cases submitted by a state or the UN Security Council, or on the initiative of the court prosecutor. Hence humanitarian organisations do not have the possibility to refer a case to the Court. They can provide information to prosecutors on their own initiative with the guarantee that this will be treated confidentially, but nothing obliges prosecutors to take the information into consideration, or to open an inquiry on the basis of evidence communicated to them. The court can, by contrast, oblige anyone to appear before the Court and testify publicly. At the prosecutor's discretion, special measures, such as *in camera* hearings or testimony given by electronic or other means (e.g. video links) may be applied in order the protect victims and witnesses. Nevertheless, the possibility, and more importantly the obligation, to testify raise a delicate problem for humanitarian workers because it interferes directly with their potential access to victims.

In most conflict zones requests for, or insistence on, access to non-combatants (civilian population, wounded soldiers or prisoners of war) are addressed to the *de facto* authority. At central level this means government authorities, or the staff headquarters of the regular army or rebel force. But approaches also have to be made at the local level, negotiating with the military commander in charge of an area and sometimes quite simply with individual soldiers controlling access to a road or a bridge. In practice the provision of assistance requires the local authorities to agree that care may be given to the wounded and the sick, and to grant permission for the deployment of the necessary means to do so by approving the circulation of people and vehicles, the use of communication equipment such as radio or satellite phones, the transport of medical and logistical material, the installation of temporary infrastructure, and the hiring of local personnel. Under these conditions, the local combatants are the masters of the situation and the way in which an aid intervention is implemented is necessarily subject to their good will.

The armed forces have numerous reasons for blocking access of aid organisations to conflict zones or for forbidding them from crossing a front line. Aid operations unavoidably interfere with the conduct of military operations, are regularly suspected of providing cover for espionage, and undeniably constitute a resource for the enemy when assisting victims of the opposing side. In spite of this, humanitarian volunteers are not systematically excluded from combat zones, as the need to assist the wounded and the sick is usually recognised by belligerents. Hence whether desirable or not, establishing an aid operation necessitates the construction of a *modus vivendi* with the various fighting forces involved, and is largely determined by the ability of humanitarian teams to explain the reasons for their presence.

Dealing with roadblocks and checkpoints, and negotiating with soldiers and militia from all sides are part of the daily lot of missions in conflict zones. But so too are violence and war crimes. Aid personnel are sometimes direct witnesses to events such as attacks against civilian populations and deportations, and have on occasion discovered mass graves. Sometimes they are also indirect witnesses of crimes, treating people who have been tortured or raped, or observing a pattern of systematic mutilation or deliberate wounding of non-combatants and children. And sometimes, quite simply, they hear about violence and war crimes in the stories of patients and victims. This is the reality of humanitarian action. Aid workers are obliged to negotiate – which does not mean taking sides – with criminals or potential criminals in zones where arbitrary decisions are taken and where the rule of law has been abolished *de facto,* and where the teams are in a position to identify grave crimes or to suspect that they have taken place.

The establishment of the ICC, and the obligation to testify before it, is likely to affect the relationship between aid workers and combatants. This becomes singularly complicated if aid personnel are likely to be in a position to send the people they are dealing with to prison a few years down the track by testifying during a trial before an international court. Imagine the case of a medical team who asks the head of an armed group for permission to go into a village where there has been fighting and the possibility of a large number of wounded. Authorisation is given. On the way in, members of the team pass militiamen coming in the opposite direction. Once they get there, they discover, lying beside the wounded, the bodies of many civilians who have clearly been killed at point-blank range. The stories of the terrified wounded leave no doubt that people have been summarily executed. If, at a later date, the members of this team testify before an international tribunal, they will potentially render more difficult the work of those who are trying to reach victims in conflict zones. If this testimony serves to determine the responsibility of those who have committed such criminal acts, it will become known that humanitarian volunteers can contribute to ensuring the trial and condemnation of combatants. The fact that the latter have been judged guilty of grave crimes will only be regarded as a secondary element.

This problem already exists at another level of responsibility, that of governments or political bodies, which have sometimes shown little appreciation for the presence of witnesses on the battlefield. But with the ICC, there is the added problem of individual criminal responsibility. Thus a Russian soldier in Chechnya, a faction head in Congo, or an American officer in Afghanistan, indeed all those who might have a concern, founded or not, that they may one day have to account for their actions in front of a court, will see in the provisions of the ICC a powerful incentive to remove any humanitarian presence.[1]

The International Committee of the Red Cross (ICRC) has addressed this problem by obtaining a formal exemption from the obligation to testify by virtue of the confidentiality required for its actions. In July 1999, the ICTY ruled that 'the ICRC has the right, in application of customary international law, not to divulge in legal proceedings information relating to its action' and considered that confidentiality was 'absolutely essential to the accomplishment of the ICRC's mandate'. On the basis of these arguments, the ICRC then requested that this exemption be included in the rules governing the ICC's actions. In fact, the rules establish that any information reaching a representative

---

[1] It should be noted that the United States' policy is to try to establish the immunity of its own nationals. This is being sought through the signature of bilateral agreements with a number of countries that would effectively countermand their obligation under Article 98 of the Treaty of Rome to assist the ICC.

of the ICRC in the exercise of his/her functions is covered by professional secrecy. This exemption was granted exclusively to the ICRC. As its action includes certain tasks for which it has an official mandate under international law, it is difficult to imagine how the systematic exercise of this mandate could be reconciled with an obligation to serve as a witness. It should be noted, however, that the principal reason invoked by the ICRC was that 'access by its delegates to the victims of armed conflicts depends on the confidence of the parties to the conflict' and as a consequence 'the ICRC will not bear witness against them in case of later criminal proceedings.' Described as such, the problem of access to victims is also applicable to other organisations whose purpose is to bring humanitarian aid. Confidentiality could be invoked by them in the same terms since this interpretation is not linked to activities exclusive to the ICRC's mandate, such as visiting prisoners of war or detention facilities.

Other categories of professionals present in the field are confronted with similar difficulties. Some journalists are concerned that the possibility of being obliged to act as witnesses in trials against potential sources of information leads to a loss of credibility and a weakening of their role. They consider that this situation constitutes a direct threat to their ability to perform their professional function. Jonathan Randal, a journalist for the *Washington Post*, has been refusing since January 2002 to appear before the ICTY in The Hague despite being summoned to do so, hence running the theoretical risk of a prison sentence. His stance has been supported by his employer and by several journalistic bodies. An appeal decision in December 2002 finally established that a journalist could not be obliged to appear except when there is 'a direct and crucial link to the essential questions of a case' and if 'the element of proof cannot be obtained from any other source'. As this was not the case here, Randal's presence was excused. However, the ICTY is not thereby renouncing the principle that a journalist is obliged to appear since it lays out the criteria under which this obligation can be enforced.

For the moment the conflict between the obligation to testify and the discretion required for negotiating access to victims remains theoretical. At the legal level the present texts provide no way of foreseeing what attitude the prosecutor would take if a member of a humanitarian organisation, summoned to appear before the Court, were to invoke the general necessity to protect humanitarian activity in support of a request to testify anonymously or to refrain from testifying. One MSF volunteer has already testified before an international court. In 1997 Dr Rony Zachariah himself decided to accept a request to provide evidence to the investigators at the Arusha Tribunal. He had the benefit of legal assistance provided by MSF. His testimony, however, did not seek to establish or to deny the responsibility of the person on trial, but rather to clarify the situation prevailing in Rwanda at the time of the facts.

The statutes and rules governing the ICC are intended to protect the security, well-being and dignity of victims and witnesses, but do not *a priori* affect aid personnel. The prosecutor may make a commitment not to divulge the information obtained from a witness if this 'confidential' information would make it possible to gather new evidence or if the witness fears for his/her own safety or that of family members who cannot be offered protection by the Court. Several Bosnian witnesses were thus granted anonymity by the ICTY in the trial of a guard in an 'ethnic-cleansing' camp because the Court considered that it was unable to offer them sufficient protection. But there is nothing to oblige the prosecutor to make use of these confidentiality measures in relation to humanitarian volunteers, and no requirement to accept a request for confidentiality motivated by a general concern to preserve access to victims within the framework of humanitarian activity. In fact, the prosecutor must also respect the rights of the accused, which implies access to witnesses, hence rendering anonymity an exceptional measure. Humanitarian volunteers are unable to claim a special status because this does not exist at the legal level. We might then ask what would happen if a volunteer did not wish to testify in public because this testimony could have negative consequences for the teams in the field. The answer remains unclear although theoretically the volunteer would be liable to sanctions.

Humanitarian NGOs must therefore anticipate the likelihood of a situation of this type. Faced with a request from the prosecutor for the names and addresses of volunteers, both national and expatriate, NGOs should inform all their personnel that such a possibility exists, obtain individual consent, and envisage providing legal assistance to anyone who might be summoned to appear before the Court. The same problem arises if aid personnel are solicited for information about people who have confided in them within the context of general public testimonies for which a commitment to respect anonymity was given.

The dilemma posed by the existence of the ICC cannot be resolved by taking an institutional or formal position. Humanitarian volunteers are potentially faced with a paradoxical situation: either we compromise our ability to aid victims by testifying, or we protect criminals in order to continue to provide assistance. Within MSF, as within other organisations, there is a stream of positive feeling towards the idea of working through the legal system (a sort of 'pro-jurisdictionality') that considers humanitarian action as falling within the framework of international law, and regards humanitarian commitment as inseparable from the fight against impunity for those who commit grave crimes. MSF is a member of the NGO coalition in favour of the creation of the ICC. During the preparatory meetings, MSF, contrary to the ICRC, excluded the idea of requesting any exemption from the obligation to testify by virtue of the exceptional nature of the humanitarian role. MSF expressed publicly that 'international justice is an essential response to the trivialisation of war crimes, of crimes against humanity and of genocide.' From this point of view, it seems natural that we should adopt a positive approach to justice by providing information that could be used within the framework of judicial procedures when we are confronted with crime and violence on a large scale. From there flows the idea to proceed with the systematic collection of data concerning abuses of international humanitarian law and to register precise details of dates, places and circumstances. The objective is to formalise and professionalise '*témoignage*' (witnessing and documenting people's experiences) in order to sustain the justice process with relevant information.

In opposition to this concept, it is important to stress that the production of testimony intended for courts or other institutions can only weaken both the position of the witness and humanitarian action itself. The value of witnesses lies in their ability to report what they have seen and not in their motivation for relating the facts. Any attempt to give a pre-determined form to this testimony, as well as any initiative intended to encourage it or to consolidate it by gathering specifically selected data, directs the form and contents of the evidence and renders its use as a means to an end. This would only weaken the testimony before a court whose work consists of establishing the reality of the facts and which bears responsibility for them. In the same way, an approach aimed at establishing the nature and the gravity of crimes committed would go counter to our vocation as aid workers whose main concern is the interests of the victims. Such an approach would set us up as informal auxiliaries to the justice process, a role that requires specific responsibilities.

NGOs such as Human Rights Watch whose main vocation is to investigate human rights abuses see active collaboration with the ICC as a logical follow-on to their work. In order to ensure that their investigations can be considered in the judicial procedure, these organisations are likely to commit themselves to adopt a specific code of conduct for their researchers similar to that of the Court's official investigators. This would then serve to validate the inquiries carried out by these NGOs. They envisage, very logically, modelling their activities on what the ICC would expect from them by serving as a link between the Court and the victims and by facilitating the Court's access to the latter. They are preparing to include in their investigations the distribution of forms on which to register in the procedure as either a victim or a witness, or to claim compensation. They are also considering drawing up a list of people to communicate to the Court, on condition, of course, that those concerned give their consent.

It is clear that if aid agencies were to introduce this type of procedure it would have a negative effect on humanitarian work and on the transparency of humanitarian action. We might then ask ourselves what are the reasons pushing us to play such distinct roles simultaneously, and realise that they are rooted in the belief that the law is the ground of 'a more just international order'. Simple moral duty then enjoins us to contribute actively to this attempt at universal jurisdiction because it will finally allow us, if we believe in the words of its eulogists, to prevent and to limit suffering and crimes.

It is not my intention to comment on this self-proclamation of the law as the basis of a new moral order, but rather to remark that succumbing to the temptation – illusory – that humanitarian actors can take a role in socio-political transformation by supporting this 'new crisis-response paradigm that constitutes international justice' would, by pledging them to juridical practices, dispossess them of their ability to bring aid. Rather than inscribing aid activity within the framework of the ICC's expectations, it might, on the contrary, be pertinent to consider a scenario in which its requirements would prove damaging to the efforts being employed to assist the victims. We would then have to envisage giving our support to one of our volunteers who refuses to testify despite the legal obligation – a refusal founded, of course, on an individual decision of conscience in the face of a specific situation.

16

The Modern Missionaries of Islam

Abdel-Rahman Ghandour

Since the late 1980s, Western humanitarian organisations have been encountering a new type of NGO that defines itself as 'Islamic'. The International Islamic Relief Organisation (Saudi Arabia), Human Appeal International (Ajman, United Arab Emirates), the Islamic African Relief Agency (IARA, Sudan), Islamic Relief Worldwide (UK), the Imam Khomeini Relief Committee (Iran), and the Benevolence International Foundation (US) are just a few examples of these global players. More than one hundred operate internationally and over 10,000 operate locally. At the beginning of the new millennium – a time when most of the world's refugees are still Muslim – Islamic humanitarian organisations are at work in every crisis area where Muslims are affected.

Islamic NGOs: opposition forces and tools of the state

Some of these NGOs existed before the 'awakening' of political Islam but others sprang from the new movement and aim to redress the 'breakdown of the state' in the Arab-Islamic world. They are run by dedicated Islamists and act as magnets for protest against local powers who are seen as impious, corrupt and therefore illegitimate. Many countries like Egypt, Algeria, and Turkey have been observing the approach of this Islamic – and sometimes Islamist – social wave with apprehension. Egypt is particularly adept in its efforts to prevent these protest movements from overly disrupting established order and challenging existing power. The Red Crescent, the Muslim equivalent of the Red Cross, is one of the tools states use to counter Islamic NGOs as they attempt to monopolise humanitarian action in Islamic lands. Although the Red Crescent is still resisting the tidal wave of Islamic NGOs, local secular or traditional NGOs throughout the Muslim world are slowly being overtaken at the national level.

Paradoxically, while Islamic NGOs have met with a certain amount of success in their own countries through competing with the state and the Red Crescent, their influence at the international level derives from the support of Muslim states. This is particularly the case with exporters of Islamic ideology like Sudan, Iran and Saudi Arabia – and to a lesser extent Kuwait – who seek to extend their influence through the medium of Islamic NGOs.

Since the attacks of 11 September 2001 the major Western powers have subjected the Arab and Muslim world to much tighter surveillance but Islamic NGOs continue to expand. They all share the same impressive strength of conviction, determination, and efficiency. Their projects are far from modest and include the provision of drinking water systems in refugee camps, construction and management of hospitals, schools and orphanages, and large-scale food distribution. They now occupy a significant part of the field of humanitarian action that was once the exclusive preserve of Western organisations.

This spectacular expansion may be explained by several factors. Islamic NGOs are endowed with considerable funds – some budgets surpass 150 million euros – that come from state subsidies (in the Gulf countries, Libya, and Iran) and from Islamic banks, wealthy patrons, and informal financial networks. Donations from the general public, solicited by direct marketing techniques, are also increasing. Islamic NGOs also benefit from invaluable political support at the centres and peripheries of power in certain countries like Saudi Arabia, Iran and Kuwait. Finally, they are driven by the religious fervour of their members, echoing a return to religion seen twenty years ago in the Arab-Islamic world. This fervour is fuelled by the central notion of charity contained in the message of Islam which, of all the monotheist religions, has most systemised the duty of charity. *Zakat* (obligatory alms) is the third pillar of Islam, after the profession of faith and prayers. It stipulates that once a year every Muslim, male or female, who has the means to do so, must give 2.5 percent of their wealth (and not just their income) to the needy who are specified as the poor, the sick, orphans, and travellers. The Shia practice of *Khoms* – literally 'one-fifth' – enjoins them to distribute 20 percent of their wealth to the poor and the vulnerable through the intermediary of a religious authority (a *Marjaa*). Furthermore, Islam recommends *Sadaqa*, the distribution of supplementary alms, as the donor sees fit. The *Waqf* (religious legacy) has enabled many NGOs to benefit from premises or materials and enhance their efforts to assist those in need. Islamic NGOs thus have a range of charitable instruments at their disposal, all of which are reinforced by the central injunction of Islam – the duty of justice and equity.

The rise of Islamic NGOs

Four events closely linked in time have acted as catalysts for the rise of Islamic charitable work. First, the Iranian Islamic Revolution in 1979 sought both to export its ideas, through non-governmental organisations among other channels, and to offer an alternative, Muslim model to Western political and cultural domination, including in the field of humanitarian action. The revived memory of the humiliation of the Crusades, colonialism and Christian missionary activity legitimised the rejection of the western model of humanitarianism.

Second, the Soviet occupation of Afghanistan in 1979 triggered a surge of solidarity throughout the *Umma* (community of believers) in resistance to the atheist Soviet empire. Afghanistan constituted the initial stage of a voyage of discovery for Islamic charitable organisations, their romantic era. For the first time, they were faced with the challenge of exercising solidarity by putting Islamic theories into practice on foreign soil. They had almost unlimited means at their disposal but little practical experience.

Third, the explosion of oil prices in 1979 meant that huge funds were suddenly available to several Middle Eastern regimes who took the opportunity to reinforce their legitimacy by distributing part of their wealth to less fortunate Muslims. These states were reluctant to intervene in certain conflicts in which Muslim populations were particularly affected, but were able to reduce the pressure of public opinion by donating colossal sums of money to Islamic NGOs. The Bosnian crisis of the 1990s was an example of this form of charitable engagement: civil society throughout the Muslim world mobilised in outrage at what they saw through the media, yet in Islam as in the West, charity merely masked a lack of political will to address the causes of the crisis.

Finally, the Israeli invasion of Lebanon in 1982 and the Arab world's failure to support resistance to it tipped many Palestinian and Lebanese militants into Islamism and also breathed new life into Islamic charitable movements. With the Islamisation of the Palestinian resistance and the emergence of Hamas as a major political and social movement in the occupied territories, Palestine became a prime site for the development of Islamic NGOs.

Bread, the Koran and the sword

Islamic NGOs by no means form a monolithic whole. Four major strategies can be identified in the methods they employ to establish their presence on the international stage. The first is clearly subversive and its followers are prepared to use any means available, including violence, to exploit certain Islamist political demands and 'help' the Muslims they believe to be oppressed. The combination of the *jihad* of souls – i.e., spiritual salvation through Islam – and the *jihad* of bodies – caring for Muslims' minds and bodies by day and combating their enemies by night – was a dominant feature of the first Islamic NGOs to operate in Afghanistan. Bosnia in the mid-1990s was a training ground for interaction with other humanitarian organisations and marked the disappearance of the public version of the double *jihad*. Even so, certain Islamic NGOs engaged in subversive activity in Bosnia, although the vast majority of Muslim donors were unaware of it. This subversive strategy is now confined to a minority of organisations. NGOs like Human Concern International and Mercy Relief International (suspected of complicity in the attack on the US embassy in Nairobi in 1998) still practice it and facilitate the transit of weapons, combatants and money with the aim of perpetrating violence.

The second strategy may be described as 'dawatist' (from the term *al-dawa*, 'the call' or preaching). Although its promoters claim it is a defensive approach, Western humanitarian actors perceive it as aggressive. In practice, it replicates the missionary techniques employed by European powers in the 18th and 19th centuries and seeks to bolster the faith of Muslims and convert non-Muslims. Most Islamic NGOs may be classed as 'dawatist'; the al-Haramain Foundation (Saudi Arabia), al-Dawa al-Islamiya (Sudan), and the al-Rasheed Trust (Pakistan) are prominent examples. The construction of mosques, the distribution of religious texts, and the establishment of Koranic schools accompany their relief work.

The third strategy is based on conciliation and involves attempts to build operational partnerships with

Western humanitarian actors and develop a language of harmony and inclusiveness. Islamic Relief Worldwide (UK) and Muslim Helfen (Germany) are 'conciliatory' organisations. The final strategy is the 'chameleon' approach. Employed by the majority of Islamic NGOs, it is based on ambivalence and adaptation to circumstances. The International Islamic Relief Organisation (IIRO) and Human Appeal International are typical of these chameleon NGOs; they skilfully manipulate a flexible strategy that, depending on the situation and the participants, may be conciliatory or 'dawatist' at times and possibly subversive at others.

This is a somewhat superficial classification and it should be noted that several tendencies coexist within any organisation. Within the Abu Dhabi-based Zayed Foundation, for example, Wahhabis and partisans of the Muslim Brotherhood work alongside the 'People of Goodness' (*Ahl al-Kheir*), benefactors who believe that the very idea of charity is a project in itself and should be stripped of all political intentions. Conciliation is in the ascendancy today and is the preferred strategy for at least two reasons. It helps to ease the growing suspicion surrounding all Islamic humanitarian activity and its possible implication in Islamist violence, particularly since the attacks of 11 September 2001. These suspicions have considerably reduced the amount of funding available and restrict operational conditions. Conciliation is also the gateway to a vast international aid system whose rules and standards are largely inspired by Western values.

The battle for souls: Christian and Muslim missionaries

Because a majority of Islamic humanitarian organisations operate in isolation in the humanitarian field and reject dialogue with their Western counterparts as a matter of principle – most of their volunteers speak Arabic and refuse to use English – they fill a particular niche in communities throughout the Muslim world. Their activity is no longer confined to war-torn 'Islamic lands' like Afghanistan, Sudan, Somalia, Bosnia, Chechnya, Kosovo, and Kashmir, and they have now set their sights on regions where Islam is not the dominant religion (Central Africa, Southeast Asia). The most dedicated Islamic NGOs intend to fully exercise their role as the modern missionaries of Islam in these new promised lands, aiming as much to re-Islamise 'token' Muslims as to make new converts.

'Dawatist' NGOs, as already noted, are the most numerous. They endow Islamic NGOs with a specific image and maintain a high profile in areas where Western NGOs are active. In fact, religious-based charitable work – whatever form it may take – has never been in such robust health. Humanitarian action inspired by Christianity, particularly the Protestant variety, is experiencing a striking revival in Latin America and central and South-East Asia as well as in Black Africa. The proliferation of Christian evangelising NGOs – World Vision (US) being the leader – in Sudan, Kenya, Uganda, Rwanda, the Democratic Republic of Congo, Congo-Brazzaville, and Gabon, and the intensification of their proselytising action, indicates that the phenomenon of Islamic NGOs can only be understood in a much broader context. In Sudan, notably, a sometimes insidious, sometimes ferocious rivalry is unfolding as NGOs are caught between Christian missionaries seeking new converts and 'dawatists' whose aim is to Islamise the considerable number of Africans who do not yet belong to one of the great monotheist religions. When Islamic humanitarian actors are confronted with the militancy of their western alter egos, it is natural for them to think that they are simply fighting to defend Islam.

Humanitarian against humanitarian?

How can Islamic NGOs fit into the classic independent humanitarian environment when it is dominated on the one hand by Western Christian organisations intent on saving souls, and on the other by secular NGOs who cannot reconcile the secularism of 'their' humanitarian activity with the Islamic interpretation of charity? Is there an on-site collision between these two 'blocs' who find themselves face to face but share neither the same language nor the same discourse?

Relations between secular Western NGOs and Islamic organisations are blighted by simplistic and stereotypical representations. The former often view the latter as aggressively proselytising organisations and auxiliaries of Islamist states, led by hostile and extremist volunteers who are humanitarian in name only. Islamic volunteers have just as stereotyped an image of Western international NGOs who are seen as crude embodiments of Christian missions, reeking of a Christian clerical authority that has never come to terms with the separation of church and state.

Islamic non-governmental organisations are deeply suspicious of the secular claims advanced by some of today's international NGOs. Islamists have difficulty integrating the idea of secularism into their representations of the West and the concept of a secular NGO is even more problematic. Moreover, it is hard for them to distinguish between a secular organisation and one run by atheists. They neither understand nor accept that the humanitarian gesture, whatever its origin, can be situated outside the sphere of religious values, and cannot envisage associating with secular managers representing organisations that adopt an international approach devoid of any religious inspiration.

On a personal level, a Western humanitarian volunteer who expresses atheism in the course of a conversation can only plunge the Islamic listener into profound shock. In the same way, citing atheism as a principle to avoid accusations of being a missionary organisation can be counter-productive for Western NGOs. Whatever the situation, even when the atmosphere is extremely tense, the Islamic volunteer will always prefer to deal with a 'Christian' rather than an atheist 'possessing neither faith nor law'. Because their concept of society is governed by religious precepts, Islamists cannot easily accept the idea that secular international NGOs are the products of Western societies in the process of shedding their Christian faith. This they would regard as a terrible consequence of the radical loss of essential moral values. Sexual promiscuity and alcohol and drug consumption by Western aid workers – who often display contempt for local cultures – are perceived as symptoms of a disintegrating society that has lost its fundamental values by renouncing its religious faith. This distorted image provides Islamic NGOs with an alternative example that allows them to mobilise the support of their social base

– although the technical expertise that fascinates them is drawn from their Western counterparts. These representations poison relations between Western and Islamic NGOs. Indeed, if religious NGOs are considered by Islamic NGOs as clearly identified historical enemies while secular NGOs are condemned out of hand, how is it possible to establish dialogue? Yet the priorities of relief work dictate ever-closer contact and sometimes provide the only opportunity for genuine Islamist militants to meet Westerners.

Médecins Sans Frontières first experienced this type of situation in the early 1990s. In 1994 IIRO volunteers working in the Kunduz region of Afghanistan did their utmost to intimidate MSF teams and force them out of an area they regarded as the sole preserve of Islamic NGOs. As a result, MSF was unable to work in the Bagh i Sherkat camp. A few weeks later, MSF began operating in a refugee camp under construction near Khanabad but the sudden arrival of the Iranian Red Crescent, quickly followed by Arab Islamic NGOs, produced tensions that forced MSF to abandon the area. In Sudan too, there have been many clashes involving Western NGOs on one side and authorities and Islamic NGOs on the other. In 1995, in the Wadi-al-Bashir camp at Omdurman, Sudanese Islamic NGOs like al-Dawa al-Islamiya and the Islamic African Relief Agency worked alongside Christian national organisations like the Sudanese Council of Churches, and Western non-religious organisations like MSF and GOAL (Ireland). Al-Dawa al-Islamiya incited the population, mainly composed of displaced and newly-Islamised Muslims, all of them destitute, to drive out the non-Islamic NGOs. The experience of the MSF regional bureau in the United Arab Emirates provides another example of this permanent tension. Since its establishment in 1995 and despite many attempts to improve relations, Islamic NGOs based in the UAE have never stopped publicly denigrating MSF, notably accusing it of being the incarnation of an expansionist Christian West that seeks to impose its culture and beliefs on others.

Not all problems of coexistence, however, stem from certain Islamic NGOs and the responsibility must be shared. Western NGOs harbour an almost instinctive suspicion of Islamic NGOs, a mistrust that precludes the possibility of dialogue. Islamic NGOs are seldom invited to on-site coordination meetings, whether in Beirut, Peshawar, Khartoum, Sarajevo or Pristina. The unfortunate experience of one manager of an Islamic NGO, cited with bitterness by an Irish official of Islamic Relief Worldwide, is typical of the pernicious attitude that prevails. This individual, who did not have a good grasp of English, attended a humanitarian relief coordination meeting in Pristina in 1999 and was subjected to sarcastic remarks by his Western colleagues. He did not attend any further meetings. Western and Islamic humanitarian actors only rarely engage in dialogue in the established forums and it is cause for concern that Western aid workers do not seem bothered by this.

A humanitarian trap for Islamic NGOs

By turning their attention to crisis-hit non-Muslim populations (i.e. by not following a 'dawatist' agenda) as in India and Mozambique, Islamic NGOs are trying to show that the Islamic version of charitable relief work is well-intentioned and of benefit to everybody. By devoting more effort to the provision of emergency aid,

Islamic NGOs are forging a qualitative bond and drawing closer to the world of independent humanitarian organisations. Some Islamic NGOs, buoyed by their success in Islamic lands – in contrast to the loss of popularity suffered by more politicised Islamic groups – now have ambitions to join the 'major league'. In order to gain access to the power, legitimacy, and resources enjoyed by leading Western NGOs, they are being forced to revise their strategies. A growing number – especially those based in the West and subject to 'democratic constraints' – are now adopting a strategy that combines two contrasting forms of legitimacy. They are juggling with two types of discourse and two types of action. One advocates straightforward Islamic solidarity to convey the cultural values appropriate to, and protective of, the lives and dignity of vulnerable Muslims. The other promotes modern humanitarianism and the principles of universality, impartiality, and inclusiveness cherished by the contemporary West. Although certain groups are meeting with some success in imposing this double legitimacy and synthesising an identity of their own – as in the case of certain Western-based Islamic NGOs like Islamic Relief Worldwide – others, like the Islamic African Relief Agency (IARA, Sudan), risk losing their identity in a brittle fusion. In fact, there are two opposing logics at work: one, represented by the major Western aid organisations, constantly demands more professionalism and guarantees of 'good conduct'. The other, represented by Muslim donors, ceaselessly demands more guarantees that relief work must be both efficient and conducted according to strict Islamic principles corresponding to the 'duties of a Muslim'.

These external constraints are now combining with pressures from within the Islamic humanitarian world. The greatest pressure stems from the risk of getting caught up in an institutional logic. Some of the more highly developed Islamic NGOs are becoming victims of their own success: they are gradually losing contact with the foundations of their religious legitimacy and are moving into the ruthless field of competition. Four forms of rivalry have slowly emerged – ideological competition between NGOs of different Islamic strands (such as Wahhabism, the Muslim Brotherhood, Jamaat Tabligh, and Khomeinism) who are trying to impose 'their' Islam; political rivalry between NGOs used by states to export the Islamic faith; competition between the classic Middle Eastern Islamic NGOs – who still regard Islamic solidarity as their primary legitimacy – and Western Islamic NGOs who seek to develop a form of humanitarianism that artfully combines Islamic and Western values; and finally, a sometimes ferocious and extremely pragmatic struggle between all the Islamic organisations for recognition, expertise, and resources.

This competition was clearly apparent during the Kosovo crisis. The United Arab Emirates' Red Crescent equipped tents in the Kukes displaced persons camp with air conditioning, and provided 10,000 displaced Kosovars with three hot meals a day, hot running water, and nappies for babies. It also completely equipped a nearby hospital. Journalists voted this camp the best refugee reception site in the area. Kosovars deserted other camps and fought to get into Kukes. Some Islamic NGOs followed the Red Crescent's example and made great efforts to provide high quality aid. For the first time, they had shifted from the rhetoric of cultural alienation to a pragmatic logic of competition with

Western NGOs in the provision of services to victim-clients.

The need for funding also leads to a problem well known in the West. Many Islamic NGOs are involved in programs for which it is easy to raise funds, such as Palestine, but do very little in other regions with large Muslim populations. Sub-Saharan countries, for example, need aid but receive less media attention and hence less NGO attention than elsewhere. This latter form of competition is perhaps the most symptomatic: it demonstrates that even Islamic NGOs are not immune to the classic obsession that permanently threatens the world of humanitarian action – the placing of institutional interests above those of the victims.

The elevation of Islamic NGOs to the major league of Western NGOs is slowly ensuring that they share the same preoccupations. A Muslim journalist interviewed Adnan Basha, director-general of the International Islamic Relief Organisation, and, obviously hoping to steer him onto the subject of confrontations with Western humanitarian organisations, invited him to name the principal obstacles to his organisation's work. Basha's response was surprisingly pragmatic. 'There are many [obstacles and problems]... among the greatest are the lack of funds; lack of technical expertise in emergency relief work; the lack of collaboration and cooperation with other aid agencies; the legal problems arising from complicated regulations in certain countries in which we operate; the risk of death run by our volunteers in the field.' The list might have come from any Western aid worker and shows that Islamic NGOs are gaining in maturity. When the reality of the situation on the ground catches up with an Islamic NGO, it overrides more ideological or political considerations.

Most humanitarians working for modern international relief organisations, whether Western or Islamic, subscribe to an operational logic with which they are confronted and to which they must – to a certain extent – come to terms. Contemporary, secular Western NGOs still too often have the leading role in this extremely politicised environment. It is easier to present oneself as a champion of universal humanitarianism if one occupies a position of cultural dominance. Let us imagine the reverse scenario for a moment, one in which the world had been dominated by an Islamic culture until recently; in which the Christian West had barely recovered from the Muslim crusades and had just shed the yoke of Arab-Muslim colonialism. In what camp would we find the humanitarian NGOs claiming a universal vocation, and in what camp the simple NGOs extolling religious solidarity and sometimes prepared to adopt more extreme measures to defend a threatened identity? Would the roles not be reversed?

17

Of Medicines and Men

Annick Hamel

In antiquity, the term 'victim' referred to a human being or animal immolated as a sacrifice to some divinity. In the term's modern meaning, a victim is someone who 'suffers harm through somebody's fault..., who has suffered from the interests or passions of others'. Wars, natural catastrophes, and fraud are recognised as producers of victims. But there are tens of millions of others today who are not accorded this status, despite meeting the criteria of both definitions of the term above. They are the sick who are not treated as they could and should be. Because they do not constitute a 'lucrative market', they cannot obtain the treatment they require and must make do with medicines that are ineffective and sometimes dangerous. Not belonging to the politically and economically dominant groups, they are in many ways the 'sacrificed' to the political economy of health.

Volunteers from Médecins Sans Frontières are constantly confronted with this social violence in the course of their work.. Each year, several million people, most of them children, die from common diseases that are often curable but almost always fatal if left untreated. This injustice does not arise by chance, nor is it inevitable. It the result of financial, political, economic, and social decisions made at national and international levels. It is one facet of the 'hidden fatality' wrought by the balance of socio-economic forces.

Logics of exclusion

The deficiencies of the therapeutic arsenal

Every day, doctors working in poor countries find themselves unable to provide their patients with treatment that could save them. Faced with illnesses as widespread and deadly as malaria and AIDS, they often only have at their disposal medicines that are ineffective, dangerous or unaffordable. Other drugs have simply been withdrawn from the market for lack of any solvent demand. Production, for example, of oily chloramphenicol, the antibiotic best suited to treating forms of meningitis that are epidemic in Africa, was halted in 1995. Destined solely for use by poor, sick Africans, the medicine was no longer profitable to the pharmaceutical company manufacturing it. Production of oily chloramphenicol was resumed one year later by a not-for-profit laboratory, but is now at risk once more, because the laboratory has been acquired by a commercial firm.

The 60 million Africans exposed to trypanosomiasis (sleeping sickness) are scarcely any better off. If left untreated, sleeping sickness is fatal in almost 100 percent of cases, and the therapeutic regime dates from forty years ago. Melarsoprol, an arsenic derivative, is used to treat the most advanced stage of the disease but has side effects that are fatal in 5 percent of patients. Furthermore, this drug is now ineffective for 25 percent of patients due to the resistance trypanosome has developed. Thus, almost one third of all patients treated with melarsoprol is condemned to die.

In 1990, eflornithine, an anti-cancer drug, was found to be effective in treating sleeping sickness. Less toxic than arsenic derivatives, it is the sole recourse where resistance to melarsoprol is present. In 1995, the laboratory producing eflornithine – which was abandoned as a cancer treatment – stopped manufacturing and marketing it because its (African) market was not profitable and its target (sleeping sickness) was not a 'growth area'. Under pressure from Médecins Sans Frontières and the World Health Organisation (WHO), the pharmaceutical laboratory agreed to resume production in 2001. This positive outcome only constitutes a short-term solution: no drug is presently under development to replace eflornithine when it becomes ineffective due to resistance.

Developing appropriate treatments demands permanent investment in drug research and development. This holds true for all pathologies and all treatments. Yet between 1975 and 1999, only thirteen of the 1,393 medicines put on the market were for treating tropical diseases, which kill millions of people each year. Moreover, the majority of these thirteen medicines emerged from veterinary or military research. In other words, it is only by accident that they have helped the sick in developing countries.

When it comes to AIDS, by contrast, it is not an absence of research and development that is penalising the most disadvantaged patients. While antiretroviral drugs are available in rich industrialised countries, considerably improving the length and quality of life of patients, their cost – several thousand euros a year – makes them inaccessible to patients in poorer countries. Yet the latter are by far the most numerous: 30 million of the 42 million people infected with the HIV virus live in Africa. Lacking the possibility to benefit from these drugs, the poor are proposed information, prevention and abstinence.

There are between 300 and 500 million new cases of malaria registered each year that result in 1 to 2 million deaths, yet the only treatment patients can usually obtain is chloroquine, which has become ineffective. Chloroquine was developed in 1934 and became one of the most common anti-malarial drugs. At the time, it combined all the qualities of an ideal drug: effectiveness, low production cost, and ease of use. But after fifty years its efficiency is close to zero due to the resistance developed by the parasite. The second-line drug, sulfadoxine-pyrimethamine, is now also becoming less and less active, and can no longer be regarded as a serious alternative to chloroquine. Effective drug combinations do exist and are capable of curing patients, but most African countries have not incorporated them into national treatment protocols. Chloroquine still often features in the front line of treatment regimes recommended by the health ministries.

Discriminatory health policies

By maintaining these obsolete treatment protocols, African health ministries – who are fully aware of chloroquine and sulfadoxine-pyrimethamine resistance and the effectiveness of the combination therapies – are depriving the vast majority of their populations of the possibility of receiving correct treatment. The relatively high cost of the drug combinations is a genuine obstacle, but does not constitute a sufficient reason to continue giving patients useless drugs, unless as an expression of profound contempt for the poorest patients. For even if absent from the public domain, these effective drugs are on sale in the private sector. They are authorised by health ministries and are available to patients who can afford them. Sometimes part of their cost is even refunded to members of 'corporatist' mutual insurance schemes (particularly those covering state employees), thus highlighting the priorities of the health authorities. Financing possibilities exist, moreover, that would make it possible for these drug combinations to be available in the public sector, to which the great majority of the sick turn for help.

The health ministries that restrict the range of therapeutic assistance in this way take advantage of certain international support. Under the slogan 'health for all in the year 2000', international bodies such as the WHO and UNICEF advocated establishing 'primary health care' strategies that neglected individual care in favour of prevention. By so doing, they gave their backing to health policies on the cheap: prevention is a vague notion embracing not only well-tried measures such as vaccination, but also behavioural recommendations, such as health education, devoid of any practical effectiveness. The establishment of collective facilities and improvements in living conditions, whose impact on health is well proven, were overlooked. According to the utopia still prevailing, prevention is supposed to reduce the number of sick, and hence the cost of care, in countries with limited financial and human resources. This dogma allows states, under pressure from international financial institutions and with the support of WHO, to implement structural adjustment policies that cut public spending in supposedly unproductive sectors such as education and health. The choices leave millions of sick people – especially those with AIDS – to die while waiting for the advent of an ideal world where, thanks to prevention, there are no more sick.

Advocacy of prevention at the expense of treatment likewise makes it possible to back health systems that confine their therapeutic services to the most affluent patients. Ever since the 'Bamako Initiative' launched by WHO in 1987, the benefits of patients contributing financially to the cost of their treatment have been regularly extolled. Since then it has been accepted that paying for health care leads to responsible and rational management of resources, while simultaneously ensuring, by some unspecified mechanism, an improved quality of care. This initiative, the famous 'cost recovery system' has been being progressively introduced in every country, including states completely shattered by wars in progress or ones that have barely terminated: Burundi, Sudan, Liberia, and Sierra Leone. An effective malaria treatment costs on average 1.2 euro, and a Caesarean around 100 euros. Since the average income of most people in these countries is less than 1 euro per day, women die because they cannot pay for a Caesarean. Some luckier ones, not having confessed their poverty on admission, are imprisoned inside the hospital itself once the Caesarean is performed until the family, neighbours, or associations club together to pay the costs of the operation. It is fortunate for those who claim success in this system that deaths linked to the introduction of cost recovery do not figure in statistics: sick people who know they will be turned away by the health centre or hospital because they cannot pay the bill no longer even bother to go there. Many health professionals have adopted the ideological discourse of these international institutions. Gradually, doctors and nurses are accepting that their main work no longer consists of treating the sick but in managing systems that prioritise prevention and cost reduction at the expense of treatment and curative care. Individual curative care is becoming marginalised, making way for general measures of prevention and financial rationalisation aimed at avoiding the sick. This marginalisation of care makes it possible for doctors and nurses, as the years go by, to accept as inevitable that the treatments they provide are less and less effective, indeed devoid of any therapeutic power whatever, and that the poor are left standing at the doors of their dispensaries.

The primacy of financial considerations

These logics of exclusion are aggravated by recent developments in the international trade and financial system. It was in 1994 that the Marrakech Agreement setting up the World Trade Organisation (WTO) was signed. The Agreement on Trade-related Aspects of Intellectual Property Rights (TRIPS Agreement), an annex to the Marrakech Agreement, strengthens the protection accorded to inventions and discoveries – including those in field of drugs. Every innovation can be patented, i.e. protected, giving its inventor a 20-year monopoly on its exploitation, sale and distribution.

Any monopoly makes it possible to abuse the dominant position. Prices of inventions are not set in accordance with production costs, with a profit margin added on, but in accordance with what the market can pay, considering the service provided. Hence, the monetary value of drugs that prolong the lives of the sick can be limitless. Precise information on the real cost of drugs is difficult to find, reinforcing the opaqueness surrounding the way prices are set. This is true of the triple antiretroviral therapies used to treat AIDS whose price reaches several thousand euros a year. Research costs, although often invoked, in no way justify the prices charged. In fact, it was government or university researchers who first identified the most frequently used antiretroviral drugs – zidovudine, didanosine, abacavir, stavudine, zalcitabine – and the concept of antiproteases. For some of these drugs, it was also public money that funded some of the clinical trials. Yet the fact remains that the prices charged condemn millions of people to certain death. For while the sick of rich countries enjoy social welfare systems that ensure that society, after financing the research costs, bears the exorbitant price of these drugs as a matter of solidarity, the sick of poor countries have no social welfare systems, and only the most affluent sufferers can afford these treatments. The others die.

Drugs appear nowadays, in fact, as ordinary goods. Over the past few decades, the pharmaceutical industry has undergone major restructuring which has made it highly dependent on financial markets. Big laboratories have been increasingly obliged to select their investments on the basis of predicted profitability. Concerned for their profits and those of their shareholders, they have an obvious interest in producing and marketing drugs that will guarantee them a quick return on their investment, i.e. drugs targeting 'profitable' diseases and patients with money. The pharmaceutical companies are thus far more inclined toward developing antidepressants than anti-malarials, and even more so toward finding new uses for already existing drugs (the 'me-toos'), rather than innovative treatments for sleeping sickness.

The public sector invests significant sums in fundamental medical research, including that concerned with tropical diseases. But once this fundamental research has been completed, the public sector leaves the task of developing of the final product largely to the market sector. Since the logic of the pharmaceutical companies is based essentially on profit forecasts, they will not use the research to develop drugs unless these provide them with quick and sizeable profits. In the end, the public funds finance private interests whose logic is completely disconnected from the policy imperatives of health.

A perceptible evolution

Realising the extremely high human cost of these injustices, a certain number of actors have decided to organise and react. The scale of the AIDS epidemic in developing countries, which is the most visible part of the disaster, has finally provoked questions about the more general issue of treatment for the poorest sick people on the planet.

Emergence of new social and economic actors

Following the example set in Western countries a few years earlier, African, Asian, and Latin American AIDS sufferers formed associations in the late 1990s to demand treatment, not hesitating to confront their governments. The first associations were created in Brazil, Thailand and South Africa. In Costa Rica, an association of the sick instituted legal proceedings in 1997 against the public health system, which at the time did not provide antiretroviral therapy. The court found in favour of the association, and the Costa Rican government found itself obliged to treat its sick.

In developing countries, the situation of the pharmaceutical industry has also evolved. Some countries have benefited and continue to benefit from extensions of the deadline set for them to comply with the TRIPS agreement. They are not obliged to respect patents on certain drugs until these extended deadlines expire. Some, such as Brazil, Thailand and India, have made use of these transition periods to strengthen their productive capacity. These countries, which had already built up successful pharmaceutical industries, are now capable of producing ever more sophisticated drugs, copying protected compounds or developing new methods for producing compounds still under patent. These generic drugs are the same quality as protected drugs but can cost 20 to 100 times less. In generic form, the triple antiretroviral therapies now cost less then 300 euros a year. Moreover, the appearance on the market of these competitively priced therapies has led some big laboratories to considerably reduce the price they charge for those of their drugs going to poor countries, adjusting it to that of the generics.

The impact of the Pretoria lawsuit

The assertion of a right to health care reached its high point in the Pretoria lawsuit of 2001. On 5 March legal proceedings instituted by thirty-nine pharmaceutical companies against the South African government opened in the country's capital. By adopting a law in 1997 favouring recourse to generic drugs, the government had been guilty, in the laboratories' eyes, of infringing intellectual property rights. On 19 April 2001 the thirty-nine laboratories withdrew their complaint without requiring the South African government to change its law.

It was the mobilisation of civil society (South African associations and non-governmental organisations, supported by international NGOs), virulent criticism in the press (including the financial press), internal opposition from some of their own employees and shareholders, and desertion by Western governments that induced the laboratories to back down and forced the very powerful Pharmaceutical Manufacturers' Association of South Africa (PMASA) to withdraw its complaint and pay the costs of the proceedings.

The Pretoria ruling projected the issue of access to treatment for the world's poorest into the realm of public debate. The question of the distribution of drugs at the global level, hitherto confined to relatively specialised circles, was brought into the open by social movements that forced most international bodies to shift their position. Having long claimed that treating the sick in poor countries was impossible, the United Nations, G8 countries, European Union, African Union (the former Organisation for African Unity), and other organisations now acknowledge the need to combine prevention policies with genuine access to effective treatment. Some countries, including the United States, continue to prefer prevention to treatment.

The creation by the UN of the Global Fund to Fight AIDS, Tuberculosis and Malaria, which aims to collect contributions from Western countries to tackle these three diseases in developing countries, recognised the rich countries' duty of solidarity with poor countries. Similarly, the World Trade Organisation, through the Doha Declaration adopted in November 2001, now accepts the idea that private interests must be reconciled with general interest in the area of intellectual property. This declaration states that the TRIPS agreement should be implemented in a way that guarantees the right of WTO members to protect public health and, in particular, to promote universal access to therapeutic drugs. Theoretically, patent law cannot, therefore, deprive the majority of patients of the treatments they need. The imperatives of public health allow resort to copies of protected drugs, and the least advanced countries are not obliged to comply with patent legislation until 2016.

WHO is now finally restoring the treatment of AIDS sufferers to the place it deserves. WHO now supports the necessity of making effective treatment available to sick people, even when the price of drugs appears prohibitive for countries with limited financial resources. Rather than eliminating these drugs from its *List of Essential Drugs* from the outset, as it did previously, it is now seeking to get the cost of treatment reduced, notably by identifying generic equivalents.

Challenges for the future

Beyond these positive developments only a political commitment and a search for lasting solutions will offer any serious hope of one day seeing all sick people receive the vital treatment they require.

Essential political decisions

The South African example shows that the availability of a legal tool (such as the law of 1997) does not suffice to guarantee the sick better access to drugs. In order to benefit from the safeguard clauses incorporated in the TRIPS agreement and strengthened by the Doha Declaration, states must have the political will to adopt and implement the appropriate concrete measures. The South African government has still not taken these steps, and thus persists in depriving the poorest people of vital treatment. More seriously still, President Thabo Mbeki continues to prevaricate on the need to treat AIDS sufferers, provoking activist organisations to lodge a complaint against his government for non-assistance to persons in danger.

The establishment of 'cost recovery' systems, in other words payment for care at the point of delivery, is also the result of political decisions. The quest for equality in access to health care raises the question of more cost sharing between rich and poor countries. Supporting cost recovery policies in the absence of any real systems of solidarity for sick people with limited means amounts to excluding them from the health care system. The sacrifice of thousands of people that this choice implies should be recognised as such and publicly debated. As for humanitarian organisations, there is a great risk that they will find themselves caught up in such policies without opposing or even revealing the sacrifice they engender. By being integrated in the functioning of these systems, humanitarian actors will actually participate in this process of exclusion.

Finding lasting solutions

The fall in the price of some patented drugs, mainly as a result of competition from generic copies, only represents a temporary solution. All countries presently producing generics will have to bring their laws into conformity with agreements on intellectual property by 2006 at the latest. They will have to respect drug patents, and will thus no longer be entitled to produce copies of protected drugs, except in exceptional circumstances and only for their own home market. Hence they will be forced to stop supplying generics to those countries – generally the poorest ones – that are unable to produce these drugs themselves but have received permission from the WTO to import them until 2016. The World Trade Organisation, aware of this inconsistency which effectively deprives the poorest countries of the chance to resort to generic drugs after 2006, advised its Council in 2002 to find a solution. To date, the process remains blocked due to the attitude of the United States, which wants to limit to three the number of diseases that could be recognised as a public health problem justifying resort to generic drugs. Yet by regarding anthrax as a public health problem in 2001, the United States government was able to threaten to resort to generic ciprofloxacine in efforts to lower the price of the brand drug. Despite declarations in favour of protecting public health, the European Union's proposals in the negotiations differs little from that of the United States, since it too aims to limit the number of diseases covered. Even if a solution is found for the period following 2006, the present haggling indicates that concern to limit infringements of intellectual property will push proposals to abandon the spirit of the Doha Declaration, which recognised that the right to health takes precedence over property rights. The only viable solution is to establish a genuine system of differential pricing based on equity and not on *ad hoc* measures which are sometimes a matter of charity and sometimes of public relations policy, and which are inherently provisional. This system should result in vital treatment being accessible to all the sick, independently of their financial resources.

The future of those suffering from tropical diseases such as leishmaniosis or trypanosomiasis is yet more uncertain. The pursuit of profits will never permit the development of new drugs providing effective treatment for these patients, who offer no guarantee of a return on investment. Potential solutions that offer some hope of treating the sick necessarily lie outside the logic of profitability. By creating a not-for-profit body whose social objective is researching and developing new drugs for the most neglected diseases (Drugs for Neglected Diseases Initiative, DNDI), Médecins Sans Frontières and various research institutes (Institut Pasteur, Indian Council for Medical Research, Brazil's Oswaldo Cruz Institute and others) are endeavouring to open up a path and provide a practical demonstration of the feasibility of such a goal. But this not-for profit body will not really be able to develop new drugs unless the solidarity between countries of the North and the South, between rich and poor and between the public and private sectors is real and effective.

The 2003 G8 summit in Evian does not augur well for the future concerning either research and development or access to essential drugs at affordable prices. Rather than adopting measures aimed at treating the largest number of patients (recourse to generic drugs, local production and technology transfer), the eight richest countries gave preference to the least efficient and durable practices (reinforcing private sector participation, sporadic donations). In this fashion these governments further distanced themselves from objectives set in previous G8 summits to control and reduce the major epidemics.

The issue of access to medical treatment for the planet's poorest inhabitants has now found a place in the arena of public debate. This debate should expand to embrace all the processes that conspire to deprive the majority of humanity of vital care. In addition to the question of access to health facilities and effective drugs, it must not fail to consider the quality of care provided. It is now a matter of urgency that this debate should lead to concrete measures and actions – at present all too few – by all those involved in health, starting with national and international political authorities, so that equity in the face of disease becomes more than just a slogan.

The Contributors

Michel Agier, anthropologist, research director at the Development Research Institute (IRD) and member of the Centre d'Etudes Africaines of the EHESS. Has published *L'Invention de la Ville. Banlieues, townships, invasions et favelas* (Paris, Ed. des Archives Contemporaines, 1999) and *Aux bords du monde, les refugies* (Paris, Flammarion, 2002). In 1999 he became responsible for a research project on the socialisation and identity reconstruction of displaced populations and refugees in Colombia and Black Africa.

Chawki Amari, journalist, columnist for various Algerian daily papers (*La Tribune, Le Matin, El Watan...*). Since 1997 he has lived in France where he regularly collaborates with the *Courrier International*. He is also the representative for Algeria of a defence association of cartoonists in the world, 'Cartoonist Relief Network'.

Françoise Bouchet-Saulnier, Doctor in Law, legal counsel for MSF, coordinates the activities of the MSF Foundation and has written several books including *Droits de l'Homme, droit humanitaire et justice internationale* (Paris, Actes Sud, 2002) and *Dictionnaire Pratique du Droit Humanitaire* (Paris, La Découverte, 2000).

Rony Brauman, medical doctor, president of MSF from 1982 to 1994, became research director of the MSF Foundation in 1996 and is associate professor at the Institut d'Etudes Politiques de Paris. He has written extensively on the implications and limitations of humanitarian action. Among his books are *L'Action Humanitaire* (Flammarion, Dominos, 2000) and *Humanitaire, le dilemme* (Paris, Textuel, 1996).

François Calas, member of MSF, has regularly taken part since 1992 in humanitarian missions in Central Asia, particularly in Afghanistan.

Eric Dachy, a specialist in child psychiatry, has been a collaborator with MSF since 1991. He has participated in numerous emergency missions (ex-Yugoslavia, Russia, DRC) and written works on the ethical and political aspects of humanitarian action. He has also co-ordinated a special issue of *Les Temps Modernes* dedicated to humanitarian aid (2003).

Abdel-Rahman Ghandour, doctor in political science and graduate of the IEP in Paris, of the American University in Beirut and of the School of Oriental and African Studies in London, has been head of mission for MSF in Sudan and Iran and directed the MSF office in the UAE for four years. In 2001 he became political adviser in Nairobi to the UN Secretary-General's special representative for the Great Lakes region. He is also the author of *Djihad Humanitaire* (Flammarion, 2002) on Islamic charitable organisations.

Gil Gonzalez-Foerster, independent journalist, also head of mission of several NGOs, including Action Contre La Faim, for which he led in 2001 a survey on the reconstruction of East Timor.

Thorniké Gordadzé, research fellow at the Centre d'Etudes et de Relations Internationales (CERI/FNSP) and author of numerous works on state formation and identity processes in the Caucasus.

Annick Hamel, a nurse graduated from the IEP of Paris, is MSF's co-ordinator of the campaign for access to essential medicines. She is the author of numerous articles on the problems of making care available for the most destitute populations.

Jean-Hervé Jézéquel, *agrégé* and doctor in history, associate member of the Centre d'Etudes Africaines of the EHESS and a specialist on West Africa. He has carried out several study missions for MSF.

Marc Lavergne, doctor in geography and director of research at the CNRS (Ethnology and Comparative Sociology Laboratory, Paris X, Nanterre). An Arabic speaker, he has directed several research and scientific co-operation institutions in Beirut, Khartoum and Amman. Among other publications, he edited *Le Soudan Contemporain* (Paris, Karthala, 1989) and *L'Oman Contemporain – Etat, Territoire, Identité* (with Brigitte Dumortier; Paris, Karthala, 2003).

Marc Le Pape, researcher at the CNRS (Centre d'Etudes Africaines/EHESS), member of the administrative council of MSF. He has co-edited 'Les Politiques de la haine. Rwanda-Burundi, 1994-95' (with Claudine Vidal, *Les Temps Modernes*, July-August 1995), *Une guerre contre les civils – Réflexions sur les pratiques humanitaires au Congo Brazzaville 1998-2000* (with Pierre Salignon, Paris, Karthala, 2001) and *Côte d'Ivoire, l'année terrible* (with Claudine Vidal, Paris, Karthala, 2002).

Christine Messiant, researcher at the Centre d'Etudes Africaines at the EHESS. She has published numerous works on Angola and Southern Africa including *Les chemins de la guerre à la paix* (with Roland Marchal, Paris, Karthala, 1997).

David Rieff, independent journalist, author of *Crimes de guerre, ce que nous devons savoir* (with Roy Gutman, Paris, Autrement, 2003) and *A Bed for the Night. Humanitarianism in Crisis* (2003).

Pierre Salignon, lawyer, head of programmes for MSF. He has also co-directed *Une guerre contre les civils – Réflexions sur les pratiques humanitaires au Congo-Brazzaville. 1998-2000* (Paris, Karthala, 2001).

Fiona Terry, doctor in political science, research director at the MSF Foundation. Among her books is *Condemned to repeat? The paradox of humanitarian action* (Ithaca, NY, Cornell University Press, 2002).

Fabrice Weissman, IEP Paris graduate, research director at the MSF Foundation. Author of various works and publications on humanitarian aid and political economy of conflicts.

Index

**MEDECINS
SANS FRONTIERES**

Médecins Sans Frontières is a private, international, non-profit, humanitarian organisation whose objective is to provide medical aid to populations in crisis, without discrimination.

The organisation relies on volunteer health and other professionals and is independent of all states or institutions, as well as of all political, economic and religious influences.

MSF was founded in 1971 by doctors determined to offer emergency assistance wherever wars and disasters occur in the world. Its guiding principles are laid down in a charter to which all members of the organisation subscribe.

During more than three decades of humanitarian action around the world, MSF has gained a wide range of expertise, tested techniques and strategies of intervention that allow it to pool rapidly the resources necessary to provide efficient and effective aid.

Largely supported by private donors, MSF is able to maintain great flexibility in its interventions and total independence in its choice of operations. Furthermore, in bearing witness to violations of fundamental humanitarian principles and denouncing them publicly, MSF volunteers implement a vital part of their humanitarian commitment.

The international MSF network consists of five operational sections (France, Belgium, the Netherlands, Switzerland and Spain), thirteen partner sections and an international office, based in Brussels.

In 2002, nearly 3,000 Médecins Sans Frontières from more than 70 different nationalities worked in 78 countries of the world.

THE CHARTER OF
MÉDECINS SANS FRONTIÈRES

MSF is a private international organisation. Most of its
members are doctors and health workers, but many
other support professions contribute to MSF's smooth
functioning. All of them agree to honour the following
principles:

- Médecins Sans Frontières offers assistance to
populations in distress, to victims of natural or
man-made disasters and to victims of armed
conflict, without discrimination and irrespective of
race, religion, creed or political affiliation.

- Médecins Sans Frontières observes neutrality and
impartiality in the name of universal medical ethics
and the right to humanitarian assistance and
demands full and unhindered freedom in the
exercise of its functions.

- Médecins Sans Frontières' volunteers undertake to
respect their professional code of ethics and to
maintain complete independence from all political,
economic and religious powers.

- As volunteers, members are aware of the risks and
dangers of the mission they undertake, and have
no right to compensation for themselves or their
beneficiaries other than that which Médecins Sans
Frontières is able to afford them.

THE INTERNATIONAL NETWORK OF MÉDECINS SANS FRONTIÈRES

AUSTRALIA
Médecins Sans Frontières
Suite C, Level 1
263 Broadway
Glebe NSW 2037 or GPO Box
847 Broadway NSW 2007

tel. : +61 2 95 52 49 33
fax : +61 2 95 52 65 39
office@sydney.msf.org

AUSTRIA
Arzte Ohne Grenzen
Josefstaedter Strasse, 19
1082 Wien (or Postfach 53)

tel. : +43 1 409 72 76
fax : +43 1 409 72 76-40
office@msf.at

BELGIUM
Médecins Sans Frontières
Dupréstreet, 94
1090 Brussels Jette

tel. : +32 2 474 74 74
fax : +32 2 474 75 75
zoom@brussels.msf.org

BELGIUM
International Office
Médecins Sans Frontières
39 rue de La Tourelle
1040 Brussels

tel. : +32 2 280 18 81
fax : +32 2 280 01 73
office-intnl@bi.msf.org

CANADA
Médecins Sans Frontières
720, Spadina Avenue, suite 402
Toronto, Ontario ON M5S-2T9

tel. : +1 416 964 06 19
fax : +1 416 963 87 07
msfcan@msf.ca

DENMARK
Médecins Sans Frontières
Bernstorffsvej 20
2900 Hellerup

tel. : +45 39 62 63 01
fax : +45 39 62 61 04
info@.msf.dk

FRANCE
Médecins Sans Frontières   tel. : +33 (0)1 - 40 21 29 29
8, rue Saint-Sabin   fax : +33 (0)1 - 48 06 68 68
75544 Paris Cedex 11   office@paris.msf.org

GERMANY
Ärzte Ohne Grenzen   tel. : +49 (30) 22 33 77 00
Am Köllnishen Park, 1   fax : +49 (30) 22 33 77 88
10179 Berlin   office@bonn.msf.org

HOLLAND
Artsen Zonder Grenzen   tel. : +31 20-520 87 00
Max Euweplein, 40   fax : +31 20-620 51 70
P.O. Box 10014   hq@amsterdam.msf.org
1001 EA Amsterdam

HONG KONG
Médecins Sans Frontières   tel. : +852 2 338 82 77
Shop 5B, Lai chi kok Bay Garden,   fax : +852 2 304 60 81
Lai King Hill Road, N° 272   office@.msf.org.hk
Kowloon, Hong Kong
(or GPO Box 5083)

ITALY
Médecins Sans Frontières   tel. : +39 06 448 69 21
Via Volturno, 58   fax : +39 06 448 69 22
Rome 00185   msf@msf.it

JAPAN
Médecins Sans Frontières   tel. : +813 33 66 85 71
Takadanobaba 3-28-1   fax : +813 33 66 85 73
Shinjuku-ku, Tokyo 169   msf@japan.msf.org

LUXEMBOURG
Médecins Sans Frontières   tel. : +35 2 - 33 25 15
70 route de Luxembourg   fax : +35 2 - 33 51 33
L-7240 Bereldange   info@msf.lu
or B.P 38   L-7201 Walferdange

NORWAY
Médecins Sans Frontières
Radhusgate 30 A
0151 Oslo

tel : +47 22 33 45 55
fax: +47 22 33 45 51
office-osl@oslo.msf.org

SPAIN
Médicos Sin Fronteras
Nou de la Rambla, 26
08001 Barcelona

tel. : +34 3 - 304 61 00
fax : +34 3 - 304 61 02
oficina@barcelona.msf.org

SWEDEN
Médecins Sans Frontières
Godlansgatan, 84
S-116 38 Stockholm

tel. : +46 8 - 55 60 98 00
fax : +46 8 - 55 60 98 01
office-sto@msf.org

SWITZERLAND
Médecins Sans Frontières
78, rue de Lausanne
1202 Genève
Case Postale 116, 1211 Genève 21

tel. : +41 22-849 84 84
fax : +41 22-849 84 88
office-gva@geneva.msf.org

UNITED ARAB EMIRATES
Nasr Street (Behind Khalifa
Committee)
Oteiba Building - Office 203
Abu Dhabi (or PO Box 47226)

tel. : +971 2 6317 645
fax : +971 2 6215 059
msfuae@emirates.net.ae

UNITED KINGDOM
Médecins Sans Frontières
67-74 Saffron Hill
London, EC1N 8QX

tel. : +44 20 7404 6600
fax : +44 20 7404 4466
office-ldn@london.msf.org

UNITED STATES
Doctors Without Borders
333, 7th Avenue, 2nd floor
New York, NY 10001-5004

tel. : +1 212 679 68 00
fax : +1 212 679 70 16
doctors@newyork.msf.org